2018 SQA Specimen & Past Papers with Answers

National 5
HISTORY

2017 & 2018 Exams
and 2017 Specimen Question Paper

HODDER
GIBSON
AN HACHETTE UK COMPANY

This book contains the official SQA 2017 and 2018 Exams, and the 2017 Specimen Question Paper for National 5 History, with associated SQA-approved answers modified from the official marking instructions that accompany the paper.

In addition the book contains study skills advice. This has been specially commissioned by Hodder Gibson, and has been written by experienced senior teachers and examiners in line with the new National 5 syllabus and assessment outlines. This is not SQA material but has been devised to provide further guidance for National 5 examinations.

Hodder Gibson is grateful to the copyright holders, as credited on the final page of the Answer section, for permission to use their material. Every effort has been made to trace the copyright holders and to obtain their permission for the use of copyright material. Hodder Gibson will be happy to receive information allowing us to rectify any error or omission in future editions.

Hachette UK's policy is to use papers that are natural, renewable and recyclable products and made from wood grown in sustainable forests. The logging and manufacturing processes are expected to conform to the environmental regulations of the country of origin.

Orders: please contact Bookpoint Ltd, 130 Park Drive, Milton Park, Abingdon, Oxon OX14 4SE. Telephone: (44) 01235 827827. Fax: (44) 01235 400454. Lines are open 9.00–5.00, Monday to Saturday, with a 24-hour message answering service. Visit our website at www.hoddereducation.co.uk. Hodder Gibson can also be contacted directly at hoddergibson@hodder.co.uk

This collection first published in 2018 by
Hodder Gibson, an imprint of Hodder Education,
An Hachette UK Company
211 St Vincent Street
Glasgow G2 5QY

Typeset by Aptara, Inc.

Printed in the UK

A catalogue record for this title is available from the British Library

ISBN: 978-1-5104-5597-9

2 1

2019 2018

MIX
Paper from
responsible sources
FSC™ C104740
FSC
www.fsc.org

Introduction

National 5 History

This book of SQA past papers contains the question papers used in the 2017 and 2018 exams (with answers at the back of the book). A specimen question paper reflecting the requirements, content and duration of the revised exam in 2018 is also included. All of the question papers included in the book provide excellent, representative practice for the final exams.

Using these papers as part of your revision will help you to develop the vital skills and techniques needed for the exam, and will help you to identify any knowledge gaps you may have.

It is always a very good idea to refer to SQA's website for the most up-to-date course specification documents. Further details can be found in the National 5 History section on the SQA website: www.sqa.org.uk/sqa/47447.html.

The course requirements

The Assignment – how to be successful

The Assignment is an essay written under exam conditions and then sent to the SQA to be marked.

The Assignment counts for 20 marks out of a total of 100, so doing well in it can provide you with a very useful launch pad for future success.

How long does my essay have to be?

There are NO word limits in the Assignment – it is whatever you can write in one hour!

What should I write about?

First, it makes sense to choose a question from the topics you have been learning about. It is also sensible to choose a question from a past exam paper.

Second, your essay title should be based on a question that allows you to use your evidence to answer the question. You must avoid titles that are just statements such as "The Slave Trade" or "Appeasement". They do not allow you to use information to provide an overall answer to your title question.

Finally, try NOT to make up questions that are too complicated or that ask two questions within the same title.

What is the Resource Sheet?

Your Resource Sheet provides a framework and notes for your essay.

It shows the marker

- that you have researched, selected and organised your information
- that you have thought about your work and reached a decision about the question in your title
- which sources you have used and demonstrates how you have used them.

Your Resource Sheet MUST be sent to the SQA with your finished essay.

Your Resource Sheet should NOT be just a collection of facts, figures and quotes. It should outline the main parts of your essay and remind you what to write. Remember that this has a limit of 200 words.

The exam paper

The question paper is made up of three **sections**:

Section 1 – Historical Study: Scottish
Section 2 – Historical Study: British
Section 3 – Historical Study: European and World

In each **section** you will select **one** part to answer questions on:

Section 1 – Historical Study: Scottish

Part 1: The Wars of Independence, 1286–1328
Part 2: Mary Queen of Scots and the Scottish Reformation, 1542–1587
Part 3: The Treaty of Union, 1689–1715
Part 4: Migration and Empire, 1830–1939
Part 5: The Era of the Great War, 1900–1928

Section 2 – Historical Study: British

Part 1: The Creation of the Medieval Kingdoms, 1066–1406
Part 2: War of the Three Kingdoms, 1603–1651
Part 3: The Atlantic Slave Trade, 1770–1807
Part 4: Changing Britain, 1760–1914
Part 5: The Making of Modern Britain, 1880–1951

Section 3 – Historical Study: European and World

Answering the Exam Questions

The first rule is simple and is the most important thing that will get you marks:

Answer the question that you are asked, NOT what you would like it to ask.

The Exam paper has six types of questions.

TYPE 1 – the **"Describe"** question, worth **4 marks**.

In this type of question you must describe what happened by using four pieces of your own knowledge, known as **recall**. There is no source to help you with information so your answer will be based on your own recall.

TYPE 2 – the **"Explain"** question, worth **6 marks**.

To be successful with this type of question you must give six reasons why something happened. Once again, there is no source to help you. Use recall that is correct and accurate.

(**Note:** question types 3, 4 and 5 are very similar in nature, but remember to pay close attention to the wording of the question – and make sure you answer it!)

TYPE 3A – the **"To what extent ..."** question, worth **9 marks**.

To be successful with this type of question you must write a balanced answer. That means you must decide how important a particular factor was in explaining why something happened. Include at least five pieces of relevant information and give a short conclusion which sums up your answer to the question, including a reason to support your conclusion.

TYPE 3B – the **"How successful"** question, worth **9 marks**.

To be successful with this type of question you must write a balanced answer. That means you must decide

how successful a particular factor was in explaining why something happened. Include at least five pieces of relevant information and give a short conclusion which sums up your answer to the question, including a reason to support your conclusion.

TYPE 3C – the **"How important"** question, worth **9 marks**.

To be successful with this type of question you must write a balanced answer. That means you must decide how important a particular factor was in explaining why something happened. Include at least five pieces of relevant information and give a short conclusion which sums up your answer to the question, including a reason to support your conclusion.

TYPE 4 – the **"Evaluate the usefulness ..."** question, worth **5 marks**. This question will ask "Evaluate the usefulness of a source as evidence of ...."

Evaluate means **to judge** how good a source is as evidence for finding out about something. The short answer is that it will always be partly useful but it will never be entirely useful in giving all the information you need.

In this type of question it is never enough just to **describe** what is in a source. It might be helpful to base your answer around the following guide questions.

- **WHO** produced the source? Why is the AUTHORSHIP of the source relevant and therefore useful in assessing the value of a source?

- **WHAT** type of source is it? What is the purpose of the source?

- **WHEN** was the source produced and how might that help in the evaluation of the source?

- **WHAT'S NOT THERE?** What important information is missing from the source that makes you think the source was not as useful as it could be? You will also need to consider what *is* there when thinking about what is omitted.

TYPE 5 – the **"Compare"** question, worth **4 marks**.

You will always get two questions that ask you to compare two sources in your exam. To be successful with this type of question you must make clear connections between sources but do not just describe the two sources.

These questions are easy to spot because they are the only ones that will refer to TWO sources. For this type of question you must say whether you think the sources agree or not and then support your decision by making two comparisons using evidence from the sources.

TYPE 6 – the **"How fully ..."** question, worth **6 marks**.

To be successful with this type of question you must select information from the source which is relevant to the question – usually there will be three points of information in the source for you to use. Use recall that is accurate and relevant to make your answer more balanced. You will never get a source that gives the full story so it is up to you to say that the source PARTLY explains or describes something but there is more information needed to give the full story. That's where you show off your recalled extra knowledge.

Good luck!

Remember that the rewards for passing National 5 History are well worth it! Your pass will help you get the future you want for yourself. In the exam, be confident in your own ability. If you're not sure how to answer a question, trust your instincts and just give it a go anyway – keep calm and don't panic! GOOD LUCK!

Study Skills – what you need to know to pass exams!

General exam revision: 20 top tips

When preparing for exams, it is easy to feel unsure of where to start or how to revise. This guide to general exam revision provides a good starting place, and, as these are very general tips, they can be applied to all your exams.

1. Start revising in good time.

Don't leave revision until the last minute – this will make you panic and it will be difficult to learn. Make a revision timetable that counts down the weeks to go.

2. Work to a study plan.

Set up sessions of work spread through the weeks ahead. Make sure each session has a focus and a clear purpose. What will you study, when and why? Be realistic about what you can achieve in each session, and don't be afraid to adjust your plans as needed.

3. Make sure you know exactly when your exams are.

Get your exam dates from the SQA website and use the timetable builder tool to create your own exam schedule. You will also get a personalised timetable from your school, but this might not be until close to the exam period.

4. Make sure that you know the topics that make up each course.

Studying is easier if material is in manageable chunks – why not use the SQA topic headings or create your own from your class notes? Ask your teacher for help on this if you are not sure.

5. Break the chunks up into even smaller bits.

The small chunks should be easier to cope with. Remember that they fit together to make larger ideas. Even the process of chunking down will help!

6. Ask yourself these key questions for each course:

- Are all topics compulsory or are there choices?
- Which topics seem to come up time and time again?
- Which topics are your strongest and which are your weakest?

Use your answers to these questions to work out how much time you will need to spend revising each topic.

7. Make sure you know what to expect in the exam.

The subject-specific introduction to this book will help with this. Make sure you can answer these questions:

- How is the paper structured?
- How much time is there for each part of the exam?
- What types of question are involved? These will vary depending on the subject so read the subject-specific section carefully.

8. Past papers are a vital revision tool!

Use past papers to support your revision wherever possible. This book contains the answers and mark schemes too – refer to these carefully when checking your work. Using the mark scheme is useful; even if you don't manage to get all the marks available first time when you first practise, it helps you identify how to extend and develop your answers to get more marks next time – and of course, in the real exam.

9. Use study methods that work well for you.

People study and learn in different ways. Reading and looking at diagrams suits some students. Others prefer to listen and hear material – what about reading out loud or getting a friend or family member to do this for you? You could also record and play back material.

10. There are three tried and tested ways to make material stick in your long-term memory:

- Practising – e.g. rehearsal, repeating
- Organising – e.g. making drawings, lists, diagrams, tables, memory aids
- Elaborating – e.g. incorporating the material into a story or an imagined journey

11. Learn actively.

Most people prefer to learn actively – for example, making notes, highlighting, redrawing and redrafting, making up memory aids, or writing past paper answers. A good way to stay engaged and inspired is to mix and match these methods – find the combination that best suits you. This is likely to vary depending on the topic or subject.

12. Be an expert.

Be sure to have a few areas in which you feel you are an expert. This often works because at least some of them will come up, which can boost confidence.

13. Try some visual methods.

Use symbols, diagrams, charts, flashcards, post-it notes etc. Don't forget – the brain takes in chunked images more easily than loads of text.

14. Remember – practice makes perfect.

Work on difficult areas again and again. Look and read – then test yourself. You cannot do this too much.

15. Try past papers against the clock.

Practise writing answers in a set time. This is a good habit from the start but is especially important when you get closer to exam time.

16. Collaborate with friends.

Test each other and talk about the material – this can really help. Two brains are better than one! It is amazing how talking about a problem can help you solve it.

17. Know your weaknesses.

Ask your teacher for help to identify what you don't know. Try to do this as early as possible. If you are having trouble, it is probably with a difficult topic, so your teacher will already be aware of this – most students will find it tough.

18. Have your materials organised and ready.

Know what is needed for each exam:

- Do you need a calculator or a ruler?
- Should you have pencils as well as pens?
- Will you need water or paper tissues?

19. Make full use of school resources.

Find out what support is on offer:

- Are there study classes available?
- When is the library open?
- When is the best time to ask for extra help?
- Can you borrow textbooks, study guides, past papers, etc.?
- Is school open for Easter revision?

20. Keep fit and healthy!

Try to stick to a routine as much as possible, including with sleep. If you are tired, sluggish or dehydrated, it is difficult to see how concentration is even possible. Combine study with relaxation, drink plenty of water, eat sensibly, and get fresh air and exercise – all these things will help more than you could imagine. Good luck!

NATIONAL 5

2017

National Qualifications 2017

X737/75/11

History

TUESDAY, 9 MAY

1:00 PM – 2:45 PM

Total marks — 60

SECTION 1 — SCOTTISH CONTEXTS — 20 marks

Attempt ONE part.

SECTION 2 — BRITISH CONTEXTS — 20 marks

Attempt ONE part.

SECTION 3 — EUROPEAN AND WORLD CONTEXTS — 20 marks

Attempt ONE part.

Write your answers clearly in the answer booklet provided. In the answer booklet you must clearly identify the question number you are attempting.

Use **blue** or **black** ink.

Before leaving the examination room you must give your answer booklet to the Invigilator; if you do not, you may lose all the marks for this paper.

SECTION 1 — SCOTTISH CONTEXTS
PARTS

SECTION 2 — BRITISH CONTEXTS
PARTS

SECTION 3 — EUROPEAN AND WORLD CONTEXTS
PARTS

MARKS

SECTION 1 — SCOTTISH CONTEXTS — 20 marks

Part A — The Wars of Independence, 1286–1328

Answer the following **four** questions using recalled knowledge and information from the sources where appropriate.

1. Explain the reasons why many Scots were unhappy to accept the Maid of Norway as their queen.

5

Source A is from a textbook written by a modern historian in 2009.

Source A

> After the Scots asked for his help, King Edward I called for a parliament to be held in May 1291 to settle the future of the Scottish crown. The location he chose was Norham Castle on the English side of the River Tweed. He said that the proceedings would not start until the Guardians and the claimants to the throne had acknowledged his position as overlord of Scotland. The Scots were stunned.

2. Evaluate the usefulness of **Source A** as evidence of problems the Scots faced when judging the Great Cause.

5

(You may want to comment on what type of source it is, who wrote it, when they wrote it, why they wrote it, what they say and what has been missed out.)

3. Describe the actions Edward I took to assert his authority over Scotland in 1296.

5

Source B is about what happened to William Wallace after the Battle of Falkirk.

Source B

> For many years, little was known about Wallace's activities between his defeat at Falkirk and his death. He certainly left Scotland. Historians found a "safe conduct" which was given to Wallace in 1300 by the King of France. Wallace travelled to France as part of his campaign to free John Balliol. Wallace apparently planned to visit the Pope to get him on Balliol's side. His campaign failed however and Wallace was back in Scotland well before 1305 where he continued to fight against Edward's rule.

4. How fully does **Source B** describe what happened to William Wallace after the Battle of Falkirk? (Use the source and recall to reach a judgement.)

5

[Now go to SECTION 2 starting on *Page eight*]

MARKS

SECTION 1 — SCOTTISH CONTEXTS — 20 marks

Part B — Mary Queen of Scots, and the Scottish Reformation, 1542–1587

Answer the following **four** questions using recalled knowledge and information from the sources where appropriate.

5. Explain the reasons why Mary, Queen of Scots left Scotland for France in 1548.   **5**

6. Describe the events that led to Scotland becoming a Protestant country in 1560.   **5**

Source A is from a textbook written by a modern historian in 2013.

Source A

> On the night Darnley was killed, everyone in the palace was woken by a deafening noise that shook the entire area. Mary asked what cannon were firing as she thought they were under attack. But no one knew what was happening. All over town, people hurried outside to discover what dreadful disaster had occurred. Those who lived in Kirk o' Field stared in disbelief at the house where Darnley was staying, which was now rubble.

7. Evaluate the usefulness of **Source A** as evidence of the death of Darnley in 1567.   **5**

   (You may want to comment on what type of source it is, who wrote it, when they wrote it, why they wrote it, what they say and what has been missed out.)

Source B describes the events relating to the abdication of Mary, Queen of Scots in 1567.

Source B

> Many of the Scottish nobles were outraged that Mary had married the Earl of Bothwell. Some of the Protestant nobles decided to rebel against Mary and Bothwell, including her half-brother the Earl of Moray. The Protestant nobles raised an army and so did Mary and her new husband. The two armies met at Carberry on 15th June 1566. The nobles said they would withdraw if Mary gave up Bothwell but she refused. Bothwell escaped to Denmark and Mary surrendered to the Scottish nobles.

8. How fully does **Source B** describe the events relating to the abdication of Mary, Queen of Scots? (Use the source and recall to reach a judgement.)   **5**

[Now go to SECTION 2 starting on *Page eight*]

SECTION 1 — SCOTTISH CONTEXTS — 20 marks

Part C — The Treaty of Union, 1689–1715

Answer the following **four** questions using recalled knowledge and information from the sources where appropriate.

Source A describes the causes of tension between Scotland and England up to 1707.

Source A

> Relations between Scotland and England were very poor in these years. In England there was a lot of resentment at the level of support for the Jacobites in Scotland. The Scots were angry at not being consulted by the English over the Act of Settlement of 1701. As the smaller partner in the union of crowns the Scots felt their interests were ignored. The Scots were also annoyed that they had not been consulted over entry into the war of Spanish Succession.

9. How fully does **Source A** describe the causes of tension between Scotland and England up to 1707? (Use the source and recall to reach a judgement.)   **5**

10. Describe the arguments used by the opponents of Union in Scotland.   **5**

11. Explain the reasons why many Scots were in favour of Union with England.   **5**

Source B is from a textbook written by a modern historian in 1996.

Source B

> Many Kirk ministers were very concerned about the possibility of union. But when Parliament passed an Act for the Security of the Kirk many of them changed their tune. The Equivalent was the biggest incentive for many as it led to the sum of over three hundred thousand pounds sterling to be sent in cash to Scotland. English guarantees over the independence of the Scots legal system also soothed most fears within the Scottish legal profession.

12. Evaluate the usefulness of **Source B** as evidence of the reasons why the Scots Parliament passed the Treaty of Union.   **5**

    (You may want to comment on what type of source it is, who wrote it, when they wrote it, why they wrote it, what they say and what has been missed out.)

[Now go to SECTION 2 starting on *Page eight*]

MARKS

SECTION 1 — SCOTTISH CONTEXTS — 20 marks

Part D — Migration and Empire, 1830–1939

Answer the following **four** questions using recalled knowledge and information from the sources where appropriate.

13. Describe the impact the Empire had on Scotland between 1830 and 1939.   **5**

Source A describes the importance of the Catholic Church to Irish immigrants in Scotland.

Source A

> Seventy five percent of Irish immigrants to Scotland were Catholic and by 1902 there were 234 priests ministering to the Irish community in Glasgow. The church enabled them to keep their religious identity in Scotland through worshipping in their traditional way. It was the centre of social life for many Irish immigrants, offering a friendly environment where people could meet and be made welcome. The church also established youth groups. The church also attempted to tackle some of the issues Scottish society faced, such as the problem of poverty.

14. How fully does **Source A** describe the importance of the Catholic Church to Irish immigrants in Scotland? (Use the source and recall to reach a judgement.)   **5**

Source B is from a textbook written by a modern historian in 2007.

Source B

> Jewish immigrants usually lacked the experience needed to work in heavy industry but instead they supplied goods and services. The Census of 1891 showed that in the Gorbals in Glasgow, where most of the working class Jews lived, 195 Jews worked in the clothing industry. Another 116 made a living selling door to door or running small shops. Many had practised these occupations in their native country so they brought these skills with them.

15. Evaluate the usefulness of **Source B** as evidence of the work done by immigrants in Scotland.   **5**

    (You may want to comment on what type of source it is, who wrote it, when they wrote it, why they wrote it, what they say and what has been missed out.)

16. Explain the reasons why many Scots were attracted to start new lives overseas.   **5**

[Now go to SECTION 2 starting on *Page eight*]

MARKS

SECTION 1 — SCOTTISH CONTEXTS — 20 marks

Part E — The Era of the Great War, 1900—1928

Answer the following **four** questions using recalled knowledge and information from the sources where appropriate.

17. Describe the conditions Scottish soldiers faced in the trenches.   5

18. Explain the reasons why rationing was introduced during the Great War.   5

Source A describes the changing role of women during the Great War.

Source A

> The Great War was a crucial time for women. This is because it gave women an opportunity to prove themselves in a male-dominated society, doing more than cleaning the house and looking after children. With so many men going to war, there was a large gap in employment and women responded by replacing men in the workplace. The Women's Royal Air Force was created, where women worked on planes as mechanics. Some of the less well known roles of women in the war included selling war bonds.

19. How fully does **Source A** describe the changing role of women during the Great War? (Use the source and recall to reach a judgement.)   5

Source B is from a textbook written by a modern historian in 1989.

Source B

> The Great War had a considerable impact on Scotland's fishing industry. By 1919 the hundreds of fishing boats that had been working for the Royal Navy were free again to go fishing. It meant there were far more boats chasing the same amount of fish, and many boats could not make enough money to stay in business. On top of that it was far more difficult to sell fish. Before the war most of the herring that were caught were sold to Germany and Russia.

20. Evaluate the usefulness of **Source B** as evidence of the effects of the Great War on Scotland's industries.   5

(You may want to comment on what type of source it is, who wrote it, when they wrote it, why they wrote it, what they say and what has been missed out.)

[Now go to SECTION 2 starting on *Page eight*]

MARKS

SECTION 2 — BRITISH CONTEXTS — 20 marks

Part A — The Creation of the Medieval Kingdoms, 1066–1406

Answer the following **three** questions using recalled knowledge and information from the sources where appropriate.

21. Explain the reasons why David I was influenced by the Normans during his reign.

6

22. To what extent were illegal castles Henry II's greatest problem when he became king in 1154?

8

    (You must use recalled knowledge to present a **balanced assessment** of the influence of different factors and come to a **reasoned conclusion**.)

Source A is from a chronicle, written by a monk in 1381.

Source A

> King Richard II was eager to end the revolt and so agreed to meet the peasants. Whilst at the meeting, a fight broke out and the peasants' leader, Wat Tyler was killed. The peasants immediately took up their weapons to fight but the king rode toward them and persuaded them to put their weapons away. The king promised the peasants that they would be treated fairly and so they agreed to go home.

23. Evaluate the usefulness of **Source A** as evidence of the reasons for the failure of the Peasants' Revolt.

6

    (You may want to comment on what type of source it is, who wrote it, when they wrote it, why they wrote it, what they say and what has been missed out.)

[Now go to SECTION 3 starting on *Page fourteen*]

MARKS

SECTION 2 — BRITISH CONTEXTS — 20 marks

Part B — War of the Three Kingdoms, 1603–1651

Answer the following **three** questions using recalled knowledge and information from the sources where appropriate.

Source A is from the Protestation of 1621, a statement from the House of Commons of England.

Source A

> After many years of growing discontent we the members assemble in Parliament to make our protest formally. The privileges of Parliament are our ancient birth right. Matters concerning the king, state, defence, the church and the making of laws are for debating in Parliament only. And that, if any of its members are questioned for anything said or done in Parliament, the same is to be applied to the king.

24. Evaluate the usefulness of **Source A** as evidence of the arguments between Parliament and King James VI and I.   6

    (You may want to comment on what type of source it is, who wrote it, when they wrote it, why they wrote it, what they say and what has been missed out.)

25. Explain the reasons why Charles I was unpopular in Scotland.   6

26. To what extent were financial disputes between Charles I and Parliament the main reason for the outbreak of the Civil War?   8

    (You must use recalled knowledge to present a **balanced assessment** of the influence of different factors and come to a **reasoned conclusion**.)

[Now go to SECTION 3 starting on *Page fourteen*]

MARKS

SECTION 2 — BRITISH CONTEXTS — 20 marks

Part C — The Atlantic Slave Trade, 1770–1807

Answer the following **three** questions using recalled knowledge and information from the sources where appropriate.

27. To what extent was increased employment the main benefit the slave trade brought to Britain?

    (You must use recalled knowledge to present a **balanced assessment** of the influence of different factors and come to a **reasoned conclusion.**)

    8

28. Explain the reasons why the slave trade had a negative impact on the Caribbean islands.

    6

Source A is from an Abolitionist speech made by William Wilberforce to the House of Commons on the 12th May 1789.

Source A

> Let anyone imagine to himself 600 of these unfortunates chained two and two. The right ankle of one is connected with the left ankle of another by a small iron fetter. The slaves are so miserable at leaving their country, that they set sail at night, unaware of their departure. For exercise, these miserable people, loaded down by chains and suffering from disease, are forced to dance by the terror of the whip.

29. Evaluate the usefulness of **Source A** as evidence used by the abolitionists to argue against the slave trade.

    6

    (You may want to comment on what type of source it is, who wrote it, when they wrote it, why they wrote it, what they say and what has been missed out.)

[Now go to SECTION 3 starting on *Page fourteen*]

MARKS

SECTION 2 — BRITISH CONTEXTS — 20 marks

Part D — Changing Britain, 1760–1914

Answer the following **three** questions using recalled knowledge and information from the sources where appropriate.

30. To what extent was a lack of clean water the main reason for poor health in towns during the nineteenth century?   8

    (You must use recalled knowledge to present a **balanced assessment** of the influence of different factors and come to a **reasoned conclusion.**)

Source A is an extract from the Factory Act passed by the government in 1833.

Source A

> - No children under the age of 9 are permitted to work in textile mills
> - Children aged 9–13 must not work more than 8 hours each day
> - Children aged 14–18 must not work more than 12 hours each day
> - Children under 18 must not work at night
> - Government factory inspectors will be given the power to demand entry to textile mills and enforce these rules

31. Evaluate the usefulness of **Source A** as evidence of the ways working conditions in factories were improved by 1900.   6

    (You may want to comment on what type of source it is, who wrote it, when they wrote it, why they wrote it, what they say and what has been missed out.)

32. Explain the reasons why the Chartists failed to achieve their aims.   6

[Now go to SECTION 3 starting on *Page fourteen*]

MARKS

SECTION 2 — BRITISH CONTEXTS — 20 marks

Part E — The Making of Modern Britain, 1880–1951

Answer the following **three** questions using recalled knowledge and information from the sources where appropriate.

33. To what extent were the reports of Booth and Rowntree the main reason for changing attitudes to poverty around 1900?

    (You must use recalled knowledge to present a **balanced assessment** of the influence of different factors and come to a **reasoned conclusion**.)

    8

34. Explain the reasons why the Liberal Reforms of 1906–1914 improved the lives of some British people.

    6

Source A is a government advertisement published in May 1948.

Source A

> YOUR NEW
> NATIONAL HEALTH SERVICE
>
> On 5th July the new National Health Service starts for the benefit of the public all over Britain.
>
> Anyone can use it — men, women and children. There are no age limits. You can use any part of it, or all of it, as you wish. Your right to use the National Health Service does not depend upon any weekly payments.
>
> Choose your doctor now.

35. Evaluate the usefulness of **Source A** as evidence of the introduction of the National Health Service in 1948.

    (You may want to comment on what type of source it is, who wrote it, when they wrote it, why they wrote it, what they say and what has been missed out.)

    6

[Now go to SECTION 3 starting on *Page fourteen*]

[BLANK PAGE]

DO NOT WRITE ON THIS PAGE

MARKS

SECTION 3 — EUROPEAN AND WORLD CONTEXTS — 20 marks

Part A — The Cross and the Crescent: the Crusades, 1071—1192

Answer the following **four** questions using recalled knowledge and information from the sources where appropriate.

Sources **A** and **B** are about Pope Urban II's speech in 1095.

Source A

> In 1095, Pope Urban II held a meeting in France. At the meeting, the Pope said that Jerusalem must be recaptured and protection given to Christian churches and shrines there. The Pope warned that every Christian in the west must fight or the Muslims could advance into Europe. He appealed to the knights to stop their violent behaviour towards each other and use their military skills against God's enemy in the east.

Source B

> Pope Urban II's speech at Clermont shocked all those who heard it. The Pope said a Christian army must be called to stop the Muslims before they captured every city they attacked. Pope Urban told the knights of Europe to stop fighting amongst each other and unite against the infidel. The Pope said Jerusalem was the most important city in the world and that it must be taken back from the Muslims.

36. Compare the views of **Sources A** and **B** about Pope Urban II's call for the First Crusade in 1095. (Compare the sources overall and/or in detail.)   4

MARKS

Source C explains why Jerusalem was difficult to capture in 1099.

Source C

> The Crusaders' joy at reaching Jerusalem did not last long. The Muslims were well prepared for an attack and had strengthened the wall around the city. As well as this, the Muslims had collected the harvest early and had enough food to last for several months. The Crusaders attacked Jerusalem but the Muslims fought back and forced them to retreat. The Crusaders did not have scaling ladders or siege machines and so could not launch another attack until supplies arrived from Europe.

37. How fully does **Source C** explain the reasons why Jerusalem was difficult to capture in 1099? (Use the source and recall to reach a judgement.)   6

38. Explain the reasons why the Crusaders had problems after the First Crusade.   5

39. Describe the Battle of Arsuf in 1191.   5

MARKS

SECTION 3 — EUROPEAN AND WORLD CONTEXTS — 20 marks

Part B — "Tea and Freedom": the American Revolution, 1774–83

Answer the following **four** questions using recalled knowledge and information from the sources where appropriate.

40. Explain the reasons why some British people sympathised with America during the American Revolution.

5

Sources A and **B** are about the Continental Army.

Source A

> The Continental Army was led by George Washington, who was an experienced soldier. The troops themselves were usually inexperienced in battle and for many it was their first time fighting. Many soldiers left to return home, leaving the army without enough men. The Continental Army always lacked sufficient cavalry and artillery. Washington was always short of money to buy much needed supplies or to pay his soldiers.

Source B

> The army needed troops even more than fortifications, and Washington appealed to Congress to provide them. Many of the soldiers needed practice with their weapons, so early in July he ordered that each man was to fire two rounds — hardly extensive training but all that supplies permitted. The Continental Army was always short of ammunition. Gunpowder was always in short supply but houses were stripped of lead for bullets.

41. Compare the views of **Sources A** and **B** about the capabilities of the Continental Army. (Compare the sources overall and/or in detail.)

4

42. Describe the events of the British defeat at Saratoga.

5

MARKS

Source C is about help given to the colonists after the British defeat at Saratoga.

Source C

> After the British defeat at Saratoga, many in Europe were keen to take advantage of British weakness. France, in particular, wanted revenge for the loss of her colonies. In order to help the colonists France offered financial support. France also gave military assistance in the form of soldiers and gunpowder to put more pressure on Britain. Spain saw an opportunity to try to retake Gibraltar to distract Britain. Finally, France and Spain joined forces and threatened to invade Britain in 1779.

43. How fully does **Source C** explain the reasons why help was given to the colonists in their war against Britain? (Use the source and recall to reach a judgement.)   6

SECTION 3 — EUROPEAN AND WORLD CONTEXTS — 20 marks

Part C — USA, 1850–1880

Answer the following **four** questions using recalled knowledge and information from the sources where appropriate.

Sources A and **B** are about the treatment of slaves on Southern Plantations.

Source A

> The cotton planter gave me meat and bread with the other slaves, which was not half enough for me to live upon. He flogged me nearly every day. He set me to work without any shirt in the cotton field, in a very hot sun. When a slave runs away, the master always adopts a more strict system of flogging. When I was caught, I got a severe flogging of one hundred lashes each time.

Source B

> The usual method of punishing slaves was using a system of floggings, beatings and in some severe cases, hanging. As well as the beatings, slaves were given the absolute minimum amount of food to survive. Some slaves were punished by being tied to trees on the plantation, often in the burning heat of the sun. However, some slaves were treated better on plantations by their masters.

44. Compare the views of **Sources A** and **B** about the treatment of slaves on Southern Plantations. (Compare the sources overall and/or in detail.)   **4**

MARKS

Source C is about the reasons for Southern secession in 1861.

Source C

> Why did the Confederate states secede? Some writers argued they seceded to escape the high taxes that they thought would come with a Republican election victory. The main reason for secession was that the Southerners had come to feel themselves a separate community. They had come more and more to dislike and despise, to hate and fear, their northern neighbours. There was also a feeling in the South that there would be more advantages to secession than staying in the union.

45. How fully does **Source C** explain the reasons for Southern secession in 1861? (Use the source and recall to reach a judgement.)   **6**

46. Describe the activities of the Freedmen's Bureau.   **5**

47. Explain the reasons why there was conflict between white settlers and Native Americans.   **5**

MARKS

SECTION 3 — EUROPEAN AND WORLD CONTEXTS — 20 marks

Part D — Hitler and Nazi Germany, 1919—1939

Answer the following **four** questions using recalled knowledge and information from the sources where appropriate.

48. Describe the appeal of Adolf Hitler to many Germans between 1929 and 1933.

5

Sources A and **B** are about the Night of the Long Knives in 1934.

Source A

> On the night of 29—30 June, units of the SS arrested the leaders of the SA as well as political opponents. The arrests carried on for two more nights. In total 77 men were executed on charges of treason. Röhm was shot and others were beaten to death. The SA was placed under the command of the army. Hitler received an oath of allegiance from all those who served in the army.

Source B

> Members of the SS stormed a hotel where the SA had gathered, pulled Röhm and his henchmen from their beds and had them arrested. Some were promptly executed. Röhm was taken to a Munich prison, along with other SA leaders, and there awaited his fate. He was given a chance to shoot himself, but did not take it. An SS officer entered his cell and shot Röhm at point blank range.

49. Compare the views of **Sources A** and **B** about the events of the Night of the Long Knives. (Compare the sources overall and/or in detail.)

4

50. Explain the reasons why there was a lack of effective opposition in Nazi Germany between 1933 and 1939.

5

MARKS

Source C is about Nazi education policies.

Source C

> Education played a very important part in Nazi Germany. Schools tried to develop a loyal following for Hitler. Geography taught pupils about the land that Germany lost in 1919 to make them understand the need for more living space. The science curriculum was changed so shooting had to be studied as well as bridge building and the impact of poisonous gasses. Girls had a different curriculum as they studied domestic science and racial studies. Both of these were to prepare a young girl to be the perfect wife and mother.

51. How fully does **Source C** explain Nazi education policies? (Use the source and recall to reach a judgement.)   **6**

MARKS

SECTION 3 — EUROPEAN AND WORLD CONTEXTS — 20 marks

Part E — Red Flag: Lenin and the Russian Revolution, 1894–1921

Answer the following **four** questions using recalled knowledge and information from the sources where appropriate.

52. Describe the events of Bloody Sunday in January 1905.   **5**

Source A is about Stolypin's reforms.

Source A

> Stolypin's government did gradually bring about a number of economic and social reforms in Russia. He ordered the Zemstvos to carry out a huge expansion of health services to the provinces. In 1912 a system of health insurance was set up for workers. Compulsory universal education within ten years became a declared aim. By 1914 the government had established 50,000 additional primary schools, administered and funded by the Zemstvos. There was also an expansion of secondary and higher educational institutions.

53. How fully does **Source A** explain the impact of Stolypin's reforms? (Use the source and recall to reach a judgement.)   **6**

54. Explain the reasons why Tsar Nicholas II abdicated in March 1917.   **5**

MARKS

Sources B and **C** are about the Russian Civil War.

Source B

> The territory held by the Bolsheviks was a great advantage to them — their control of central areas meant shorter lines of supply and communication. However the White forces stretched right out along the edges of Russia — in Siberia, the western borderlands and along the Volga in the South. The Bolsheviks were better prepared to mobilise their troops and acquire resources. In contrast the Whites were disorganised in battle. Eventually the Bolsheviks were victorious.

Source C

> During the Civil War, Russian people suffered greatly, families were torn apart and there were huge numbers of casualties. The Bolsheviks won the Civil War largely because they were well prepared and disciplined. In comparison the Whites were disorganised, lacking in the ability to properly mobilise and lead their troops. The Bolsheviks held better territory and had access to railways for their communication and supply lines.

55. Compare the views of **Sources B** and **C** about the reasons why the Bolsheviks won the Civil War. (Compare the sources overall and/or in detail.)   4

MARKS

SECTION 3 — EUROPEAN AND WORLD CONTEXTS — 20 marks

Part F — Mussolini and Fascist Italy, 1919–1939

Answer the following **four** questions using recalled knowledge and information from the sources where appropriate.

56. Describe Mussolini's economic policies up to 1939.   5

Sources **A** and **B** are about Fascist propaganda.

Source A

> Italian Fascists relied a great deal on propaganda to maintain support. Mussolini was portrayed as athletic, strong and courageous and most Italians believed this. The Fascist regime was very successful in controlling the output of radio and cinema. One admirer of him was the British Foreign Secretary, Austen Chamberlain, who was widely reported as saying that Mussolini was "a wonderful man working for the greatness of his country".

Source B

> Fascist propaganda made many claims about Mussolini. Few Italians believed the ridiculous claims that Mussolini was a brilliant athlete and musician. While the Fascist regime did its best to control the media, in reality Italians watched American films which certainly did not support Fascist ideas. Foreigners could see through the Fascist's crude propaganda attempts and in the European press Mussolini was often presented as a figure of fun.

57. Compare the views of **Sources A** and **B** on the effectiveness of Fascist propaganda. (Compare the sources overall and/or in detail.)   4

MARKS

Source C is from a history textbook.

Source C

> Benito Mussolini's Fascist regime came to power in Italy in 1922. He quickly set about removing democratic rights and freedoms. It took Mussolini some time to fully develop his foreign policy. His main aim was to make Italy respected as a world power. To achieve this he wanted to build up the Italian armed forces to make Italy feared. Mussolini was determined that one day Italy would be the dominant power in the Mediterranean. He was particularly keen to extend Italian influence in the countries of the Balkans.

58. How fully does **Source C** explain the aims of Fascist foreign policy up to 1939? (Use the source and recall to reach a judgement.)   6

59. Explain the reasons why opposition never posed a serious threat to the Fascist state.   5

MARKS

SECTION 3 — EUROPEAN AND WORLD CONTEXTS — 20 marks

Part G — Free at Last? Civil Rights in the USA, 1918—1968

Answer the following **four** questions using recalled knowledge and information from the sources where appropriate.

Sources A and **B** describe the activities of the Ku Klux Klan.

Source A

> Dressed in their white hoods the Klan were very frightening — they looked like ghosts! They sneaked around at night when us blacks were in our beds. My father told me that I should avoid them at all costs. He said the Klansmen tied up the blacks that they caught and beat them. They left their victims with their hands tied in the air and the blood streaming out of their wounds.

Source B

> The Klan came to my house about ten o'clock. I was in bed at that time fast asleep. I jumped up, stepped to the door and looked out. As far as I could see they were all disguised, with white sheets pulled over their heads. The Klansmen came in and when I spoke they grabbed me. They took me out into the yard and struck me three times over the head with a pistol.

60. Compare the views of **Sources A** and **B** about the activities of the Ku Klux Klan. (Compare the sources overall and/or in detail.)   **4**

MARKS

Source C is about the growth of the civil rights movement after 1945.

Source C

> Soldiers in World War II experienced life in a more equal society when abroad and were determined to fight against discrimination when they returned. In the years that followed the war the campaign to gain equality for black Americans grew. Black Americans were better educated than previous generations and therefore better equipped to challenge discrimination. The success of the Montgomery Bus Boycott encouraged others to become involved in the fight for civil rights. The leadership of civil rights campaigner Martin Luther King inspired others to join the civil rights campaign.

61. How fully does **Source C** explain the reasons why there was a growth in the civil rights movement after 1945? (Use the source and recall to reach a judgement.)   6

62. Describe the events at Central High School in Little Rock, Arkansas in 1957.   5

63. Explain the reasons why race riots broke out in the ghettos of Northern cities in the 1960s.   5

MARKS

SECTION 3 — EUROPEAN AND WORLD CONTEXTS — 20 marks

Part H — Appeasement and the Road to War, 1918–1939

Answer the following **four** questions using recalled knowledge and information from the sources where appropriate.

64. Explain the reasons why France and Britain did not take military action against German rearmament up to 1938.   **5**

65. Describe the events leading to Germany's Anschluss with Austria in 1938.   **5**

Source A is about Neville Chamberlain and the policy of appeasement.

Source A

> In March 1939, Chamberlain abandoned appeasement and promised to defend Poland if the Nazis invaded. The main reason was the invasion of Czechoslovakia which proved that Hitler was a liar and that he did not just want land where Germans lived. In addition, many were influenced by Churchill's speeches which meant appeasement was losing the support of the British people. Kristallnacht proved that the Nazi regime was evil and ought to be resisted. Rearmament had strengthened Britain's armed forces too and gave Chamberlain the confidence to tackle Nazi aggression.

66. How fully does **Source A** explain the reasons why Chamberlain abandoned the policy of Appeasement? (Use the source and recall to reach a judgement.)   **6**

MARKS

Sources B and **C** are about the reasons why Stalin signed the Nazi-Soviet Non-Aggression Pact in 1939.

Source B

> The agreement shocked the world as each nation had been the sworn enemy of the other. By signing the pact the Soviet Union gained time to prepare its defences against a future German attack. Stalin also gained the opportunity to take back lands Russia lost in the aftermath of the First World War. The half-hearted attempt of the British to come to an agreement with the Soviet Union was another factor in Stalin's decision.

Source C

> The British were unenthusiastic about a possible Anglo-Soviet agreement, and this encouraged Stalin to sign the Nazi-Soviet Pact. The pact gave the Soviet Union time to prepare for eventual German invasion. The chance to extend Soviet control over lands from which Russia had been excluded since the end of the First World War was another factor. The Nazi-Soviet Pact was therefore a logical result of Stalin protecting his country's interests.

67. Compare the views of **Sources B** and **C** on the reasons why Stalin signed the Nazi-Soviet Non-Aggression Pact in 1939. (Compare the sources overall and/or in detail.)   4

MARKS

SECTION 3 — EUROPEAN AND WORLD CONTEXTS — 20 marks

Part I — World War II, 1939–1945

Answer the following **four** questions using recalled knowledge and information from the sources where appropriate.

Source A is about why Japan attacked Pearl Harbour in December 1941.

Source A

> In 1937 America restricted oil supplies to Japan. Faced with severe shortages of oil, Japan became increasingly angry with America. The Japanese were also determined to push American influence out of the Pacific and planned an attack. The attack was also intended to damage US military strength. A surprise attack took place on the US Pacific fleet at Pearl Harbour on 7 December 1941. Japan was confident of defeating the US because they had rehearsed the attack for a year until they achieved an 80% hit rate.

68. How fully does **Source A** explain why Japan attacked Pearl Harbour in December 1941? (Use the source and recall to reach a judgement.)   6

69. Describe the treatment of Jews and other minorities in Nazi occupied Europe.   5

MARKS

Sources **B** and **C** are about collaboration in Nazi occupied Europe.

Source B

> People collaborated with the Nazis in occupied Europe in many different ways. In many cases it was simply a way to survive such as doing the laundry of German soldiers to earn extra food for your family. Others were more actively involved by informing the Germans of "enemies" within the community. Then there were those who supported the Nazi regime such as the local civilians and police who were recruited into the SS death squads.

Source C

> Collaboration on a large scale occurred in Vichy France where the authorities supplied information to help the Nazis round up "undesirables". Other examples of collaboration involved civilians working for the Germans in order to earn extra money or gain extra food rations. The most infamous example of collaboration was at Babi Yar near Kiev. Over 33,000 Jews were slaughtered there in September 1941 by Nazi SS forces, assisted by the Ukrainian police.

70. Compare the views of **Sources B** and **C** about collaboration in Nazi occupied Europe. (Compare the sources overall and/or in detail.)   4

71. Explain the reasons why the Normandy landings were successful.   5

MARKS

SECTION 3 — EUROPEAN AND WORLD CONTEXTS — 20 marks

Part J — The Cold War, 1945–1989

Answer the following **four** questions using recalled knowledge and information from the sources where appropriate.

72. Describe the attitude of Hungarians to the Soviet Union by 1956.

5

73. Explain the reasons why the Berlin Wall was built.

5

Source A is about American opposition to the war in Vietnam.

Source A

> There were many in the United States who opposed joining the war in Vietnam from the beginning. They felt it was not America's job to fight a war thousands of miles from home. Many remembered the Second World War and did not want a repeat of the casualties suffered in this conflict. By 1967, as many as 160 American soldiers were being killed every week. Some Americans opposed the conflict as they felt its huge cost meant the government was unable to spend money on health and housing.

74. How fully does **Source A** explain why many Americans opposed the war in Vietnam? (Use the source and recall to reach a judgement.)

6

MARKS

Sources **B** and **C** are about the policy of Glasnost.

Source B

> At only 54 years of age, Mikhail Gorbachev, was a breath of fresh air for the Soviet Union. Gorbachev was most famous for his policies of Glasnost and Perestroika. His intention was to give a boost to the Soviet economy, which was performing badly. The aim of Glasnost was to allow open discussion of social and economic issues. Gorbachev hoped this would strengthen the Communist system.

Source C

> Mikhail Gorbachev, who was appointed in 1985, was the last General Secretary of the Soviet Union. Gorbachev was responsible for the policy of Glasnost. Gorbachev remained a committed Communist and hoped that Glasnost would increase support for the system. He wanted to find new solutions to problems by allowing people to express their views freely. Ultimately, the hope was that Glasnost could help strengthen the Soviet economy.

75. Compare the views of **Sources B** and **C** on the aims of the policy of Glasnost. (Compare the sources overall and/or in detail.)   4

[END OF QUESTION PAPER]

[BLANK PAGE]

DO NOT WRITE ON THIS PAGE

NATIONAL 5

2017 Specimen
Question Paper

National Qualifications
SPECIMEN ONLY

S837/75/11

History

Date — Not applicable

Duration — 2 hours 20 minutes

Total marks — 80

SECTION 1 — SCOTTISH CONTEXTS — 25 marks

Attempt ONE part.

SECTION 2 — BRITISH CONTEXTS — 26 marks

Attempt ONE part.

SECTION 3 — EUROPEAN AND WORLD CONTEXTS — 29 marks

Attempt ONE part.

Write your answers clearly in the answer booklet provided. In the answer booklet you must clearly identify the question number you are attempting.

Use **blue** or **black** ink.

Before leaving the examination room you must give your answer booklet to the Invigilator; if you do not, you may lose all the marks for this paper.

SECTION 1 — SCOTTISH CONTEXTS

PARTS

SECTION 2 — BRITISH CONTEXTS

PARTS

SECTION 3 — EUROPEAN AND WORLD CONTEXTS

PARTS

[BLANK PAGE]

DO NOT WRITE ON THIS PAGE

MARKS

SECTION 1 — SCOTTISH CONTEXTS — 25 marks

Part A — The Wars of Independence, 1286–1328

Answer the following **five** questions using recalled knowledge and information from the sources where appropriate.

Source A is from a textbook written by a modern historian in 2011.

Source A

> John Balliol claimed the strongest right to be King of Scots. Balliol argued this because he was descended from the eldest daughter in the family of David, Earl of Huntingdon, brother of King William the Lion. According to Balliol it didn't matter that he was a generation younger than Bruce because the feudal law of primogeniture always supported the eldest line of a family. Robert Bruce claimed he should be the next King. Bruce argued the feudal law of primogeniture did not apply to kingdoms.

1. Evaluate the usefulness of **Source A** as evidence of the succession problem following the death of the Maid of Norway.   **5**

   (You may want to comment on what type of source it is, who wrote it, when they wrote it, why they wrote it, what they say and what has been missed out.)

2. Explain the reasons why John Balliol was a failure as King of Scots.   **6**

3. Describe the actions of William Wallace during the Wars of Independence.   **4**

Source B is about the Battle of Bannockburn.

Source B

> Bruce's careful preparations for battle were ruined when Edward II moved his army to attack from the east and not from the south. However, this gave the much larger English army no room to move because they were surrounded by marshes and streams. Bruce decided to take advantage of this mistake and to attack them. The English were so jammed together and so tangled up that their leaders struggled to organise any defence. They lost all confidence in Edward II for leading them into this trap.

4. How fully does **Source B** explain why the Scots won the Battle of Bannockburn? (Use the source and recall to reach a judgement.)   **6**

MARKS

Sources **C** and **D** are about support for Robert Bruce in 1320.

Source C

> In the Declaration of Arbroath, Scottish nobles explained to the Pope why all the Scots thought Robert Bruce was their rightful king. They argued Bruce had royal blood. His actions had won him the support of the Scottish people. In addition, they argued that they wanted him as king because, by saving Scotland from being taken over by England, he proved that he was worthy of being King of Scotland.

Source D

> Even while the Declaration of Arbroath was being written, some Scottish nobles were plotting against Robert Bruce. They felt he was a ruthless thug who had murdered his main rival in a church and so he was unworthy of being King of Scots. Other Scottish nobles claimed their blood ties meant they were more closely related to the Scottish royal family than Robert Bruce. These disagreements caused problems in Scotland.

5. Compare the views of **Sources C** and **D** about support for Robert Bruce in 1320. (Compare the sources overall and/or in detail.)   4

[Now go to SECTION 2 starting on *Page fourteen*]

MARKS

SECTION 1 — SCOTTISH CONTEXTS — 25 marks

Part B — Mary Queen of Scots, and the Scottish Reformation, 1542—1587

Answer the following **five** questions using recalled knowledge and information from the sources where appropriate.

6. Describe the events of the "Rough Wooing".   4

Source A is about why Protestantism spread in Scotland in the 1540s and 1550s.

Source A

> In Germany, the ideas of Martin Luther had started the Reformation movement. Some Scots began to criticise the teachings of the Catholic Church. During the Rough Wooing, English invaders had further encouraged this. This was done by the distribution of English translations of the Bible which helped the growth of Protestantism in Scotland. The Catholic Church continued to use the Latin Bible. Religious pamphlets, smuggled into Scotland from Europe, also spread Protestant ideas. The "Good and Godly Ballads" made these ideas popular, encouraging the spread of Protestantism in Scotland.

7. How fully does **Source A** explain why Protestantism spread in Scotland in the 1540s and 1550s? (Use the source and recall to reach a judgement.)   6

Sources B and **C** are about how well Mary, Queen of Scots ruled Scotland.

Source B

> Mary returned to Scotland as Queen in 1561. Mary was a Roman Catholic who believed that she should rule England instead of her Protestant cousin, Elizabeth. She neglected the government of Scotland. Mary was happy to leave the running of the country to a group of Protestant nobles. Despite the fact that Mary was a Catholic, she showed little interest in the issue of religion in Scotland.

MARKS

Source C

> To begin with Mary had been a successful ruler in Scotland. That was until she allowed her heart to rule her head by marrying her English born first cousin, Lord Darnley. She had defeated the Protestant nobles who challenged her authority and had established a successful government under her half-brother Moray. Mary was a very devout Catholic, but she decided that she would tolerate Scotland's new Protestant church.

8. Compare the views of **Sources B** and **C** about how well Mary, Queen of Scots ruled Scotland. (Compare the sources overall and/or in detail.)   **4**

Source D is from a textbook written by a modern historian in 2007.

Source D

> Some Scots simply did not want to be ruled by a woman, as they believed that only men should be in positions of power. John Knox wrote a book against women in power. Others were suspicious of Mary's religion, as she was a Catholic, and so they also opposed her. At that time in Europe, rulers had the power to decide their country's religion. Eventually, Mary's half-brother, the Earl of Moray, forced her into giving up her power in favour of her infant son.

9. Evaluate the usefulness of **Source D** as evidence of why Mary, Queen of Scots, lost power over Scotland in 1567.   **5**

   (You may want to comment on what type of source it is, who wrote it, when they wrote it, why they wrote it, what they say and what has been missed out.)

10. Explain the reasons why Mary Queen of Scots was executed in 1587.   **6**

[Now go to SECTION 2 starting on *Page fourteen*]

MARKS

SECTION 1 — SCOTTISH CONTEXTS — 25 marks

Part C — The Treaty of Union, 1689–1715

Answer the following **five** questions using recalled knowledge and information from the sources where appropriate.

11. Explain the reasons why relations between Scotland and England got worse between 1689 and 1707.

6

Sources A and **B** are about Scottish attitudes to a possible Union of the Parliaments.

Source A

> The issue of a Union of Parliaments between Scotland and England stirred up heated debate. Supporters of the Union saw it as a way of settling the Protestant Succession and closing the door to the Jacobite claimant to the throne. They weren't worried about wanting a closer relationship with England. A Union would end the danger of future wars between Scotland and England. Other Scots saw the economic benefits of gaining access to England's colonies.

Source B

> Many Scots disliked the idea of entering a Union with "the Auld Enemy". This resulted from centuries of bad feeling between the two countries. They feared that Scotland's economy would be ruined by cheap goods flooding up from England. The Jacobites encouraged opposition to the Union in the hope of restoring their king to his throne. They organised petitions against the Union and burned copies of the Treaty to stir up opposition to the Union.

12. Compare the views of **Sources A** and **B** about Scottish attitudes to a possible Union of the Parliaments. (Compare the sources overall and/or in detail.)

4

13. Describe the unrest in Edinburgh and other parts of Scotland to the proposed Treaty of Union.

4

MARKS

Source C is about why the opponents of the Treaty of Union were unable to stop it being passed.

Source C

> At first, there was widespread public opposition in Scotland to the Union. Opposition to it in Parliament was led by the Duke of Hamilton who could have become king if Scotland and England separated. Hamilton however was indecisive and unreliable. One night, without any warning, he suddenly changed sides. There was widespread belief that, like many, Hamilton had been bribed to support the Union. Hamilton's activities kept the opponents of the Union disorganised. Opponents of the Union were unable to overcome the ruthless methods used by supporters of the Union.

14. How fully does **Source C** explain why opponents of the Treaty of Union were unable to stop it being passed? (Use the source and recall to reach a judgement.)

6

Source D is from a textbook written by a modern historian in 1994.

Source D

> For most people in Scotland after the Union, life in most matters was unchanged. Some however were soon disappointed. The Church of Scotland was outraged when patronage was reintroduced into the church and Episcopalians were to be tolerated. Within a few years other significant changes were made. Many Scots thought these changes also broke the terms of the Treaty of Union. They were unhappy with the introduction of the Malt Tax as this could have had serious consequences.

15. Evaluate the usefulness of **Source D** as evidence of reasons for Scottish disappointment with the Union.

5

(You may want to comment on what type of source it is, who wrote it, when they wrote it, why they wrote it, what they say and what has been missed out.)

[Now go to SECTION 2 starting on *Page fourteen*]

MARKS

SECTION 1 — SCOTTISH CONTEXTS — 25 marks

Part D — Migration and Empire, 1830–1939

Answer the following **five** questions using recalled knowledge and information from the sources where appropriate.

Source A is about why many Irish people moved to Scotland.

Source A

> Among those who moved to Scotland, the largest group of immigrants came from Ireland. The Irish potato famine of the mid-1840s led to a sharp increase in numbers moving to Scotland. Others left for Scotland as some landlords evicted those who could not pay their rent. Transport costs were cheap making it easy to travel to Scotland. The Irish were attracted to the west of Scotland as wages were higher than those in Ireland. However, by the end of the 19th century, it wasn't just Irish who were attracted to Scotland.

16. How fully does **Source A** explain why many Irish people moved to Scotland between 1830 and 1939? (Use the source and recall to reach a judgement.)   **6**

17. Describe how Scotland benefited from the Empire between 1830 and 1939.   **4**

Sources B and **C** are about Scottish attitudes to Irish immigration.

Source B

> By the mid-nineteenth century many Irish immigrants had settled in the Glasgow area. Newspapers were eager to describe the violent activities of groups of Irish men. They were also blamed for being dirty and responsible for spreading disease. Some Irish men and women came to Scotland and worked for part of the year and then returned home. Other Irish however were accused of being too lazy to work and for relying on charity.

MARKS

Source C

> In the nineteenth century many Irish came to Scotland to escape poverty back home. When they first came over they were, in general, very clean. The Irish in Paisley are almost all poor and I can only remember one Irish shopkeeper. But when more labourers are needed, the Irish are always ready to work hard for their pay. Although they live in the worst housing, the Irish are of good character and behave very well.

18. Compare the views of **Sources B** and **C** about Scottish attitudes to Irish immigration. (Compare the sources overall and/or in detail.)   4

Source D is from a textbook written by a modern historian in 1992.

Source D

> Scots were typical of emigrants throughout history in that they moved abroad for economic reasons. Many Scots had farms which they could sell to raise funds for emigration. Countries such as Canada were keen to attract Scots. Once settled, many emigrants were happy to help pay for relatives to come and join them. The journey became much easier and cheaper with the development of faster and more efficient steam ships. Only about a quarter of Scots returned home; most made a better living abroad.

19. Evaluate the usefulness of **Source D** as evidence of why many Scots were able to emigrate between 1830 and 1939.   5

    (You may want to comment on what type of source it is, who wrote it, when they wrote it, why they wrote it, what they say and what has been missed out.)

20. Explain the reasons why so many Scots were successful in the countries to which they emigrated.   6

[Now go to SECTION 2 starting on *Page fourteen*]

MARKS

SECTION 1 — SCOTTISH CONTEXTS — 25 marks

Part E — The Era of the Great War, 1900–1928

Answer the following **five** questions using recalled knowledge and information from the sources where appropriate.

21. Describe the use of new technology on the Western Front during the First World War. 4

Source A is from a textbook written by a modern historian in 1984.

Source A

> In August 1914, Parliament passed the Defence of the Realm Act. This allowed the Government to introduce whatever restrictions were necessary to protect the country during wartime. British Summer Time was introduced to give more daylight working hours. Pub opening hours were limited to prevent drunkenness. People who believed, in 1914, that life in Britain would not be affected much, were quickly proved wrong. High casualties on the Western Front led to conscription, forcing unmarried men between 18 and 41 to join the armed forces.

22. Evaluate the usefulness of **Source A** as evidence of Government control of everyday life in Britain during the war. 5

    (You may want to comment on what type of source it is, who wrote it, when they wrote it, why they wrote it, what they say and what has been missed out.)

Sources B and **C** are about the impact of the First World War on employment opportunities for women.

Source B

> Women wanted to be involved in the First World War from the start. From the outbreak of war there was a steady increase in the female workforce as men enlisted. Glasgow was the first city in Britain to employ women tram drivers. The vital role they played in the war helped change many people's attitude to women. When the war ended, many women voluntarily gave up their jobs to men returning from the fighting.

MARKS

Source C

> For women in particular, the First World War brought about many changes. At the beginning of the war, thousands of women were unemployed. Despite women's contribution to the war effort, it didn't change deep-seated beliefs many people had about the role of women. At the end of the war many newspapers became critical of women workers. Many women wanted to keep their jobs but when the fighting ended, large numbers of women were sacked.

23. Compare the views of **Sources B** and **C** about the impact of the First World War on employment opportunities for women. (Compare the sources overall and/or in detail.)   4

Source D is about the decline of Scottish industries in the 1920s.

Source D

> Before the First World War, the Scottish economy was very dependent on the traditional industries. When the war ended, there was a sharp drop in demand for Clyde-built warships. This decline in shipbuilding in the 1920s had a damaging effect on the iron and steel industries. Many of the companies had depended on shipbuilding for their orders. Despite increased competition from abroad, Scotland's manufacturers failed to invest in new technology. Not surprisingly, overseas markets lost during the war often preferred to stay with their new suppliers.

24. How fully does **Source D** explain the reasons for the decline of Scottish industries in the 1920s? (Use the source and recall to reach a judgement.)   6

25. Explain the reasons why women gained the vote in 1918.   6

[Now go to SECTION 2 starting on *Page fourteen*]

MARKS

SECTION 2 — BRITISH CONTEXTS — 26 marks

Part A — The Creation of the Medieval Kingdoms, 1066–1406

Answer the following **four** questions using recalled knowledge and information from the sources where appropriate.

Source A is from a chronicle written by William's priest in 1077.

Source A

> William went to various parts of his new kingdom. Wherever he went, the people surrendered to him. The remaining English Earls were confirmed in their lands and titles. There was limited resistance from the native population. To overcome this, his loyal Norman lords undertook a programme of castle building to maintain their hold on the kingdom. He gave rich fiefs to the men he had brought over from France but no Frenchman was given anything that had been unjustly taken from an Englishman.

26. Evaluate the usefulness of **Source A** as evidence of William's attempts to control England after 1066.

    (You may want to comment on what type of source it is, who wrote it, when they wrote it, why they wrote it, what they say and what has been missed out.)

    5

27. To what extent was the corruption in the legal system the most important problem facing Henry II?

    (Use recalled knowledge to introduce, then present a **balanced assessment** of the influence of different factors and come to a **reasoned conclusion**.)

    9

28. Explain the reasons why the Church was important in the Middle Ages.

    6

MARKS

Source B describes the effects of the Black Death on England.

Source B

> One in three of the population of England died. If the same proportion of people killed by the Black Death in England were affected today, then about 17 million people would die. Lords, who relied on their peasants to farm their land, became desperate to retain them. This meant Lords were forced to pay more to keep each peasant on their land. The labour shortage meant they were in greater demand, so some peasants left their own Lord's land in search of higher pay elsewhere.

29. How fully does **Source B** describe the effects of the Black Death on England? (Use the source and recall to reach a judgement.)

6

[Now go to SECTION 3 starting on *Page twenty-four*]

MARKS

SECTION 2 — BRITISH CONTEXTS — 26 marks

Part B — War of the Three Kingdoms, 1603–1651

Answer the following **four** questions using recalled knowledge and information from the sources where appropriate.

30. To what extent were financial grievances the main cause of dispute between King James I and Parliament?

    (Use recalled knowledge to introduce, then present a **balanced assessment** of the influence of different factors and come to a **reasoned conclusion**.)

    9

31. Explain the reasons why Charles I became unpopular in Scotland between 1629 and 1640.

    6

Source A is from a letter written by Sir John Eliot, a Member of Parliament, in the 1630s.

Source A

> It was an ill omen that Charles' first Parliament met against the background of a terrible outbreak of plague in London. Members of Parliament complained that the terms of Charles' marriage contract included unacceptable concessions to English Catholics. In addition we were suspicious of Charles' foreign policy which meant Parliament was reluctant to grant him funds. The king tried his best to manipulate Parliament. This didn't stop me launching a fierce criticism of Charles' favourite, Buckingham's mismanagement of the Cadiz expedition.

32. Evaluate the usefulness of **Source A** as evidence of growing opposition in England to the reign of King Charles I.

    5

    (You may want to comment on what type of source it is, who wrote it, when they wrote it, why they wrote it, what they say and what has been missed out.)

MARKS

Source B describes events between 1640 and 1642 that led to the outbreak of civil war.

Source B

> Charles called Parliament in April 1640. He then dismissed it because MPs refused to give him what he wanted. In November 1640 Charles was forced to recall Parliament. He still didn't get the money he wanted. Charles faced growing criticism in Parliament from Pym and other Puritan MPs regarding his religious policies. In May 1641 Parliament accused the King's chief Minister, Strafford, of treason and executed him. Many MPs were unhappy with the way Pym twisted the laws to get Strafford executed, which led to further disputes in Parliament.

33. How fully does **Source B** describe the events between 1640 and 1642 that led to the outbreak of the civil war? (Use the source and recall to reach a judgement.)   6

[Now go to SECTION 3 starting on *Page twenty-four*]

MARKS

SECTION 2 — BRITISH CONTEXTS — 26 marks

Part C — The Atlantic Slave Trade, 1770—1807

Answer the following **four** questions using recalled knowledge and information from the sources where appropriate.

Source A is from a diary written by a slave ship's doctor in 1788.

Source A

> Some wet and windy weather had caused the port holes to be shut. This led to diarrhoea and fevers among the slaves. I often went down below deck among them. After some time the apartments became so extremely hot, as to be only bearable for a very short time. The floor of the place where the slaves lay was covered in blood and diarrhoea which had come from them because of their sickness. It looked like a slaughter house.

34. Evaluate the usefulness of **Source A** as evidence of the conditions faced by slaves during the Middle Passage.

    (You may want to comment on what type of source it is, who wrote it, when they wrote it, why they wrote it, what they say and what has been missed out.)

5

MARKS

Source B is about the impact the slave trade had on the Caribbean islands.

Source B

> The slave trade had a long lasting effect on the islands of the Caribbean. The slaves outnumbered the white population about 20 to 1 which created a fear of rebellion among the white population. This fear of a slave uprising led to the introduction of a legal system which supported slavery. Slave laws were introduced which allowed slave owners to brutally punish or even execute slaves. Slaves were vital to work on the plantations. The concentration on sugar production did lasting damage to the Jamaican economy.

35. How fully does **Source B** describe the impact the slave trade had on the Caribbean islands? (Use the source and recall to reach a judgement.)   6

36. Explain the reasons why resistance was difficult for slaves on the plantations.   6

37. To what extent was Olaudah Equiano the main reason for the success of the abolitionist campaign?   9

    (Use recalled knowledge to introduce, then present a **balanced assessment** of the influence of different factors and come to a **reasoned conclusion**.)

[Now go to SECTION 3 starting on *Page twenty-four*]

MARKS

SECTION 2 — BRITISH CONTEXTS — 26 marks

Part D — Changing Britain, 1760–1914

Answer the following **four** questions using recalled knowledge and information from the sources where appropriate.

38. To what extent were medical advances the main reason for improved health by 1900?   9

    (Use recalled knowledge to introduce, then present a **balanced assessment** of the influence of different factors and come to a **reasoned conclusion**.)

Source A describes the impact of factories upon the working conditions of textile workers.

Source A

> People used to working in their own homes found working in a factory very different. The powered machines went on hour after hour and many workers struggled to keep up with them. Owners had very strict rules and workers had to do what they were told to do. There was, however, no shortage of workers wanting employment in factories. Wages were usually better than farm work, but only when the factory was working. If business became slow then workers were laid off, with no income at all.

39. How fully does **Source A** describe the impact of factories upon the working conditions of textile workers? (Use the source and recall to reach a judgement.)   6

MARKS

Source B is from the diary of a Scottish railway engineer written in the 1840s.

Source B

> We had to build the line to Perth over Lord Seafield's land. Lady Seafield very decidedly told us that she hated railways. "Cheap travel", she said, "brought together such an objectionable variety of people." Lord Seafield said the railway would frighten away the grouse from his moors. "Besides", he went on, "what would become of the men who have for many years been employed to float timber down the River Spey to the sea. Would a railway replace them?"

40. Evaluate the usefulness of **Source B** as evidence of different attitudes to the building of railways in 19th century Scotland.   5

     (You may want to comment on what type of source it is, who wrote it, when they wrote it, why they wrote it, what they say and what has been missed out.)

41. Explain the reasons why more people gained the vote by 1867.   6

[Now go to SECTION 3 starting on *Page twenty-four*]

MARKS

SECTION 2 — BRITISH CONTEXTS — 26 marks

Part E — The Making of Modern Britain, 1880–1951

Answer the following **four** questions using recalled knowledge and information from the sources where appropriate.

Source A is from a report written by a social investigator about conditions in London in 1892.

Source A

> The building was spread over two floors. The two room apartment on the ground floor is occupied by Fletcher, a pedlar, his wife and six of his children. Eight feet square—that is about the average of many of these rooms. On the first floor are the Lawson and Bewley families. In most of the apartments the walls and ceilings are black with filth. In these buildings it is a common occurrence to find sewage running down the walls.

42. Evaluate the usefulness of **Source A** as evidence of poverty in Britain in the 1890s.   **5**

    (You may want to comment on what type of source it is, who wrote it, when they wrote it, why they wrote it, what they say and what has been missed out.)

MARKS

Source B is about the limitations of the Liberal welfare reforms of 1906—1914.

Source B

> The Liberal reforms were just a beginning. They were a long way short of solving all the problems. Medical care was only provided for the worker, it did not cover his wife or children. Other benefits were only to last for a short period of time. The amounts paid as benefits were not enough to live on. Old Age Pensions were paid for the first time in 1909. However as the pension only applied to people over 70, many elderly still received no help.

43. How fully does **Source B** describe the limitations of the Liberal welfare reforms of 1906—1914? (Use the source and recall to reach a judgement.)   6

44. Explain the reasons why the Labour Government introduced the Welfare State in 1948.   6

45. To what extent was the NHS the most beneficial social reform introduced by the Labour Government after 1948?   9

    (Use recalled knowledge to introduce, then present a **balanced assessment** of the influence of different factors and come to a **reasoned conclusion**.)

[Now go to SECTION 3 starting on *Page twenty-four*]

MARKS

SECTION 3 — EUROPEAN AND WORLD CONTEXTS — 29 marks

Part A — The Cross and the Crescent: the Crusades, 1071—1192

Answer the following **five** questions using recalled knowledge and information from the sources where appropriate.

Source A is about the importance of castles in the twelfth century.

Source A

> During Henry II's reign, castles were built of stone and with extra walls and towers. These castles became a key symbol of power. They were also the administrative centres of each town. The numerous rooms inside a castle meant that it was an ideal base for the local garrison carrying out guard duty. During the civil war many castles had been built illegally. There was no doubt however that they were useful during times of attack when food, drink and other supplies could be stored there.

46. How fully does **Source A** describe the importance of castles in the twelfth century? (Use the source and recall to reach a judgement.)

6

MARKS

Sources **B** and **C** describe what happened to Jewish communities during the First Crusade.

Source B

> After a few weeks of travelling, Peter the Hermit and his followers came upon a Jewish community. Many Crusaders were poor and hungry so they began stealing food and possessions from the Jews. As the Crusaders thought the Jews were the enemy of Christ, most believed they could treat them as they wished. Some forced the Jews to change religion and become Christian. Others, against the orders of Peter the Hermit, slaughtered the Jews.

Source C

> A rumour spread among the Crusaders that whoever killed a Jew would have all their sins forgiven. Immediately, Peter the Hermit's army began attacking and killing Jewish men, women and children. Although some Jews tried to fight back they had few weapons and were easily defeated. In the riot that followed, Jewish houses were robbed and valuables stolen. Those Jews who survived the massacre were forced to give up their faith and become Christians.

47. Compare the views of **Sources B** and **C** about what happened to Jews during the First Crusade. (Compare the sources overall and/or in detail.)   4

48. To what extent were Muslim divisions the main reason for the success of the First Crusade?   9

    (Use recalled knowledge to introduce, then present a **balanced assessment** of the influence of different factors and come to a **reasoned conclusion**.)

49. Explain the reasons why the Crusaders lost control of Jerusalem in 1187.   6

50. Describe the Battle of Jaffa in 1192.   4

MARKS

SECTION 3 — EUROPEAN AND WORLD CONTEXTS — 29 marks

Part B — "Tea and Freedom": the American Revolution, 1774–1783

Answer the following **five** questions using recalled knowledge and information from the sources where appropriate.

51. To what extent were Britain's attempts at raising revenue from the colonies the main reason why the American Wars of Independence broke out in 1775?

    (Use recalled knowledge to introduce, then present a **balanced assessment** of the influence of different factors and come to a **reasoned conclusion**.)

    9

52. Explain the reasons why some colonists remained loyal to Britain during the war.

    6

Source A is about the condition of the American army in 1777.

Source A

> The Revolutionary War was waged by small armies on both sides. The American forces were often led by inefficient, even incompetent, commanders who fought muddled campaigns. The men gathering in Boston were very enthusiastic. They were however badly armed and lacking supplies. The American commander, George Washington, could rely on no more than 5,000 regular soldiers. Most men were part-time and served for only a few months at a time. Britain's professional army was larger but not large enough to subdue the Americans.

53. How fully does **Source A** describe the condition of the American army in 1777? (Use the source and recall to reach a judgement.)

    6

MARKS

54. Describe the events leading up to the British surrender at Saratoga in 1777.   **4**

Sources B and **C** are about the events of the Battle of Yorktown, 1781.

Source B

> In 1781, Cornwallis moved into Virginia and began to build a base at Yorktown. By late summer, Cornwallis's position at Yorktown was deteriorating fast. While American forces prevented him from moving inland, a large French fleet carrying 3,000 troops had sailed up to join the siege. The fate of Cornwallis was sealed when the French defeated the British fleet in Chesapeake Bay. On 19 October, Cornwallis surrendered his entire army of 7,000 men.

Source C

> To launch his campaign in Virginia, Cornwallis's army carried out raids, harassing the American forces wherever he could. In August 1781, Cornwallis's British forces set up camp at Yorktown. Yorktown however turned out to be a poor position and his situation became more serious. American troops moved quickly into the area to surround him and keep him there. The British could not help Cornwallis's army to escape, or bring in reinforcements.

55. Compare the views of **Sources B** and **C** about the events of the Battle of Yorktown. (Compare the sources overall and/or in detail.)   **4**

MARKS

SECTION 3 — EUROPEAN AND WORLD CONTEXTS — 29 marks

Part C — USA, 1850–1880

Answer the following **five** questions using recalled knowledge and information from the sources where appropriate.

56. Explain the reasons why settlers moved West after 1850.

6

Source A is about the events that led to the outbreak of the Civil War.

Source A

> The Compromise of 1850 was created by Henry Clay and others to deal with the balance between slave and free states. The Kansas-Nebraska Act of 1854, however, increased tensions. This allowed continued expansion to the West. The real issue occurred in Kansas. Pro-slavery people of Missouri began to pour into Kansas to help force it to be a slave state. The fight over slavery even erupted on the floor of the Senate. Anti-slavery campaigner Charles Sumner was beat over the head by South Carolina's pro-slavery Senator Preston Brooks.

57. How fully does **Source A** describe the events that led to the outbreak of the Civil War? (Use the source and recall to reach a judgement.)

6

58. Describe the work of the Freedmen's Bureau after 1865.

4

MARKS

Sources **B** and **C** are about what happened during Reconstruction.

Source B

> Many school houses were burned down. Hostility was shown to the school teachers like me who taught in schools for blacks. Two school board directors were warned to leave the Board. One of them did. They came at night and gave these warnings. I asked them while they were whipping me what I had done. They said I wanted to make these blacks equal to the white men; that this was a white man's country.

Source C

> The violence that the whites committed was directed not only at black people but anyone who furthered their cause. Teachers in schools for black Americans became key figures so they were frequently intimidated. These attacks usually took place at night: leaving behind a burning cross they whipped, mutilated and murdered black people. Black Americans were reluctant to resist as they wanted to be seen by others as peaceful and law-abiding.

59. Compare the views of **Sources B** and **C** about what happened during Reconstruction. (Compare the sources overall and/or in detail.)   4

60. To what extent was the discovery of gold the main reason for growing tension between the Native Americans and the white settlers?   9

    (Use recalled knowledge to introduce, then present a **balanced assessment** of the influence of different factors and come to a **reasoned conclusion**.)

MARKS

SECTION 3 — EUROPEAN AND WORLD CONTEXTS — 29 marks

Part D — Hitler and Nazi Germany, 1919–1939

Answer the following **five** questions using recalled knowledge and information from the sources where appropriate.

61.   Describe the events of the Beer Hall Putsch of 1923.   4

62.   To what extent was discontent with the Weimar Republic the main reason for the Nazi rise to power by January 1933?   9

   (Use recalled knowledge to introduce, then present a **balanced assessment** of the influence of different factors and come to a **reasoned conclusion**.)

Sources **A** and **B** are about the Nazi views on race.

Source A

> The Nazi theory of racial superiority was not original even though Hitler had stated, in *Mein Kampf*, that differences between the races was a matter of scientific fact. There could be no argument that the Aryan people of northern Europe were superior in every way. This was not just a matter of physical superiority but also of intellectual strength. It was logical that superior people like this should be in control of all other races.

Source B

> The stereotype of the blond haired and blue-eyed warrior took a powerful hold on many young Germans who were taught that the Aryans of Germany and Scandinavia were the Master Race. According to Nazi propaganda, which continually stressed the importance of "pure blood", biological research had shown that there was a distinction between races. This gave these superior races the authority to rule over the peoples of the world.

63.   Compare the views of **Sources A** and **B** about Nazi views on race. (Compare the sources overall and/or in detail.)   4

64.   Explain the reasons why it was so difficult to oppose the Nazi Government after 1933.   6

Source C is about changes to education in Nazi Germany.

Source C

> There were many changes at school. Some were barely noticed, others were introduced as though with a great fanfare of trumpets. None questioned the introduction of new Nazi textbooks. In line with National Socialist education policies, the number of PE periods was increased at the expense of religious education. When competitive field games were added to the curriculum our teacher spelled it out to us, "It is what the Führer wants for you". At the start of class we had to raise our arms in the "Heil Hitler!" salute.

65. How fully does **Source C** describe the changes to education in Nazi Germany? (Use the source and recall to reach a judgement.)   6

MARKS

SECTION 3 — EUROPEAN AND WORLD CONTEXTS — 29 marks

Part E — Red Flag: Lenin and the Russian Revolution, 1894—1921

Answer the following **five** questions using recalled knowledge and information from the sources where appropriate.

66. Describe the methods used by the Tsar to control Russia before 1905.

4

67. Explain the reasons why there was a revolution in Russia in January 1905.

6

Source A is about the reforms introduced in Russia after the 1905 Revolution.

Source A

> With the growing unrest threatening his authority, the Tsar gave in and agreed to introduce reforms. The October Manifesto established a parliament or Duma elected by the people. It also allowed the Russian people basic rights, such as freedom of speech. This helped the Tsar regain control of the country. In 1906 the Tsar appointed Peter Stolypin as Prime Minister. His land reforms allowed peasants to become owners of their own land. He also set up a peasants' bank to provide loans to help them buy the land.

68. How fully does **Source A** describe the reforms introduced in Russia after the 1905 Revolution? (Use the source and recall to reach a judgement.)

6

MARKS

Sources **B** and **C** describe the effects of the First World War on the Russian people.

Source B

> The workers are not in a patriotic mood. The high cost of living and barbaric government policies have turned the masses against the war. There are more and more strikes all over the country. Prices have gone up and people are discontented. Food is hard to get. They blame the Tsar and say "he does not care we might starve". People hate the war now and want it to end.

Source C

> Throughout much of the war, Russian cities suffered from a shortage of food. This was due to a series of bad harvests. The loss of large areas of rich farmland to the Germans did not help. The shortages meant that food prices went up and, although workers' wages increased, they did not keep pace with rising inflation. By 1917, urban workers faced terrible starvation which they blamed on the Tsar.

69. Compare the views of **Sources B** and **C** about effects of the First World War on the Russian people. (Compare the sources overall and/or in detail.)   4

70. To what extent was the leadership of Trotsky the main reason for the Reds' victory in the Civil War?   9

    (Use recalled knowledge to introduce, then present a **balanced assessment** of the influence of different factors and come to a **reasoned conclusion**.)

MARKS

SECTION 3 — EUROPEAN AND WORLD CONTEXTS — 29 marks

Part F — Mussolini and Fascist Italy, 1919–1939

Answer the following **five** questions using recalled knowledge and information from the sources where appropriate.

Sources A and **B** are about why Mussolini was able to seize power in 1922.

Source A

> The Fascist squads had a reputation for ruthless violence. This put Mussolini in the position to challenge the government, which he did in what became known as the famous "March on Rome". The government decided to send in the army to try and stop Mussolini. The King, Victor Emmanuel III, however instead of using the army, decided to give in to Mussolini's demands. He therefore appointed him head of a new Italian government.

Source B

> The Socialists and Communists launched an anti-Fascist general strike but the people failed to support them. After the strike, Mussolini decided to seize the government when he and his followers marched on the capital, Rome. Before he resigned, the prime minister called out the army when the Fascists surrounded Rome. However, the pressure proved too much for the Italian King who refused to use the military to squash Mussolini's "march".

71. Compare the views of **Sources A** and **B** about the events which led to Mussolini's seizure of power in Italy in 1922. (Compare the sources overall and/or in detail.)   **4**

MARKS

Source C is about the cult of Il Duce in Fascist Italy.

Source C

> The leadership cult in Fascist Italy started almost as soon as Mussolini came to power in 1922. By the end of 1925, his role as Duce of Fascism and Head of the Government had been secured by changes to the law. The nature of Mussolini's leadership and, above all, the quality of his political judgement, has been hotly debated. Mussolini had undoubted charisma and political intelligence with which to maintain his power over Fascism and the Italian people. However, his main talents lay in the areas of acting and propaganda.

72. How fully does **Source C** describe the cult of Il Duce in Fascist Italy? (Use the source and recall to reach a judgement.)   6

73. Explain the reasons why many Italians were unhappy with Mussolini's economic policies.   6

74. Describe the aims of Fascist foreign policy.   4

75. To what extent was fear the main reason why Mussolini was able to overcome opposition in Fascist Italy?   9

    (Use recalled knowledge to introduce, then present a **balanced assessment** of the influence of different factors and come to a **reasoned conclusion**.)

MARKS

SECTION 3 — EUROPEAN AND WORLD CONTEXTS — 29 marks

Part G — Free at Last? Civil Rights in the USA, 1918–1968

Answer the following **five** questions using recalled knowledge and information from the sources where appropriate.

76. To what extent was fear of revolution the main reason why many Americans' attitude towards immigration changed after 1918?

    (Use recalled knowledge to introduce, then present a **balanced assessment** of the influence of different factors and come to a **reasoned conclusion**.)

    9

Sources **A** and **B** are about the experience of immigrants in the USA in the 1920s.

Source A

> Italians didn't want to buy land. Few planned to stay in America for long, but wanted to return to Italy some day. They headed for the great cities where there was a far better prospect of finding employment. Italian Americans succeeded in jobs requiring little formal education, such as small business ownership. However, like other immigrants, they found other ways of making a living. Politics and sports were ladders for upward mobility.

Source B

> My family lived in the city of Chicago. When I was 14 years old I started dodging school and so didn't get much formal education. Around this time I turned to stealing. Then we joined an older gang because although they were only around 20 years old they were in the big money and drove around in fancy automobiles. My father came from Monfalcone in Italy and always hoped to return there.

77. Compare the views of **Sources A** and **B** about the experience of immigrants in the USA during the 1920s. (Compare the sources overall and/or in detail.)

    4

78. Describe how the Jim Crow laws affected black Americans.

    4

79. Explain the reasons why there was a growth in the civil rights movement between 1945 and 1968.

    6

Source C is about the appeal of the Black Panthers to many black Americans.

Source C

> The name 'Black Panther' was chosen because the panther is a strong fighter when it is cornered. They urged that it was now time to defend black Americans against this white aggression. When Huey Newton said things like "The police have never been our protectors", he voiced the distrust many black Americans felt towards the police. Little credit or publicity was given to the self-help programmes organised by the Black Panthers. In addition they also had a ten-point programme which included demands for better housing and education.

80. How fully does **Source C** describe the appeal of the Black Panthers to many black Americans? (Use the source and recall to reach a judgement.)   **6**

MARKS

SECTION 3 — EUROPEAN AND WORLD CONTEXTS — 29 marks

Part H — Appeasement and the Road to War, 1918–1939

Answer the following **five** questions using recalled knowledge and information from the sources where appropriate.

81. Explain the reasons why Germany hated the terms of the Treaty of Versailles.   **6**

Sources A and **B** are about the work of the League of Nations.

Source A

> Wilson had been the driving force behind the League of Nations. The refusal of the USA to join the League however greatly weakened its ability to succeed. In the years after the war, the League did a great deal of useful humanitarian work. The League did manage to settle disputes between smaller nations who could be leaned on. When disputes involved larger countries, the League however often failed to act.

Source B

> The Covenant was the document which outlined how the League would work. Actions against larger nations who challenged the League were inadequate and frequently half-hearted. Many members were not willing to use sanctions, which weakened the League. The League however did achieve some success in solving arguments between lesser countries. The failure of several big powers, including the USA , to join the League badly damaged its effectiveness.

82. Compare the views of **Sources A** and **B** about the work of the League of Nations. (Compare the sources overall and/or in detail.)   **4**

83. Describe the aims of Nazi foreign policy.   **4**

84. To what extent were military concerns the main reason why Chamberlain followed a policy of appeasement?   **9**

   (Use recalled knowledge to introduce, then present a **balanced assessment** of the influence of different factors and come to a **reasoned conclusion**.)

MARKS

Source C is about the events that led to the outbreak of war between Britain and Germany in 1939.

Source C

> The loss of the Sudetenland to Germany in October 1938 left the rest of Czechoslovakia weak and vulnerable to attack. In March 1939, German troops marched into Czechoslovakia. This action broke the Munich Agreement. Slovakia broke away and became a pro-German 'puppet state'. Bohemia and Moravia became a German protectorate. Up to this point Hitler had justified his demands in terms of self-determination. This was impossible after his actions in March 1939. Germany's aggression led to Great Britain and France abandoning the policy of appeasement.

85. How fully does **Source C** describe the events in 1939 leading to the outbreak of war between Britain and Germany? (Use the source and recall to reach a judgement.) 6

MARKS

SECTION 3 — EUROPEAN AND WORLD CONTEXTS — 29 marks

Part I — World War II, 1939–1945

Answer the following **five** questions using recalled knowledge and information from the sources where appropriate.

86. Explain the reasons why Hitler ordered the invasion of Russia in June 1941.   6

87. Describe the Battle of Midway in June 1942.   4

Sources **A** and **B** are about the work of the French Resistance.

Source A

> Resistance movements in occupied countries carried on the fight against Germany's armed forces. Their methods included sabotage of the German rail network. They also distributed anti-German propaganda. This resistance took place in all countries occupied by the Germans. The help they gave the Allies was extremely important. Some historians believe without their help the Allies would have been defeated. If members of the Resistance were caught they would almost certainly be tortured and executed.

Source B

> As a result of the German invasion in 1940 a resistance movement grew in France. Over the course of the war, the French Resistance scored key victories against the German occupation forces. Resistance members organised themselves in secret groups. They destroyed trains carrying German troops and military equipment. These accomplishments carried a heavy price as many members of the Resistance paid for their bravery with their lives.

88. Compare the views of **Sources A** and **B** about the work of the French Resistance. (Compare the sources overall and/or in detail.)   4

89. To what extent were German mistakes the main reason for the Allied success at Normandy in 1944?   9

  (Use recalled knowledge to introduce, then present a **balanced assessment** of the influence of different factors and come to a **reasoned conclusion**.)

Source C is about the fall of Berlin.

Source C

> Friday 20th April was Hitler's birthday. The Soviets sent him a birthday present in the form of an artillery barrage right into the heart of Berlin. The Western Allies launched a massive air raid. The radio announced Hitler had come out of his bomb-proof bunker. He spoke to young boys who had 'volunteered' to join the SS and die for their Führer in defence of Berlin. What a cruel lie! They didn't volunteer, but had no choice. Boys who were found hiding were hanged as traitors by the SS.

90. How fully does **Source C** describe events leading to the fall of Berlin? (Use the source and recall to reach a judgement.)   6

MARKS

SECTION 3 — EUROPEAN AND WORLD CONTEXTS — 29 marks

Part J — The Cold War, 1945–1989

Answer the following **five** questions using recalled knowledge and information from the sources where appropriate.

Sources A and **B** are about why a Cold War broke out between the superpowers.

Source A

> Once World War Two was over, relations between the two allies deteriorated, to be replaced by a climate of suspicion between America and the Soviet Union. Soviet and American leaders held opposing ideological views and attempted to spread their beliefs to other countries. Tensions continued to grow over the next few years. America's decision to develop and use the atomic bomb against the Japanese without consulting the Soviets placed further strain on relations.

Source B

> As soon as the war ended, the Soviet Union and the Americans developed open hostility towards each other. The meetings at Yalta and Potsdam did little to improve relations between the two countries. The new American President Truman and Soviet leader Stalin seemed hostile to one another, and this emphasised their ideological divisions. The tension at Potsdam was increased by America's use of the atomic bomb against Japan.

91. Compare the views of **Sources A** and **B** about the reasons why a Cold War broke out between the Soviet Union and the USA. (Compare the sources overall and/or in detail.)

4

MARKS

Source C is about the events which led to the crisis in Berlin in 1961.

Source C

> By 1960 the situation in East Berlin was very dangerous. A new East German labour law, which stopped workers from going on strike, had led to growing unrest in the factories. Agriculture reforms had led to higher prices and food shortages. All of this led to a massive increase in the numbers of refugees fleeing to the West. At a meeting of the Warsaw Pact states, Khrushchev had been informed about the situation. In the six months up to June 1961, 103,000 East Germans had fled through Berlin.

92. How fully does **Source C** describe the events which led to the crisis in Berlin in 1961? (Use the source and recall to reach a judgement.)   6

93. Explain the reasons why the USA became involved in a crisis over Cuba in 1962.   6

94. To what extent were Vietcong tactics the main reason for their success in winning the war in Vietnam?   9

    (Use recalled knowledge to introduce, then present a **balanced assessment** of the influence of different factors and come to a **reasoned conclusion**.)

95. Describe the steps taken to reduce tension between the USA and the USSR between 1968 and 1989.   4

[END OF QUESTION PAPER]

[BLANK PAGE]

DO NOT WRITE ON THIS PAGE

NATIONAL 5

2018

WEDNESDAY, 16 MAY

1:00 PM – 3:20 PM

Total marks — 80

SECTION 1 — SCOTTISH CONTEXTS — 26 marks

Attempt ONE part.

SECTION 2 — BRITISH CONTEXTS — 29 marks

Attempt ONE part.

SECTION 3 — EUROPEAN AND WORLD CONTEXTS — 25 marks

Attempt ONE part.

Write your answers clearly in the answer booklet provided. In the answer booklet you must clearly identify the question number you are attempting.

Use **blue** or **black** ink.

Before leaving the examination room you must give your answer booklet to the Invigilator; if you do not, you may lose all the marks for this paper.

SECTION 1 — SCOTTISH CONTEXTS

PARTS

SECTION 2 — BRITISH CONTEXTS

PARTS

SECTION 3 — EUROPEAN AND WORLD CONTEXTS

PARTS

[BLANK PAGE]

DO NOT WRITE ON THIS PAGE

MARKS

SECTION 1 — SCOTTISH CONTEXTS — 26 marks

Part A — The Wars of Independence, 1286–1328

Attempt the following **four** questions using recalled knowledge and information from the sources where appropriate.

1. Explain the reasons why the succession of Margaret, the Maid of Norway, caused problems for Scotland after 1286.

6

Source A is about the events that led to the defeat and capture of John Balliol.

Source A

> During John's reign, his attempts to break free of Edward's increasing control of Scotland proved hopeless. John lost patience and summoned his own parliament which agreed that homage and fealty should be withdrawn. The Scots knew better than to appeal to Edward's good nature and chose a course of action which would guarantee war: they concluded a treaty with France. To begin with, the Scots displayed a near suicidal optimism and invaded England. Edward began by slaughtering most of the citizens of Berwick for their bold resistance.

2. How fully does **Source A** describe the events that led to the defeat and capture of John Balliol? (Use the source and recall to reach a judgement.)

6

3. To what extent were the mistakes made by the English the most important reason why the Scots won the Battle of Stirling Bridge in 1297?

9

   (Use recalled knowledge to **introduce** then present a **balanced assessment** of the influence of different factors and come to a **reasoned conclusion**.)

MARKS

Source B is from a chronicle written by a Scottish writer around 1335.

Source B

> The castle of Forfar was occupied by Englishmen. Some of King Robert's followers hurried to the castle with ladders and secretly climbed over the stone wall and took the castle. Then they slaughtered all they found. They handed the castle over to King Robert who offered them a good reward. The king had the castle wall broken down, destroyed the well and then the whole castle. The wise, strong and bold king moved onto Perth with his army and soon set siege to it.

4. Evaluate the usefulness of **Source B** as evidence of the methods used by King Robert to drive the English out of Scotland between 1307 and 1314.

    (You may want to comment on what type of source it is, who wrote it, when they wrote it, why they wrote it, what they say and what has been missed out.)

5

[Now go to SECTION 2 starting on *Page fourteen*]

MARKS

SECTION 1 — SCOTTISH CONTEXTS — 26 marks

Part B — Mary Queen of Scots, and the Scottish Reformation, 1542–1587

Attempt the following **four** questions using recalled knowledge and information from the sources where appropriate.

5. Explain the reasons why the Catholic Church faced difficulties in Scotland in the 1540s and 1550s.

6

Source A describes the regencies of Moray and Morton in Scotland.

Source A

> In 1567, James VI became king but was too young to rule so Moray became James' first regent. He had to cope with the fact that Mary still had supporters who wanted to return her to the throne even after her abdication. Moray spent his time securing Protestantism in Scotland by passing laws to strengthen the religion. This helped reduce support for Mary among the nobles. In 1572, Morton became regent and also strongly supported Protestantism. He forced ministers to declare loyalty to the King as Governor of the Kirk.

6. How fully does **Source A** describe the regencies of Moray and Morton? (Use the source and recall to reach a judgement.)

6

7. To what extent were relations with the nobility the main reason why Mary faced difficulties during her reign in Scotland between 1561 and 1567?

9

   (Use recalled knowledge to **introduce** then present a **balanced assessment** of the influence of different factors and come to a **reasoned conclusion**.)

Source B is from the diary of a lady-in-waiting who accompanied Mary during her imprisonment in England and was written in 1587.

Source B

> The Queen quickly, and with great courage, knelt down and showed no signs of faltering. So great was her bravery that all present were moved. The executioner, or rather the minister of Satan, strove to kill not only her body but her soul because he kept interrupting her prayers. When she eventually finished praying, she laid her head on the block. The executioner struck her a great blow on the neck, which was not however, entirely severed.

8. Evaluate the usefulness of **Source B** as evidence of the execution of Mary, Queen of Scots in 1587.

   (You may want to comment on what type of source it is, who wrote it, when they wrote it, why they wrote it, what they say and what has been missed out.)

5

[Now go to SECTION 2 starting on *Page fourteen*]

MARKS

SECTION 1 — SCOTTISH CONTEXTS — 26 marks

Part C — The Treaty of Union, 1689–1715

Attempt the following **four** questions using recalled knowledge and information from the sources where appropriate.

9. Explain the reasons why the Darien Scheme failed.

6

Source A is about the arguments used by the opponents of Union in Scotland.

Source A

> The Union debate produced very strong passions on both sides of the argument. Its opponents said that taxes would be sure to rise if the Union went ahead. They also claimed that as Scots would be in a minority in a new British Parliament their voices would always be drowned out by the English. Some Presbyterians warned that Union would force unwelcome changes on the Church of Scotland. Opponents of the Union also argued that it would give the English too much control over Scotland's trade.

10. How fully does **Source A** describe the arguments used by the opponents of Union in Scotland? (Use the source and recall to reach a judgement.)

6

11. To what extent was the support of the Squadrone Volante the most important reason for the passing of the Act of Union by the Scottish Parliament?

9

(Use recalled knowledge to **introduce** then present a **balanced assessment** of the influence of different factors and come to a **reasoned conclusion**.)

MARKS

Source B is from a speech by a Scottish Lord in the parliamentary journal of the House of Lords, June 1713.

Source B

> Permission should be given to bring in a Bill to end the Union. Each Kingdom should have its Rights and Privileges restored to what they had been at the time when the Union was first passed. Members should consider this question carefully. Charging Scotland with a Malt Tax is in violation of the 14th Article of the Treaty of Union in which it was clearly stated "that Scotland shall not be charged with any Malt Tax during this war".

12. Evaluate the usefulness of **Source B** as evidence of discontent with the Union after 1707.

    (You may want to comment on what type of source it is, who wrote it, when they wrote it, why they wrote it, what they say and what has been missed out.)

5

[Now go to SECTION 2 starting on *Page fourteen*]

MARKS

SECTION — SCOTTISH CONTEXTS — 26 marks

Part D — Migration and Empire, 1830–1939

Attempt the following **four** questions using recalled knowledge and information from the sources where appropriate.

Source A is from an interview with Peter Rusgis and was recorded in 1910.

Source A

> My father was 21 when he came to Scotland from Lithuania with his brother. Neither of them wanted to be forced into the Russian army as this would have meant they were away from home for several years. Scotland was far enough away so the Russians could not get hold of them. They were both frightened as conditions were bad in the Russian army so Scotland seemed a safe destination. My father had also heard that there were plenty of jobs in Scotland.

13. Evaluate the usefulness of **Source A** as evidence of the reasons why so many immigrants came to Scotland after 1830.

(You may want to comment on what type of source it is, who wrote it, when they wrote it, why they wrote it, what they say and what has been missed out.)

5

MARKS

Source B describes the relationships between immigrants and Scots between the 1830s and 1939.

Source B

> By 1914, approximately 4,500 Italians lived in Scotland. Italians established many popular businesses such as ice-cream parlours, cafés and fish and chip shops. However, there was some tension between the Catholic Italians and the Protestant Scots who objected to Italian cafés opening on Sundays. The café owners were also criticised by local people who claimed the cafés sometimes encouraged unruly behaviour. There was little integration between Scots and Italians. Many Italians intended to return to Italy once they had made money in Scotland.

14. How fully does **Source B** describe the relationships between immigrants and Scots between the 1830s and 1939? (Use the source and recall to reach a judgement.)   **6**

15. To what extent were the attractions of new lands the most important factor which led to people leaving Scotland after 1830?   **9**

    (Use recalled knowledge to **introduce** then present a **balanced assessment** of the influence of different factors and come to a **reasoned conclusion**.)

16. Explain the reasons why Scottish emigrants were often successful in their new homelands.   **6**

[Now go to SECTION 2 starting on *Page fourteen*]

MARKS

SECTION 1 — SCOTTISH CONTEXTS — 26 marks

Part E — The Era of the Great War, 1900–1928

Attempt the following **four** questions using recalled knowledge and information from the sources where appropriate.

17. To what extent was the machine gun the most effective weapon on the Western Front during the Great War?

    (Use recalled knowledge to **introduce** then present a **balanced assessment** of the influence of different factors and come to a **reasoned conclusion**.)

9

Source A describes the restrictions introduced under the Defence of the Realm Act.

Source A

> The Defence of the Realm Act (DORA) was introduced in August 1914. It stated that no-one was allowed to talk about the navy or the army in public places. You were also not allowed to spread rumours about military matters. You could not trespass on railway lines or bridges. It was added to as the war progressed and listed all the things that people were not allowed to do in wartime. In addition, British Summer Time was introduced to give more daylight hours for extra work.

18. How fully does **Source A** describe the restrictions introduced under the Defence of the Realm Act? (Use the source and recall to reach a judgement.)

6

MARKS

Source B is from a newspaper interview with Prime Minister David Lloyd George, published on 22 August 1918.

Source B

> I admire the splendid manner in which female volunteers came forward to work in administrative offices of all kinds. We would have been unable to cope during the past few months without women working in hospitals. The heroines who have flocked to work behind the front lines as ambulance drivers have faced daily danger. My message is: "Well done, carry on. You are helping to create a new world for yourselves and for your children".

19. Evaluate the usefulness of **Source B** as evidence of women's work during the Great War.   5

    (You may want to comment on what type of source it is, who wrote it, when they wrote it, why they wrote it, what they say and what has been missed out.)

20. Explain the reasons why the Suffragettes harmed the cause of votes for women.   6

[Now go to SECTION 2 starting on *Page fourteen*]

MARKS

SECTION 2 — BRITISH CONTEXTS — 29 marks

Part A — The Creation of the Medieval Kingdoms, 1066–1406

Attempt the following **five** questions using recalled knowledge and information from the sources where appropriate.

21. Describe the feudal system in medieval times.   4

Sources **A** and **B** are about the murder of Archbishop Becket in 1170.

Source A

> On the evening of December 29th, four knights arrived at Canterbury Cathedral and demanded to see Archbishop Becket. The knights attempted to arrest Becket but he refused to leave, claiming he was ready to die for God. Becket was dragged from the altar and in the scuffle that followed, was attacked by the knights. Then in an act of horror, one of the knights drew his sword and sliced off the crown of Becket's head.

Source B

> The knights attempted to seize Archbishop Becket but he would not move, stating he was willing to be a martyr for the Church. The Canterbury monks gathered around Becket and tried to protect him, but they were forced back by the knights. Becket was thrown to the floor and assaulted by the knights. To make sure he was dead, one of the knights held Becket down and cut off the top of his head.

22. Compare the views of **Sources A** and **B** about the murder of Archbishop Becket in 1170. (Compare the sources overall and/or in detail.)   4

MARKS

Source C explains why monasteries were important in medieval times.

Source C

> During medieval times, monasteries played a vital role in the wool trade, creating work for people and boosting the economy. Monasteries were also centres of learning, especially for boys preparing for a career in the Church. Although some monasteries were built far away from local communities, they were never isolated as pilgrims often stayed there overnight. The sick were also frequent visitors, hoping to be treated at the monastic infirmary. Monasteries were so important that it was not until after the 14th century that they became less popular.

23. How fully does **Source C** explain why monasteries were important in medieval times? (Use the source and recall to reach a judgement.)   **6**

24. Explain the reasons why towns grew in medieval times.   **6**

25. To what extent was the Black Death the main reason for the Peasants' Revolt in 1381?   **9**

   (Use recalled knowledge to **introduce** then present a **balanced assessment** of the influence of different factors and come to a **reasoned conclusion**.)

[Now go to SECTION 3 starting on *Page twenty-four*]

MARKS

SECTION 2 — BRITISH CONTEXTS — 29 marks

Part B — War of the Three Kingdoms, 1603—1651

Attempt the following **five** questions using recalled knowledge and information from the sources where appropriate.

26. To what extent was religion the main reason why James VI and I argued with Parliament between 1603 and 1625?

    (Use recalled knowledge to **introduce** then present a **balanced assessment** of the influence of different factors and come to a **reasoned conclusion**.)   9

Source A is about the Bishops' Wars of 1639 and 1640.

Source A

> The Bishops' Wars resulted from objections to Charles I's attempts to reform the Scottish church. The King reacted by beginning a military campaign against the Scots. However, his plans were undermined by lack of funds. The Scottish forces organised themselves quickly and efficiently, however the English forces lacked experienced commanders. The English army that finally gathered on the Scottish border in mid-1639 was untrained and poorly equipped. The King's armies were defeated but the truce did not last and led to another Bishops' War in 1640.

27. How fully does **Source A** explain the reasons why the English forces were defeated by the Scots in the Bishops' Wars of 1639 and 1640? (Use the source and recall to reach a judgement.)   6

28. Explain the reasons why there were challenges to royal authority in England during the reign of Charles I.   6

29. Describe the events of the St Giles' riot in Edinburgh in 1637.   4

MARKS

Sources **B** and **C** are about the reasons why people joined sides during the English Civil War.

Source B

> Between 1642 and 1646 England was torn apart by a civil war. The King's supporters included the gentry because they saw him as defender of the social order. Others supported him because of religious reasons with more conservative Protestants and some Catholics defending his religious policies. Then there were those who joined up purely because they sincerely believed in the cause of the King, which was to maintain his royal authority.

Source C

> Religion was an important reason for choosing sides in the civil war. The Parliamentarians were against the King's religious policies and many Puritans joined them to fight against changes to the church. However, for some religion did not matter, they were more attracted by the Parliamentarians' attitudes to challenging the class system. A few joined the civil war only to make money but the majority believed in the royal cause.

30. Compare the views of **Sources B** and **C** about the reasons why people joined sides in the English Civil War. (Compare the sources overall and/or in detail.)   4

[Now go to SECTION 3 starting on *Page twenty-four*]

MARKS

SECTION 2 — BRITISH CONTEXTS — 29 marks

Part C — The Atlantic Slave Trade, 1770—1807

Attempt the following **five** questions using recalled knowledge and information from the sources where appropriate.

31. To what extent did tribal conflict encouraged by the slave trade cause the most harm to African societies?

    (Use recalled knowledge to **introduce** then present a **balanced assessment** of the influence of different factors and come to a **reasoned conclusion**.)

9

Source A is about the impact that trade with the Caribbean had on the British economy.

Source A

> British trade with the Caribbean continued for many years. Slave-produced goods such as sugar and coffee were imported into British ports, helping them to become rich and powerful trading centres. Work was provided in many ports as men were employed as sailors, shipbuilders and dock workers. The profits made from the slave trade were also invested in the development of other British industries. Wealthy colonial families built huge mansions in many of the British cities where they traded.

32. How fully does **Source A** explain the impact that trade with the Caribbean had on the British economy? (Use the source and recall to reach a judgement.)

6

33. Describe the methods used to discipline slaves on the plantations.

4

MARKS

Sources **B** and **C** are about the methods used by the abolitionists.

Source B

> The abolitionists used a variety of methods to put a stop to the slave trade. Personal accounts changed public opinion, as the dreadful experiences of the slaves during the Middle Passage were told by survivors. Many slavers backed these up, giving similar accounts about the horrors of the trade. Abolitionists such as Clarkson toured the country with equipment used on slaves to show the public how badly they were treated.

Source C

> The Committee for the Abolition of the Slave Trade was set up by Thomas Clarkson and Granville Sharp. Clarkson travelled around Britain with instruments such as manacles and thumbscrews to gain support for the cause. John Newton, former slaver, published a pamphlet outlining the horrific conditions of the slave trade and confirming slave accounts. Some slaves, such as Olaudah Equiano, published autobiographies sharing their experiences and changing the views of the public.

34. Compare the views of **Sources B** and **C** about the methods used by the abolitionists. (Compare the sources overall and/or in detail.)   4

35. Explain the reasons why it took so long to abolish the slave trade in Britain.   6

[Now go to SECTION 3 starting on *Page twenty-four*]

MARKS

SECTION 2 — BRITISH CONTEXTS — 29 marks

Part D — Changing Britain, 1760–1914

Attempt the following **five** questions using recalled knowledge and information from the sources where appropriate.

36. To what extent did better sanitation have the biggest impact on people's health between 1760 and 1914?   9

    (Use recalled knowledge to **introduce** then present a **balanced assessment** of the influence of different factors and come to a **reasoned conclusion**.)

Sources A and **B** are about rules and punishments for workers in textile factories.

Source A

> Rules of Waterfoot Mill:
>
> Any person coming to work late shall be fined.
> Any person found talking with the other workers instead of working shall be fined.
> Any person found smoking on the premises shall be instantly dismissed.
> The overseers are responsible for enforcing these rules and shall report all fines to the masters.
> The overseers shall be the first on the premises in the morning and the last to leave the premises at night.

Source B

> Workers could not afford to lose any of their wages by being fined for things such as being late. Some employers even advanced the factory clocks by 15 minutes in the morning so that all the workers were late. There were other fines too, for offences such as talking, whistling or singing. Mill owners also had the power to sack on the spot any employee who was found to be breaking the rules.

37. Compare the views of **Sources A** and **B** about rules and punishments in textile factories. (Compare the sources overall and/or in detail.)   4

MARKS

Source C is about the laws which improved working conditions in coal mines.

Source C

> The 1842 Mines Act stated that no-one under 15 could be in charge of operating machinery or winding gear. However, this act did nothing to stop boys over the age of 10 from working underground. In 1850, it became compulsory for all mine owners to report accidents that led to death. Further progress was made in making mines safer when the Mines Act of 1862 made single mine shafts illegal. Then in 1872, miners were given the right to appoint inspectors from among themselves.

38. How fully does **Source C** explain the ways in which laws helped to improve working conditions in coal mines? (Use the source and recall to reach a judgement.)   6

39. Explain the reasons why the development of railways had such a big impact on Britain.   6

40. Describe the demands of the Chartists.   4

[Now go to SECTION 3 starting on *Page twenty-four*]

MARKS

SECTION 2 — BRITISH CONTEXTS — 29 marks

Part E — The Making of Modern Britain, 1880–1951

Attempt the following **five** questions using recalled knowledge and information from the sources where appropriate.

41. Explain the reasons why many people believed some groups of the poor deserved to be helped before 1914.

    6

42. To what extent were free school meals the most successful of the Liberal Reforms for the young?

    9

    (Use recalled knowledge to **introduce** then present a **balanced assessment** of the influence of different factors and come to a **reasoned conclusion**.)

Sources **A** and **B** are about the benefits of the 1911 National Insurance Act.

Source A

> All workers earning under £160 per year had to make a payment of 4 pence per week to the National Insurance fund. In return, insured workers received 10 shillings per week for the first 26 weeks of illness and 5 shillings a week after that. They were also entitled to free visits to the doctor and medicine. In addition, there was a maternity grant of 30 shillings for insured workers.

Source B

> Some workers resented having to make weekly National Insurance contributions, but the act had many benefits. When insured workers had a baby, they were given a grant of 30 shillings. The 1911 Act also gave insured workers 10 shillings a week for the first six months of sickness and this benefit was then halved until they were fit to return to work. Insured workers were also provided with free medical care.

43. Compare the views of **Sources A** and **B** about the benefits of the 1911 National Insurance Act. (Compare the sources overall and/or in detail.)

    4

MARKS

Source C explains why the Second World War helped to bring about a welfare state.

Source C

> In many ways, the Second World War brought people together, created a sense of community and made people determined to create a better Britain. Winston Churchill was Prime Minister of a coalition government after 1940. The government intervened in people's lives more during the war, moving further away from a 'laissez-faire' approach. Rationing was brought in and the Ministry of Food was created, to make sure that everyone got a fair share of food. Some other reforms were introduced before 1945, such as family allowances.

44. How fully does **Source C** explain why the Second World War helped to bring about a welfare state? (Use the source and recall to reach a judgement.)   6

45. Describe the Labour reforms which improved the lives of British people between 1945 and 1951.   4

[Now go to SECTION 3 starting on *Page twenty-four*]

MARKS

SECTION 3 — EUROPEAN AND WORLD CONTEXTS — 25 marks

Part A — The Cross and the Crescent: the Crusades, 1071–1192

Attempt the following **five** questions using recalled knowledge and information from the sources where appropriate.

Source A is from a textbook written by a modern historian, published in 1960.

Source A

> Castles became very important during the 11th century. Most castles were built to defend a location and so were usually made of stone and reinforced with high walls. Inside a castle were many rooms including a keep and a Great Hall, where weddings and feasts were held to celebrate special occasions. Castles were often uncomfortable with little warmth or light. Despite this, castles provided a place for knights to stay when carrying out guard duty for their lord.

46. Evaluate the usefulness of **Source A** as evidence of the use of castles in medieval times.

    (You may want to comment on what type of source it is, who wrote it, when they wrote it, why they wrote it, what they say and what has been missed out.)

    5

47. Explain the reasons why Emperor Alexius and the Crusaders had a difficult relationship during the First Crusade.

    6

Source B describes the capture of Antioch in 1098.

Source B

> The Crusaders had not been at Antioch for long when they heard the news that Kerbogha's army was on its way to attack them. Bohemond, desperate to keep Antioch for himself, bribed a Muslim guard who agreed to let the Crusaders into the city. In the middle of the night, sixty of Bohemond's men scaled the city walls. Quickly they reached the battlements and captured three towers. Before the Muslims could react, the two main gates were opened and the rest of the Crusader army rushed in.

48. How fully does **Source B** describe the capture of Antioch in 1098? (Use the source and recall to reach a judgement.)

    6

MARKS

49. Describe what happened at the Battle of Hattin in 1187.

4

Sources **C** and **D** are about the relationship between Saladin and the Muslims.

Source **C**

> When Saladin captured Jerusalem, he ended nearly 100 years of Christian control of the city. Despite this, many Muslims were unhappy with Saladin's leadership and were close to leaving his army. Saladin had been out-fought by the Crusaders at Arsuf and the Muslims believed his poor tactics at Jaffa had cost them victory. Saladin also upset the Muslims at Jerusalem by showing mercy to the Crusaders and refusing to kill them.

Source **D**

> Thousands of Muslims from Syria and Egypt flocked to join Saladin's forces. Saladin was so highly respected by the Muslims that even when he let the Crusaders go free at Jerusalem, not one Muslim complained. Although reinforcements arrived from Europe to help the Crusaders, Saladin was not concerned. At Jaffa Saladin successfully held off an attack led by Richard I and saved the grateful Muslims from defeat.

50. Compare the views of **Sources C** and **D** about the relationship between Saladin and the Muslims. (Compare the sources overall and/or in detail.)

4

MARKS

SECTION 3 — EUROPEAN AND WORLD CONTEXTS — 25 marks

Part B — 'Tea and Freedom': the American Revolution, 1774–1783

Attempt the following **five** questions using recalled knowledge and information from the sources where appropriate.

51. Describe the events of the Boston Massacre.   4

52. Explain the reasons why the American colonists went to war with Britain in 1775.   6

Source A is from a textbook written by a modern historian, published in 2005.

Source A

> The Battle of Fort Ticonderoga gave the colonists a surprising but important victory over the British. The location of the fort was vital as its position protected New York and the New England colonies from British invasion from Canada. No one was killed during the attack. The main reason that the colonists wanted the fort was because they would gain control over cannons, munitions and armaments. These cannons were later moved to Boston. The fort itself was in a rundown condition, needing reconstruction.

53. Evaluate the usefulness of **Source A** as evidence of the conflict between the colonists and the British by 1776.   5

    (You may want to comment on what type of source it is, who wrote it, when they wrote it, why they wrote it, what they say and what has been missed out.)

MARKS

Source B is about the experience of British soldiers in battle during the American Revolution.

Source B

> The British army had around 8,500 men and were vastly outnumbered by the militia they were fighting. If more troops were needed, they were hired from abroad. British troops wore red coats, white breeches and tall felt hats. Their uniform made them easy targets. It was also unsuitable for fighting in North America. British troops complained about the unfair tactics employed by the colonists. They were not used to fighting enemies whose main tactics were to hide behind walls and trees, open fire then move away.

54.   How fully does Source B describe the experience of British soldiers in battle during the American Revolution? (Use the source and recall to reach a judgement.)   6

Sources C and D are about attitudes towards the Declaration of Independence.

Source C

> On 14 July 1776, Congress took the final step by issuing the Declaration of Independence. King George III was accused by many colonists of indefensible crimes such as imposing taxes which colonists had not agreed to and damaging their trade. The worst charge was that he was responsible for an unfair justice system. The Declaration of Independence was inspirational for all Americans, both black and white.

Source D

> The Declaration of Independence was issued in July 1776. Many colonists supported King George III's policies, arguing that his taxes were justified. The King was most upset by the accusation that he had stopped America from having a just legal system as the British felt it was the fairest available. The Declaration was criticised by many as it made no comment on the large number of slaves in America.

55.   Compare the views of Sources C and D about attitudes towards the Declaration of Independence in 1776. (Compare the sources overall and/or in detail.)   4

MARKS

SECTION 3 — EUROPEAN AND WORLD CONTEXTS — 25 marks

Part C — USA, 1850–1880

Attempt the following **five** questions using recalled knowledge and information from the sources where appropriate.

Source A is from a textbook written by modern historians, published in 1998.

Source A

> The American Civil War lasted from 1861 to 1865. After the war ended, thousands of former soldiers wanted to rebuild their lives. Many of the newly freed black slaves were looking for a new life. One obvious place to go was the West. The US government also recognised the need to populate the West and to achieve this, they passed the Homestead Act in 1862. This law encouraged people to move West and allowed each family to settle on 160 acres of land.

56. Evaluate the usefulness of **Source A** as evidence of the reasons why people moved West.

    (You may want to comment on what type of source it is, who wrote it, when they wrote it, why they wrote it, what they say and what has been missed out.)

    5

57. Describe the problems faced by settlers who travelled West.

    4

58. Explain the reasons why support for the Republican Party grew in the 1850s.

    6

MARKS

Source B is about the Black Codes.

Source B

> The Black Codes were laws that were passed by the Southern States after the Civil War. They were designed to limit the freedom of ex-slaves. They gave newly freed slaves the essential right to own and inherit property. Former slaves also had the right to legal protection. However, the Black Codes tried to prevent them from using their right to vote in elections. In certain states, Black Codes banned newly freed slaves from certain jobs and made sure that they could only earn very low wages.

59. How fully does **Source B** describe the treatment of newly freed slaves by the Black Codes? (Use the source and recall to reach a judgement.)

6

Sources C and **D** are about the reaction of Native Americans to their treatment by the US Government.

Source C

> We want to die in peace feeling that our numbers will not diminish and that our name will not become extinct. We cannot accept being forced to live on land which is not suitable to our needs. Our people are decreasing in numbers here, and will continue to decrease unless they are allowed to return to their native land. There is no climate or soil which is equal to our previous home.

Source D

> After the battle of the Little Bighorn there was no prospect of a Native American military victory against the whites. The only option for us was life on a reservation which had some advantages. We were given adequate amounts of land on which to grow crops. Most accepted the change from being hunters to farmers. Food rations were sufficient and the Native American population increased.

60. Compare the views of **Sources C** and **D** about the attitudes of Native Americans to their treatment by the US Government. (Compare the sources overall and/or in detail.)

4

MARKS

SECTION 3 — EUROPEAN AND WORLD CONTEXTS — 25 marks

Part D — Hitler and Nazi Germany, 1919—1939

Attempt the following **five** questions using recalled knowledge and information from the sources where appropriate.

61. Describe the events of the Munich Beer Hall Putsch in 1923.   4

62. Explain the reasons why support for the Nazis grew by January 1933.   6

Source A is from a textbook written by modern historians, published in 2000.

Source A

> The murder of a Nazi diplomat in Paris on 7th November 1938 by a Jew sparked an episode of violent persecution in Germany. Propaganda Minister Joseph Goebbels encouraged an attack on Jewish shops, homes and synagogues. This became known as Kristallnacht (Crystal Night) because of all the glass strewn across the pavements and streets of German towns and cities. Around 100 Jews were murdered during the violence. A further 20,000 were sent to concentration camps. After Kristallnacht the Nazis introduced new measures to persecute the Jews.

63. Evaluate the usefulness of **Source A** as evidence of the treatment of Jews in Nazi Germany between 1933 and 1939.   5

(You may want to comment on what type of source it is, who wrote it, when they wrote it, why they wrote it, what they say and what has been missed out.)

MARKS

Source B describes opposition in Nazi Germany between 1933 and 1939.

Source B

> Some workers protested by refusing to give Nazi salutes. Others rebelled by not turning up for work at all. Some even damaged factory machinery or equipment. In 1939 one factory worker, Georg Elser, was so angered by the lack of workers' rights that he planted a bomb in a hall where Hitler was scheduled to speak. Elser's timing was perfect; however Hitler had finished his speech several minutes early and was no longer on the stage by the time the bomb detonated.

64. How fully does **Source B** describe opposition in Nazi Germany between 1933 and 1939? (Use the source and recall to reach a judgement.)   6

Sources **C** and **D** are about attitudes towards youth organisations for girls in Nazi Germany.

Source C

> There were separate organisations for boys and girls. For girls, the organisation prepared them for motherhood which most accepted. Girls, at the age of 10, joined the League of Young Maidens. Girls had to run 60 metres in 14 seconds, throw a ball 12 metres, know how to somersault and they enjoyed the competitiveness. When they turned 14, they had lessons on sewing and cooking which most found very useful.

Source D

> Girls aged 10-14 years joined the Young Maidens where they were taught how to become good mothers but many resented this. Compulsory route marches and swimming contests were disliked by many girls. Between the ages of 14 and 21, they joined the League of German Maidens where they were further prepared for their roles as the mothers of future Germans. There were also classes on needlework and housework which many considered unnecessary.

65. Compare the views of **Sources C** and **D** on attitudes towards youth organisations for girls in Nazi Germany. (Compare the sources overall and/or in detail.)   4

MARKS

SECTION 3 — EUROPEAN AND WORLD CONTEXTS — 25 marks

Part E — Red Flag: Lenin and the Russian Revolution, 1894–1921

Attempt the following **five** questions using recalled knowledge and information from the sources where appropriate.

66. Describe the methods used by the Tsar to control the Russian people.   **4**

Source A is about the 1905 Revolution.

Source A

> The 1905 Revolution involved a number of separate uprisings throughout Russia. In January, a wave of strikes began throughout the country involving 400,000 people. The Tsar's uncle, the Grand Duke Sergei, was assassinated in February. By summer, the demands of the protestors had become far more political. They took to the streets demanding freedom of speech, an elected parliament and the right to form political parties. In Poland and the Baltic provinces, national minorities who were opposed to the Tsarist regime also rose up to demand political and economic reforms.

67. How fully does **Source A** describe the events of the 1905 Revolution? (Use the source and recall to reach a judgement.)   **6**

68. Explain the reasons why the February Revolution broke out in 1917.   **6**

Source B is from a textbook written by a modern historian, published in 1963.

Source B

> The Tsar abdicated in March 1917 and the Duma set up a Provisional Government. It was designed to promote democracy and liberalism in Russia. However, it did not overcome the difficulties facing Russia. The Provisional Government also continued the war, even though the Russian people were completely against it and the army became much less willing to fight. Finally, the Provisional Government failed to solve the issue of land settlements which also angered the peasants.

69. Evaluate the usefulness of **Source B** as evidence of the reasons for the failure of the Provisional Government.

    (You may want to comment on what type of source it is, who wrote it, when they wrote it, why they wrote it, what they say and what has been missed out.)

    5

Sources C and D are about the effects of the Civil War on Russian peasants.

Source C

> My troops entered the village and put all the Bolshevik traitors to death, this was the usual punishment. After the executions, their houses were burned. The whole village protested but we did not care. Many villages had to be dealt with in this way but it was necessary. Then the rest of the population was ordered to deliver, without payment, all of their grain. We left them with their cattle and horses.

Source D

> Both the Reds and the Whites practised terror in areas under their control. They looked on the death penalty as an emergency measure, which was only used when absolutely necessary. The Whites adopted a policy of grain requisitioning, sending soldiers, usually armed, to get a share of the grain out of peasants' barns. They also took farm animals and horses to help them win the war.

70. Compare the views of **Sources C** and **D** about the effects of the Civil War on Russian peasants. (Compare the sources overall and/or in detail.)

    4

MARKS

SECTION 3 — EUROPEAN AND WORLD CONTEXTS — 25 marks

Part F — Mussolini and Fascist Italy, 1919–1939

Attempt the following **five** questions using recalled knowledge and information from the sources where appropriate.

Source A is from a textbook written by modern historians, published in 1998.

Source A

> The Fascists got very little support in the 1919 election, but things improved for them after this. They appealed to many small landowners who had been harmed by Socialist local government and were worried about a Socialist revolution. Young people were attracted to Fascism as it seemed to offer the prospect of adventure and action. The Fascists also gained working class support as they kept some of their original radical social policies such as fair wages and prices.

71. Evaluate the usefulness of **Source A** as evidence of the appeal of Fascism between 1919 and 1925.

    (You may want to comment on what type of source it is, who wrote it, when they wrote it, why they wrote it, what they say and what has been missed out.)

    5

72. Describe the methods used by the Italian Fascists to spread propaganda.

    4

Source B describes the activities of Fascist youth organisations.

Source B

> The Fascists were determined to win the support of every one of the younger generation. The new Fascist youth organisation was called the ONB (Opera Nazionale Balila). It was a party organisation but it was taken over by the Education Ministry in 1929. Young people learned horse riding skills. Many youngsters went skiing in the Italian Alps. Every member had to swear a personal oath of loyalty to Mussolini. Most towns had rallies on a Saturday afternoon between 3·30 and 6·00 pm.

73. How fully does **Source B** describe the activities of Fascist youth organisations? (Use the source and recall to reach a judgement.)

    6

MARKS

74. Explain the reasons why Italy invaded Abyssinia in 1935.   6

Sources **C** and **D** are about opposition to the Fascist regime.

Source **C**

> Europe in the inter-war period was divided between democracies and dictatorships. Democracy managed to survive in Britain, but Mussolini had many admirers there. Opposition to the Fascist government in Italy was quite effective. There were several reasons for this but it was mainly because the regime was not popular amongst large numbers of people. The opposition groups were only occasionally infiltrated by the police and their informers.

Source **D**

> There was opposition to the Fascists, but it never posed a threat to the regime. Many Italians wanted to stay out of politics and concentrate on family life but most supported Mussolini's foreign and economic policies. When opposition groups did appear they were unable to operate without interference from the police. Socialists and Communists were at the forefront of opposition to the government. Fascism has little support in Italy today.

75. Compare the views of **Sources C** and **D** about opposition to the Fascist regime. (Compare the sources overall and/or in detail.)   4

MARKS

SECTION 3 — EUROPEAN AND WORLD CONTEXTS — 25 marks

Part G — Free at Last? Civil Rights in the USA, 1918–1968

Attempt the following **five** questions using recalled knowledge and information from the sources where appropriate.

76. Describe the difficulties faced by immigrants to the USA in the 1920s.

4

Source A is from a textbook written by modern historians, published in 2013.

Source A

> Slavery had been abolished in the 1860s but the Southern states of the USA used Jim Crow laws to maintain a segregated society. Black children were forbidden to attend school with white children. At work, black Americans collected their pay separately from whites. There were also strict bans on whites and blacks marrying. In 1896, the Supreme Court ruled that such segregation of black people from white people was acceptable. Their ruling was called the 'separate but equal' decision.

77. Evaluate the usefulness of **Source A** as evidence of the ways in which the Jim Crow laws segregated black and white Americans.

5

(You may want to comment on what type of source it is, who wrote it, when they wrote it, why they wrote it, what they say and what has been missed out.)

78. Explain the reasons why sit-ins were an important step forward in the campaign for civil rights.

6

Source B describes events in Birmingham, Alabama in 1963.

Source B

> Birmingham was probably the most racist and segregated place in the USA. Martin Luther King led a protest march through Birmingham against the discrimination and inequality faced by black Americans in the city. The march was led by children with over 30,000 demonstrators taking part. Chief of Police, Bull Connor, ordered the arrest of protestors and many children aged 6 to 18 were jailed. On the following day water cannons were used to disperse the marchers. The events in Birmingham caused an outcry across America.

79. How fully does **Source B** describe the civil rights protest in Birmingham in 1963? (Use the source and recall to reach a judgement.)   **6**

Sources C and D describe the beliefs of Malcolm X.

Source C

> Malcolm X was a leading figure in the Nation of Islam. Malcolm was a racist who hated white Americans, in much the same way that members of the KKK hated black Americans. His answer to the discrimination faced by black Americans was to call for segregation of the races — to separate black Americans from the 'white enemy'. In promoting 'Black is Beautiful', Malcolm argued that black Americans were a superior people to other races.

Source D

> Malcolm X never once argued for segregation of white Americans from black Americans. He believed that black Americans should be in control of black communities and equally believed in white power for white people. Malcolm never believed that black people were superior to anyone else. Malcolm didn't hate white Americans, he just distrusted them, not because of their skin colour but because of the way they treated his people.

80. Compare the views of **Sources C** and **D** about the beliefs of Malcolm X. (Compare the sources overall and/or in detail.)   **4**

NATIONAL 5 HISTORY   130   SQA EXAM PAPER 2018

MARKS

SECTION 3 — EUROPEAN AND WORLD CONTEXTS — 25 marks

Part H — Appeasement and the Road to War, 1918–1939

Attempt the following **five** questions using recalled knowledge and information from the sources where appropriate.

81. Explain the reasons why the German people were so opposed to the Treaty of Versailles.

6

Source A is about the work of the League of Nations.

Source A

> The 1920s are known as the Golden Age of the League of Nations. The League improved health by starting a global campaign to exterminate mosquitoes and the spread of malaria. It also tried to settle disputes between nations. When Czechoslovakia and Poland fought over Teschen, the League resolved the conflict by splitting the area between the two countries. In 1921 it held a vote to settle a disagreement between Germany and Poland over control of Silesia. When Greece invaded Bulgaria in 1925, the League successfully ordered Greece to withdraw.

82. How fully does **Source A** describe the successes of the League of Nations before 1933? (Use the source and recall to reach a judgement.)

6

83. Describe the steps taken by Hitler to strengthen Germany's military position between 1933 and 1938.

4

MARKS

Source B is from a textbook written by modern historians, published in 2006.

Source B

> Time and again Britain backed down in the face of Nazi aggression. This policy can be traced back to the way Germany was treated at Versailles, with many in Britain later regretting how harsh the Treaty had been. After the horrors of the Great War, public opinion influenced British governments more than ever before, because people longed for peace. Furthermore, the British economy was depressed throughout the 1930s and appeasement was an attractive way of avoiding expensive conflict.

84. Evaluate the usefulness of **Source B** as evidence of the reasons why Britain chose to follow a policy of appeasement.

    (You may want to comment on what type of source it is, who wrote it, when they wrote it, why they wrote it, what they say and what has been missed out.)

5

Sources C and D are about the reaction of Neville Chamberlain to Germany's occupation of Czechoslovakia in March 1939.

Source C

> The British public reacted with fury. However, Chamberlain's reaction to the German occupation of Czechoslovakia was weak. Although Hitler was clearly in breach of the promises he had previously made, Chamberlain would not accuse him of breaking the terms of the Munich Agreement. Chamberlain never had any intention of fighting Germany at this point and he continued trying to negotiate a peaceful settlement with Hitler.

Source D

> Chamberlain made it very clear to Hitler that he believed the promises he had made at Munich had been broken. Chamberlain put Britain on a war footing and was ready and willing to fight with Germany if necessary. The German occupation of Czechoslovakia marks the moment that Chamberlain finally took strong action against Hitler. On 31st March, Britain pledged to defend the independence of Poland.

85. Compare the views of **Sources C** and **D** about the reaction of Neville Chamberlain to Germany's occupation of Czechoslovakia in March 1939. (Compare the sources overall and/or in detail.)

4

MARKS

SECTION 3 — EUROPEAN AND WORLD CONTEXTS — 25 marks

Part I — World War II, 1939–1945

Attempt the following **five** questions using recalled knowledge and information from the sources where appropriate.

86. Explain the reasons why the German army was able to defeat Poland in 1939.

6

Source A is from a textbook written by a modern historian, published in 2011.

Source A

> The German plan was to attack through Holland and Belgium, with the main blow against France to be launched a little later through the Ardennes. This was a hilly and heavily forested area on the German-Belgian-French border. Contrary to a generally held belief, the Germans had fewer tanks than the Allies (2,500 against 3,500) at this point. The German tanks were concentrated into Panzer formations but the French tanks were scattered rather than organised into powerful formations like the Germans.

87. Evaluate the usefulness of **Source A** as evidence of the German invasion of France in 1940.

5

(You may want to comment on what type of source it is, who wrote it, when they wrote it, why they wrote it, what they say and what has been missed out.)

Source B is about the Battle of Midway, June 1942.

Source B

> At 10·26 am on the 4th June 1942 the course of World War Two in the Pacific changed. At that moment 37 bombers from the USS Enterprise engaged in a dive-bombing attack on two Japanese aircraft carriers. Within minutes both ships were on fire due to the explosion of fuel lines and aircraft petrol tanks. Within six hours the remaining two Japanese carriers had also been destroyed. By the time the battle ended, 3,057 Japanese had died. Midway was that rarest of fights — a truly decisive battle.

88. How fully does **Source B** describe the Battle of Midway in June 1942? (Use the source and recall to reach a judgement.)

6

MARKS

89. Describe the conditions for prisoners in forced labour camps in Nazi occupied Europe.   4

Sources **C** and **D** describe the Normandy landings in June 1944.

Source C

> The 6th of June 1944 saw the start of the largest naval, air and land operation in history. The Normandy landings, which pushed German forces out of north-west Europe, are often remembered as a predominantly American operation. The German forces were defeated in northern France due to the better tactical skills of the Allies. However, despite the Allies becoming bogged down in Normandy, they eventually secured one of history's most memorable victories.

Source D

> Despite being led by an American General, D-Day was a huge Allied effort with Britain taking the lead in planning and resourcing it. Although a long and costly campaign, it played a crucial role in ending the war. The rapid Allied advance through France was faster than the German advance through France four years earlier. The German forces were not easy to defeat, nevertheless the Allies prevailed due to their superior resources.

90. Compare the views of **Sources C** and **D** about the Normandy landings in June 1944. (Compare the sources overall and/or in detail.)   4

MARKS

SECTION 3 — EUROPEAN AND WORLD CONTEXTS — 25 marks

Part J — The Cold War, 1945–1989

Attempt the following **five** questions using recalled knowledge and information from the sources where appropriate.

91.   Explain the reasons why NATO was set up in 1949.   6

Source A is from a textbook written by a modern historian, published in 1997.

Source A

> The Soviet Union exploded an atomic bomb in 1949. From this point there was the possibility of nuclear war between the Soviet Union and America. In 1962 Castro agreed to the placing of 64 nuclear missiles on 9 bases in Cuba. In October, 43,000 Soviet servicemen arrived in Cuba, along with hundreds of tanks and anti-aircraft missiles to operate and defend the bases. The equipment was unloaded at night and the servicemen arrived on cruise ships dressed as holidaymakers.

92.   Evaluate the usefulness of **Source A** as evidence of the Cuban missile crisis.   5

   (You may want to comment on what type of source it is, who wrote it, when they wrote it, why they wrote it, what they say and what has been missed out.)

Source B is about American military tactics in Vietnam.

Source B

> By the end of 1968 there were more than half a million American troops in Vietnam. Their involvement in this conflict would prove to be very controversial indeed. The Americans used napalm which caused horrific burns on its victims. Anti-personnel bombs exploded in mid-air and spewed out thousands of pellets and needles onto the land below. Helicopters were also used to transport platoons in and out of the jungle very quickly. Operation Flaming Dart was a bombing campaign targeting North Vietnamese bases in 1965.

93.   How fully does **Source B** describe American military tactics in Vietnam? (Use the source and recall to reach a judgement.)   6

MARKS

94. Describe the tactics used by the Vietcong.   4

Sources C and **D** are about the attitudes towards the strategic arms limitation treaties.

Source C

> By the 1970s both the Soviet Union and the United States were willing to make agreements with each other to limit weapons. Both countries believed that these treaties would limit the threat of nuclear destruction. There was a desire in both countries to save money rather than spending it on more weapons. There was a belief that arms reduction could lead to increased cooperation between the two superpowers.

Source D

> In 1972 the SALT 1 Treaty limited the number of Anti-Ballistic Missiles and prevented the addition of more long range missiles. Nixon and Brezhnev did not care about how much this would cost. Many were concerned that agreements such as this would not reduce the threat of nuclear war. Both countries continued to view each other with suspicion and were reluctant to cooperate on areas such as joint space missions.

95. Compare the views of **Sources C** and **D** on the attitudes towards the strategic arms limitation treaties. (Compare the sources overall and/or in detail.)   4

[END OF QUESTION PAPER]

[BLANK PAGE]

DO NOT WRITE ON THIS PAGE

NATIONAL 5

Answers

NATIONAL 5 HISTORY
2017

Section 1, Context A, The Wars of Independence, 1286–1328

1. *Candidates can be credited in a number of ways up to a maximum of 5 marks.*

Candidates must show a causal relationship between events.

Up to a **maximum of 5 marks in total, 1 mark** should be given for each accurate, relevant reason, and a **second mark** should be given for reasons that are developed. Candidates may achieve full marks by providing five straightforward reasons, three developed reasons, or a combination of these.

Possible reasons may include:

1. she was a girl – people did not believe females were suitable to be monarchs so were not happy to accept her as queen
2. as a female she would not be able to lead an army in battle so would not fulfil her role as monarch/defend her realm which worried people
3. she was a small child so would need someone else to rule on her behalf – people knew this could cause rivalries among the nobles for this role so they were worried
4. she could be kidnapped by an unscrupulous noble in order to gain control over the country so her safety caused concern
5. she would not be able to control powerful nobles so a danger of civil war would remain which made many very unhappy
6. she would have to marry and a Scottish husband would lead to rivalry among the nobles
7. choosing a foreign husband would lead to Scotland being ruled by a foreigner
8. she herself was foreign and she was living far away in Norway, which some found unacceptable
9. there would have to be negotiations with her father before she could come to Scotland/about her future marriage – this would involve foreign interest which worried many Scots
10. nobles such as Bruce felt that they had a better claim so did not want her to be queen

2. *Candidates can be credited in a number of ways up to a maximum of 5 marks.*

Candidates must make a judgement about the usefulness of the source and support this by making evaluative comments on identified aspects of the source.

1 mark should be given for each relevant comment made, up to a **maximum of 5 marks in total.**

- A maximum of **4 marks** can be given for evaluative comments relating to the author, type of source, purpose and timing.
- A maximum of **2 marks** may be given for comments relating to the content of the source.
- A maximum of **2 marks** may be given for comments relating to points of significant omission.

Examples of aspects of the source and relevant comments:

Aspect of the source	Possible comment
Author: Modern historian	Useful because he has expert knowledge/has studied a range of relevant sources
Type of Source: Textbook	Useful because it contains straightforward factual information without bias/well researched
Purpose: To inform	Useful because it provides detailed information
Timing: 2009	Useful because it has the benefit of hindsight

Content	Possible comment
King Edward called for a parliament to be held in May 1291 to settle the future of the Scottish crown	Useful as it is accurate (Edward was in charge of the event rather than the Scots)
The location he chose was Norham Castle on the English side of the Tweed	Useful as it is accurate (Edward's intention was to disadvantage the Scots)
He said that the proceedings would not start until the Guardians and the claimants to the throne had acknowledged his position as overlord of Scotland	Useful as it is accurate (Edward did want to be the ruler of Scotland)

Possible points of significant omission may include:

1. Scottish nobles/representatives did not think they could make such an agreement – only a king could do so
2. some claimants agreed very quickly (eg Bruce) and made it difficult for others to refuse (eg Balliol)
3. civil war a possibility due to rival factions/13 claimants in all including Edward
4. Edward brought an army with him to Norham to intimidate the Scots

3. *Candidates can be credited in a number of ways up to a maximum of 5 marks.*

Candidates may take different perspectives on the events and may describe a variety of different aspects of the events. **1 mark** should be given for each accurate relevant key point of knowledge. A **second mark** should be given for each point that is developed, up to a maximum of **5 marks**. Candidates may achieve full marks by providing five straightforward points, by making three developed points, or a combination of these.

Possible points of knowledge may include:

1. sacked Berwick
2. slaughtered the townspeople as a warning against resistance
3. defeated Scots noble-led army at Dunbar
4. marched his army throughout Scotland from Dunbar as far as Elgin and back
5. took control of Scottish castles eg Stirling, Edinburgh, Perth
6. dethroned Balliol/stripped Balliol of his king's insignia
7. took Balliol to London as his prisoner/took other hostages to ensure loyalty
8. made important Scots sign allegiance to him/Ragman Rolls
9. took away the Stone of Scone to England to stop another king being crowned
10. took away important Scottish legal documents/Black Rood of St Margaret

4. *Candidates can be credited in a number of ways up to a maximum of 5 marks.*

Candidates must make an overall judgement about how fully the source explains the events. **1 mark** may be given for each valid point interpreted from the source or each valid point of significant omission provided.

Up to **3 marks** should be given for their identification of points from the source that supports their judgement. Candidates should be given up to **4 marks** for their identification of points of significant omission, based on their own knowledge, that support their judgement.

A maximum of 2 marks may be given for answers in which no judgement has been made.

Possible points which may be identified in the source include:
1. Wallace left Scotland
2. he travelled to France as part of his campaign to free John Balliol
3. Wallace planned to visit the Pope to get him on Balliol's side
4. Wallace was back in Scotland well before 1305 where he continued to fight against Edward's rule

Possible points of significant omission may include:
5. resigned as Guardian of Scotland in 1298
6. declared an outlaw by Scottish parliament (in March 1305 at Edward's behest)
7. handed over to English by John Menteith in August 1305
8. taken to London and tried for treason
9. executed by being hanged, drawn and quartered

Section 1, Context B, Mary Queen of Scots, and the Scottish Reformation, 1542–1587

5. *Candidates can be credited in a number of ways up to a maximum of 5 marks.*

Candidates must show a causal relationship between events.

Up to a **maximum of 5 marks in total, 1 mark** should be given for each accurate, relevant reason, and a **second mark** should be given for reasons that are developed. Candidates may achieve full marks by providing five straightforward reasons, three developed reasons, or a combination of these.

Possible reasons may include:
1. Scotland broke the Treaty of Greenwich with England (promise for Mary to marry Henry VIII's son) so Mary would have been in danger from the English ('Rough Wooing')
2. Mary had to be moved around the country many times so it was becoming difficult to keep her safe from the attacking English
3. a plan was developed to smuggle Mary out of Scotland to France because the English continued to try and enforce the treaty even after Henry VIII had died (1547)
4. the French wanted Mary to marry the heir to the French throne so Mary had to leave Scotland to live in France
5. in August 1548 Mary set sail for France because Scotland and France had signed the Treaty of Haddington which promised Mary in marriage to the French heir to the throne
6. moving Mary to France was a precondition for French military aid against the English

6. *Candidates can be credited in a number of ways up to a maximum of 5 marks.*

Candidates may provide a number of straightforward points or a smaller number of developed points, or a combination of these. Up to a maximum of **5 marks, 1 mark** should be given for each accurate relevant point of knowledge, and a **second mark** should be given for any point that is developed. Candidates may achieve full marks by providing five straightforward points, by making three developed points, or a combination of these.

Possible points of knowledge may include:
1. some Scots began to question the teachings of the Catholic Church
2. criticism of the wealth of the Catholic Church in Scotland
3. English translations of the Bible were distributed
4. religious pamphlets were brought over from abroad
5. Protestant preachers like John Knox started preaching/returned to Scotland in 1559
6. resentment of French/Catholic influence over Scotland
7. criticism of how some Protestant preachers were treated eg Wishart
8. death of Catholic Queen Mary of Guise in 1560
9. Parliament in August abolished the mass, ended the authority of the Pope and adopted the Protestant Confession of Faith

7. *Candidates can be credited in a number of ways up to a maximum of 5 marks.*

Candidates must make a judgement about the usefulness of the source and support this by making evaluative comments on identified aspects of the source.

1 mark should be given for each relevant comment made, up to a **maximum of 5 marks in total.**
- A maximum of **4 marks** can be given for evaluative comments relating to the author, type of source, purpose and timing.
- A maximum of **2 marks** may be given for comments relating to the content of the source.
- A maximum of **2 marks** may be given for comments relating to points of significant omission.

Examples of aspects of the source and relevant comments:

Aspect of the source	Possible comment
Author: Historian	Useful because he has expert knowledge/has studied a range of relevant sources
Type of Source: Textbook	Useful because it contains straightforward factual information without bias/well researched
Purpose: To inform	Useful because it provides detailed information
Timing: 2013	Useful because it has the benefit of hindsight

Content	Possible comment
Deafening noise shook the entire area	Useful because it is accurate (the explosion was heard by many)
Mary thought they were under attack	Useful because it is accurate (Mary appeared not to know about the plot to kill Darnley)
Darnley's house reduced to a pile of rubble	Useful because it is accurate (Darnley's house did suffer extensive damage)

Possible points of significant omission may include:
1. Darnley's naked body was found in another area away from the explosion along with a servant/without any marks that would indicate that he was in an explosion
2. beside Darnley's body were found a cloak, a dagger, a chair and a coat
3. witnesses say they saw men running from the scene before the explosion
4. Mary's political enemies accused her of being involved in a plot to kill Darnley

8. *Candidates can be credited in a number of ways **up to a maximum of 5 marks**.*

Candidates must make an overall judgement about how fully the source explains the events. **1 mark** may be given for each valid point interpreted from the source or each valid point of significant omission provided.

A maximum of 2 marks may be given for answers which refer only to the source.

Possible points which may be identified in the source include:
1. Scottish nobles, outraged at Mary's marriage to Bothwell, decided to rebel against Mary and Bothwell
2. the Protestant nobles raised an army and so did Mary and her new husband
3. the nobles said they would withdraw if Mary gave up Bothwell but she refused
4. Bothwell escaped and Mary surrendered to the Scottish nobles

Possible points of significant omission may include:
5. the nobles then imprisoned Mary in Loch Leven Castle
6. the nobles forced Mary to abdicate (July 1567)
7. in July Mary miscarried twins
8. Mary's son James was to be King
9. Earl of Moray ruled as King Regent

Section 1, Context C, The Treaty of Union, 1689–1715

9. *Candidates can be credited in a number of ways **up to a maximum of 5 marks**.*

Candidates must make an overall judgement about how fully the source explains the events. **1 mark** may be given for each valid point interpreted from the source or each valid point of significant omission provided.

A maximum of 2 marks may be given for answers which refer only to the source.

Possible points which may be identified in the source include:
1. in England there was a lot of resentment at the level of support for the Jacobites in Scotland
2. the Scots were angry at not being consulted by the English over the Act of Settlement of 1701
3. as the smaller partner in the union of crowns the Scots felt their interests were ignored
4. the Scots were also annoyed that they had not been consulted over entry into the war of Spanish Succession

Possible points of significant omission may include:
5. Scots were angry at the role of England in the failure of the Darien scheme
6. England's wars with France had worsened Scotland's economic problems, especially hitting towns such as Ayr which imported French goods
7. the English were annoyed when Scots passed the Act Anent Peace and War

8. the Scottish parliament angered Westminster by appointing a Protestant successor to Queen Anne without consulting them
9. the Scots regarded the Aliens Act as an attempt to bully them
10. The Worcester Affair (execution of English captain for piracy) angered the English

10. *Candidates can be credited in a number of ways **up to a maximum of 5 marks**.*

They may take different perspectives on the events and may describe a variety of different aspects of the events.

1 mark should be given for each accurate relevant key point of knowledge. A **second mark** should be given for each point that is developed, up to a maximum of 5 marks. Candidates may achieve full marks by providing five straightforward points, by making three developed points, or a combination of these.

Possible points of knowledge may include:
1. Union would lead to a rise in taxes in Scotland
2. the Scottish MPs would be outnumbered in a new British parliament
3. Union would end Scotland's identity as an independent nation (eg currency and laws)
4. Union would threaten the independence of the Scottish church
5. Scotland would be unable to compete with the more developed English industry (at home or abroad)
6. fears that English trading interests would be prioritised

11. *Candidates can be credited in a number of ways **up to a maximum of 5 marks**.*

Candidates must show a causal relationship between events.

Up to a **maximum of 5 marks in total**, **1 mark** should be given for each accurate, relevant reason, and a **second mark** should be given for reasons that are developed. Candidates may achieve full marks by providing five straightforward reasons, three developed reasons, or a combination of these.

Possible reasons may include:
1. Protestants were happy that Union would guarantee the Protestant Succession
2. if Scotland failed to agree to Union, England might invade and enforce a worse settlement
3. Union would give the Scots access to England and her colonies and so enrich the country
4. Scotland would be more secure as they would gain English military protection
5. Many Scots were swayed by promises of temporary tax exemptions
6. the Union would give Scots greater standing in Europe
7. Scotland and England shared a similar language, religion and trade traditions

12. *Candidates can be credited in a number of ways **up to a maximum of 5 marks**.*

Candidates must make a judgement about the usefulness of the source and support this by making evaluative comments on identified aspects of the source.

1 mark should be given for each relevant comment made, up to a **maximum of 5 marks in total**.
- A **maximum of 4 marks** can be given for evaluative comments relating to the author, type of source, purpose and timing.
- A **maximum of 2 marks** may be given for comments relating to the content of the source.
- A **maximum of 2 marks** may be given for comments relating to points of significant omission.

Examples of aspects of the source and relevant comments:

Aspect of the source	Possible comment
Author: Modern historian	Useful because he has expert knowledge/has studied a range of relevant sources
Type of Source: Textbook	Useful because it contains straightforward factual information without bias/well researched
Purpose: To inform on views towards the Union	Useful because it provides detailed information
Timing: 1996	Useful because it has the benefit of hindsight

Content	Possible comment
But when Parliament passed an Act for the Security of the Kirk many of them changed their tune.	Useful as it is accurate (the Kirk was satisfied by the passing of this Act)
The Equivalent was the biggest incentive for many as it led to the sum of over three hundred thousand pounds sterling to be sent in cash to Scotland	Useful as it is accurate (the Equivalent did succeed as an incentive)
English guarantees over the independence of the Scots legal system also soothed most fears within the Scottish legal profession	Useful as it is accurate (the legal profession was satisfied by these guarantees)

Possible points of significant omission may include:

1. the Earl of Glasgow distributed £20,000 amongst the supporters of Union
2. the Squadrone Volante backed Union as they believed they would get control of the distribution of the Equivalent
3. government pensions, promotions and job positions were offered to those who voted for Union

Section 1, Context D, Migration and Empire, 1830–1939

13. *Candidates can be credited in a number of ways up to a maximum of 5 marks.*

They may take different perspectives on the events and may describe a variety of different aspects of the events.

1 mark should be given for each accurate relevant key point of knowledge. A **second mark** should be given for each point that is developed, up to a maximum of **5 marks**. Candidates may achieve full marks by providing five straightforward points, by making three developed points, or a combination of these.

Possible points of knowledge may include:

1. wealth of cities such as Glasgow increased and cities grew/population 1 million by 1911
2. built environment benefited from investment of profits made from Empire investment – fine public buildings, mansions for successful entrepreneurs
3. many jobs were created in Scotland in manufacturing goods for export to the Empire (eg railway locomotives, ships)
4. raw materials from the Empire (eg jute, sugar) were processed in Scotland
5. empire cultures introduced into Scotland (eg food, music)

6. some investment capital went overseas instead of into developing new Scottish industries
7. immigrant workers provided a cheap labour force and kept wages down
8. large available cheap labour force discouraged investment in new mechanisation (eg in mining, shipbuilding)
9. created many opportunities for Scots within the Empire (eg armed forces, civil service)

14. *Candidates can be credited in a number of ways up to a maximum of 5 marks.*

Candidates must make an overall judgement about how fully the source explains the events. **1 mark** may be given for each valid point interpreted from the source or each valid point of significant omission provided.

A maximum of 2 marks may be given for answers which refer only to the source.

Possible points which may be identified in the source include:

1. the church enabled them to keep their religious identity in Scotland through worshipping in their traditional way
2. it was the centre of social life for many Irish immigrants/offered a friendly environment where people could meet and be made welcome
3. the church also established youth groups
4. the church also attempted to tackle some of the issues Scottish society faced, such as the problem of poverty

Possible points of significant omission may include:

5. parish priests helped with writing letters, finding work and accommodation etc
6. church ran charities to help poor immigrants (eg St Vincent de Paul Society)
7. church set up and supervised schools for Catholic children
8. church set up sports organisations such as Celtic FC and Hibernian FC
9. immigrants from the north of Ireland were often Protestants so the Catholic Church did not play a part in their lives

15. *Candidates can be credited in a number of ways up to a maximum of 5 marks.*

Candidates must make a judgement about the usefulness of the source and support this by making evaluative comments on identified aspects of the source.

1 mark should be given for each relevant comment made, up to a **maximum of 5 marks in total.**

- A maximum of **4 marks** can be given for evaluative comments relating to the author, type of source, purpose and timing.
- A maximum of **2 marks** may be given for comments relating to the content of the source.
- A maximum of **2 marks** may be given for comments relating to points of significant omission.

Examples of aspects of the source and relevant comments:

Aspect of the source	Possible comment
Author: Modern Historian	Useful because he has expert knowledge/has studied a range of relevant sources
Type of Source: Textbook	Useful because it contains straightforward factual information without bias/well researched
Purpose: To inform	Useful because it provides detailed information
Timing: 2007	Useful because it has the benefit of hindsight

Content	Possible comment
They supplied goods and services/brought their skills with them from their native lands	Useful as it is accurate (Jews did not tend to work in Scotland's traditional industries)
Many worked in the clothing industry	Useful as it is accurate (the clothing industry did employ many Jewish immigrants)
Many made a living selling door-to-door or running small shops	Useful as it is accurate (Jewish immigrants did often set up their own businesses)

Possible points of significant omission may include:
1. worked in the tobacco trade/making cigarettes
2. worked in the jewellery trade
3. many other immigrants worked in agriculture
4. many other immigrants did work in heavy industries (eg coalmining)

16. *Candidates can be credited in a number of ways up to a maximum of 5 marks.*

Candidates must show a causal relationship between events.

Up to a **maximum of 5 marks in total, 1 mark** should be given for each accurate, relevant reason, and a **second mark** should be given for reasons that are developed. Candidates may achieve full marks by providing five straightforward reasons, three developed reasons, or a combination of these.

Possible reasons may include:
1. improved transport – steam ships and railways – encouraged Scots to move because they would not be without earnings for long/could return if necessary
2. some felt compelled to do missionary work/spread Christianity in the Empire
3. established Scots communities abroad were attractive to new emigrants who would feel more comfortable with their familiar culture
4. some countries offered free or cheap land (eg Canada) which attracted Scots farmers and crofters
5. land in New Zealand and the USA was known to be fertile and better than the land in Scotland so farmers were attracted there
6. agents for Empire countries held information meetings to encourage Scots to emigrate by showing the positive side of emigration
7. family and friends who had emigrated wrote letters home encouraging others to join them as they were doing well/ helped with the cost of fares
8. higher wages for skilled Scots encouraged both permanent and temporary emigration
9. wide range of work available in trades that Scots were experienced in (eg farming, mining, engineering) so they could find work easily
10. administrative empire jobs with high status were attractive to well-educated Scots

Section 1, Context E, The Era of the Great War, 1900–1928

17. *Candidates can be credited in a number of ways up to a maximum of 5 marks.*

They may take different perspectives on the events and may describe a variety of different aspects of the events.

1 mark should be given for each accurate relevant key point of knowledge. A **second mark** should be given for each point that is developed, up to a maximum of **5 marks**. Candidates may

achieve full marks by providing five straightforward points, by making three developed points, or a combination of these.

Possible points of knowledge may include:
1. the trenches were often flooded/muddy
2. the soldiers had little protection from the weather/cold in winter
3. constant strain of gunfire/explosions (eg threat of snipers, shellshock)
4. terrible smell in the trenches (eg rotting corpses, open latrines)
5. discomfort caused by lice/flies
6. problems caused by conditions such as: trench foot; trench mouth
7. danger of gas; blisters; blindness; suffocation
8. problem of rats searching for food/spreading diseases
9. difficulty of coping with seeing friends wounded or killed
10. food was monotonous/supply of food varied

18. *Candidates can be credited in a number of ways up to a maximum of 5 marks.*

Candidates must show a causal relationship between events.

Up to a **maximum of 5 marks in total, 1 mark** should be given for each accurate, relevant reason, and a **second mark** should be given for reasons that are developed. Candidates may achieve full marks by providing five straightforward reasons, three developed reasons, or a combination of these.

Possible reasons may include:
1. health was being affected by lack of food/malnutrition
2. some people were starving
3. soldiers took priority therefore there was less food on the Home Front
4. vital war workers needed fed adequately to produce weapons, etc
5. U-boats sank many supply ships which reduced the amount of food available
6. there was a limit to what civilians could grow (especially in cities)
7. food became expensive/prices of goods rose faster than peoples' wages
8. farm production affected by recruitment of labourers/ requisitioning of horses
9. failure of propaganda campaigns to limit food waste
10. rationing introduced to maintain a fair supply of food/ necessary to maintain high morale on the Home Front

19. *Candidates can be credited in a number of ways up to a maximum of 5 marks.*

Candidates must make an overall judgement about how fully the source explains the events. **1 mark** may be given for each valid point interpreted from the source or each valid point of significant omission provided.

A maximum of 2 marks may be given for answers which refer only to the source.

Possible points which may be identified in the source include:
1. it gave women an opportunity to prove themselves in a male-dominated society (doing more than cleaning the house and tending to the children)
2. (with so many men going to war there was a large gap in employment and) women responded by replacing men in the workplace
3. Women's Royal Air Force was created/women worked on planes as mechanics
4. less well known roles of women in the war included selling war bonds

Possible points of significant omission may include:
5. they worked in heavy industry
6. they worked in public transport (eg railways, trams, buses)
7. in farming and forestry/Land Army
8. they joined the newly formed women's police force
9. they joined the women's WRENS, WAACS/further details about the WRAF
10. many women worked in munitions
11. greater responsibility/promotion (eg supervisors)

20. *Candidates can be credited in a number of ways up to a maximum of 5 marks.*

Candidates must make a judgement about the usefulness of the source and support this by making evaluative comments on identified aspects of the source.

1 mark should be given for each relevant comment made, up to a **maximum of 5 marks in total.**
- A maximum of **4 marks** can be given for evaluative comments relating to the author, type of source, purpose and timing.
- A maximum of **2 marks** may be given for comments relating to the content of the source.
- A maximum of **2 marks** may be given for comments relating to points of significant omission.

Examples of aspects of the source and relevant comments:

Aspect of the source	Possible comment
Author: Modern Historian	Useful because he has expert knowledge/has studied a range of relevant sources
Type of Source: A text book/history book	Useful because it contains straightforward factual information without bias/well researched
Purpose: To inform	Useful because it provides detailed information
Timing: 1989	Useful because it has the benefit of hindsight

Content	Possible comment
the hundreds of fishing boats that had been working for the Royal Navy were free again to go fishing	Useful as it is accurate (wartime restrictions were lifted and fishing grounds reopened)
It meant there were far more boats chasing the same amount of fish/many boats could not make enough money to stay in business	Useful as it is accurate (many boats did go out of business)
On top of that it was far more difficult to sell fish. (Before the war most of the herring that were caught were sold to Germany and Russia)	Useful as it is accurate (Germany and Russia were both in chaos after the war)

Possible points of significant omission may include:
1. many industries received a boost during the war (eg shipbuilding, jute)
2. people at home were eating a lot less fish which decreased demand/European countries started to compete strongly with Scottish fleets and in 1920 the government removed the guaranteed price for herring
3. some fishing boats were in poor condition after wartime so not as productive
4. many industries declined after the war due to lack of wartime demand (eg agriculture, coal, jute)

Section 2, Context A, The Creation of the Medieval Kingdoms, 1066–1406

21. *Candidates can be credited in a number of ways up to a maximum of 6 marks.*

Candidates must show a causal relationship between events.

Up to a **maximum of 6 marks in total, 1 mark** should be given for each accurate, relevant reason, and a **second mark** should be given for reasons that are developed. Candidates may achieve full marks by providing six straightforward reasons, three developed reasons, or a combination of these.

Possible reasons may include:
1. David's mother Margaret was English/from a Saxon family which experienced Norman rule
2. David's sister was married to the King of England, Henry I
3. David spent part of his childhood in the royal court in England
4. David was married to an Anglo-Norman heiress (Matilda of Huntingdon)
5. David took part in Anglo-Norman ceremonies (eg was made a knight by Henry I)
6. David had many friends who were Anglo-Norman barons
7. David had land in England (eg Northampton/Huntingdon/Bedford)

22. Specific marking instructions for this question

Candidates can be credited in a number of ways up to a maximum of 8 marks.

Candidates must use knowledge to present a balanced assessment of the influence of different possible factors and come to a reasoned conclusion. **Up to 5 marks** are allocated for relevant points of knowledge used to support factors (but one mark should be deducted if the process is not clear in at least two factors). **1 mark** should be given for each relevant, factual key point of knowledge used to support a factor. **If only one factor is presented, a maximum of 3 marks should be given for relevant points of knowledge.**

Possible factors may include:	Relevant, factual, key points of knowledge to support this factor may include:
Illegal castles	1. Barons had built illegal castles without royal permission during the civil war 2. some Barons refused to hand the castles over to Henry (eg The Earl of York/Scarborough castle)
Illegal armies	3. Barons had hired mercenaries to fight for them/protect their land 4. illegal armies threatened Henry's control
Corrupt sheriffs	5. some sheriffs had been keeping fines paid by criminals instead of paying them to the king 6. some sheriffs had been accepting bribes from criminals
No common law	7. the law was different in every area across Henry's kingdom 8. Barons decided the law in their own area and as a result were very powerful
Land theft	9. some Barons were stealing land from their weaker neighbours 10. some Barons forged documents making false claims that they were the rightful heir to land
Large empire	11. Henry had a large empire (eg Scotland to the Pyrenees and could not be everywhere at once) 12. Henry's empire did not share many customs or traditions making it difficult to govern

Up to 3 marks should be given for presenting the answer in a structured way, leading to a conclusion which addresses the question, as follows:

1 mark for the answer being presented in a structured way, with knowledge being organised in support of different factors.

1 mark given for a conclusion with a valid judgement or overall summary.

1 mark given for a reason being provided in support of the judgement.

23. *Candidates can be credited in a number of ways **up to a maximum of 6 marks.***

Candidates must make a judgement about the usefulness of the source and support this by making evaluative comments on identified aspects of the source.

1 mark should be given for each relevant comment made, up to a **maximum of 6 marks in total.**
- A maximum of **4 marks** can be given for evaluative comments relating to the author, type of source, purpose and timing.
- A maximum of **2 marks** may be given for comments relating to the content of the source.
- A maximum of **2 marks** may be given for comments relating to points of significant omission.

Examples of aspects of the source and relevant comments:

Aspect of the source	Possible comment
Author: Monk	Useful because he would have been well placed to receive information/perhaps less useful because he is not an eyewitness
Type of Source: Chronicle	Useful because it was a detailed record of events
Purpose: To inform	Useful because it was written to inform us about the king's role in ending the Peasants' Revolt/perhaps less useful because it is biased in favour of the king
Timing: 1381	Useful because it was written at the time of the Peasants' Revolt

Content	Possible comment
The peasants' leader, Wat Tyler was killed	Useful because it is accurate (Wat Tyler did die during the Peasants' Revolt)
The king rode toward them (peasants) and persuaded them to put their weapons away	Useful because it is accurate (the king was successful in getting the peasants to lay down their arms)
The king promised the peasants that they would be treated fairly and so they agreed to go home	Useful because it is accurate (the king did manage to persuade the peasants to disperse)

Possible points of significant omission may include:
1. the king did agree to the peasants' demands
2. peasants ambushed by the king's army and arrested
3. leaders of the rebellion hanged

Section 2, Context B, War of the Three Kingdoms, 1603–1651

24. *Candidates can be credited in a number of ways **up to a maximum of 6 marks.***

Candidates must make a judgement about the usefulness of the source and support this by making evaluative comments on identified aspects of the source.

1 mark should be given for each relevant comment made, up to a **maximum of 6 marks in total.**
- A maximum of **4 marks** can be given for evaluative comments relating to the author, type of source, purpose and timing.
- A maximum of **2 marks** may be given for comments relating to the content of the source.
- A maximum of **2 marks** may be given for comments relating to points of significant omission.

Examples of aspects of the source and relevant comments:

Aspect of the source	Possible comment
Author: House of Commons	Useful because it is from eyewitnesses who were in dispute with the king
Type of Source: Official statement	Useful because it is an official government statement which outlines the concerns of parliament and will therefore be truthful/perhaps less useful as it may be biased
Purpose: To persuade	Useful because it attempts to justify the position of Parliament/perhaps less useful as it is not balanced
Timing: 1621	Useful because it is a primary source from the time when there were disputes between King James VI and I and Parliament

Content	Possible comment
Privileges of Parliament are our ancient birth right	Useful because it is accurate (Parliament was concerned that the king was trying to limit its power)
Matters concerning the king, state, defence, the church and the making of laws are for debating in Parliament only	Useful because it is accurate (Parliament did want to retain the right to debate certain state matters which the king opposed)
If any of its members are questioned for anything said or done in Parliament, the same is to be applied to the king	Useful because it is accurate (Parliament did believe the king should be accountable to Parliament as much as they were to him)

Possible points of significant omission may include:
1. James formally deleted the Protestation from the journals of Parliament
2. James dissolved Parliament demonstrating he did not agree with their protests
3. James and Parliament argued over the rights of the King with the King stressing his 'divine right' to rule
4. other issues that Parliament and the King argued over (eg the Spanish match/war in Europe)

25. *Candidates can be credited in a number of ways up to a maximum of 6 marks.*

Candidates must show a causal relationship between events.

Up to a **maximum of 6 marks in total, 1 mark** should be given for each accurate, relevant reason, and a **second mark** should be given for reasons that are developed. Candidates may achieve full marks by providing five straightforward reasons, three developed reasons, or a combination of these.

Possible reasons may include:

1. there was resentment towards the Anglican High Church ceremony that was part of Charles' coronation
2. Resentment of Charles as an absentee monarch
3. Scots suspicion that Charles wanted to be an absolute monarch
4. Charles demanded that Ministers accept and use the new Prayer Book, which was unpopular amongst the Ministers
5. there was public opposition to the introduction of the new Prayer Book (eg 1637 St Giles riots)
6. the Scottish clergy opposed the requirement to wear gowns and surplices as dictated by Laud's Canons
7. resentment at the abolition of Presbyteries and the threat of dissolution
8. Charles introduced Bishops into the Scottish Church which was opposed
9. Charles ruled that the General Assembly was not allowed to meet which caused opposition
10. Charles imposed the Act of Revocation which took back church or royal property that had been alienated since 1540, this angered the Church
11. resentment towards the money raising methods of Charles (eg Ship Money)

26. *Candidates can be credited in a number of ways up to a maximum of 8 marks.*

Candidates must use knowledge to present a balanced assessment of the influence of different possible factors and come to a reasoned conclusion. **Up to 5 marks** are allocated for relevant points of knowledge used to support factors (but one mark should be deducted if the process is not clear in at least two factors). **1 mark** should be given for each relevant, factual key point of knowledge used to support a factor.
If only one factor is presented, a maximum of 3 marks should be given for relevant points of knowledge.

Possible factors may include:	Relevant, factual, key points of knowledge to support this factor may include:
Financial disputes	1. arguments over the buying of titles, rich men were persuaded to buy titles and if they refused they were fined the same sum of money it would have cost for a title 2. in 1635 Charles ordered that everyone in the country should pay Ship Money. This tax was only meant to be paid by coastal towns but Charles insisted inland areas were also to pay, which caused resentment/led to arrests of some MPs eg Hampden 3. April 1640 Charles called for a Parliament to grant the money needed to fight a war in Scotland. Parliament refused and cited Laud and Strafford as men who were abusing the authority that had been given to them
Religious disputes	4. King Charles was married to Roman Catholic Henrietta Maria of France who was given free rein to practise her religion, this led to distrust over the religious loyalty of Charles 5. Charles preferred a High Anglican form of worship with ceremonies and rituals that made some believe he was leaning towards Catholicism, this upset the Protestants and Puritans/Charles also clashed with the Scots over the issue of the new Prayer Book this angered the Scots so much that they invaded England in 1639 6. the Appointment of Laud (who also preferred High Anglican worship) as Archbishop of Canterbury, brought about much opposition/Laud attempted to impose High Anglican forms of worship which were opposed by the Protestants eg the new Prayer Book and the wearing of vestments
Political disputes	7. in 1629 Charles refused to let Parliament meet. Members of Parliament arrived at Westminster to find that the doors had been locked with large chains and padlocks. They were locked out for eleven years 8. Parliament also demanded that Charles get rid of the Court of Star Chamber, which Charles used to rule without Parliament 9. in 1642, Charles went to Parliament with 300 soldiers to arrest his five biggest critics. Parliament had been tipped off and the five men had already fled to the safety of the city of London – this angered Parliament that the King was trying to deny them the right to speak out against him
King's character	10. Parliament considered Charles to be arrogant and conceited so they had a particularly bad relationship/Charles considered the poor relationships between his father and Parliament to be the fault of Parliament so did not trust them 11. Parliament and the King clashed over Charles' strong belief in the Divine Rights of Kings

Up to 3 marks should be given for presenting the answer in a structured way, leading to a conclusion which addresses the question, as follows:

1 mark for the answer being presented in a structured way, with knowledge being organised in support of different factors.

1 mark given for a conclusion with a valid judgement or overall summary.

1 mark given for a reason being provided in support of the judgement.

Section 2, Context C, The Atlantic Slave Trade, 1770–1807

27. *Candidates can be credited in a number of ways up to a maximum of 8 marks.*

Candidates must use knowledge to present a balanced assessment of the influence of different possible factors and come to a reasoned conclusion. **Up to 5 marks** are allocated for relevant points of knowledge used to support factors (but one mark should be deducted if the process is not clear in at least two factors). **1 mark** should be given for each relevant, factual key point of knowledge used to support a factor.
If only one factor is presented, a maximum of 3 marks should be given for relevant points of knowledge.

Possible factors may include:	Relevant, factual, key points of knowledge to support this factor may include:
Employment (marks should be awarded for any valid job related to the slave trade)	1. jobs in construction (eg factories, homes) 2. many people relied on the slave trade for employment, (eg shipbuilding, sailors, rope-makers, sail-makers) 3. other jobs (eg banking, insurance, industrial)
Industrial benefits	4. Glasgow – tobacco trade contributed to growth of industry 5. growth of industries such as copper-smelting, sugar-refining, glass-making and textiles 6. profits from the slave trade provided the capital for the Industrial Revolution
Financial/Municipal benefits	7. individuals/cities became richer due to the slave trade (eg Liverpool, Bristol, London) 8. wealthy individuals invested profits from the trade (eg schools, colleges, libraries) 9. London – provided financial services such as insurance/London banks provided long-term loans for slave trade
Consumer benefits	10. cotton, tobacco and sugar in high demand

Up to 3 marks should be given for presenting the answer in a structured way, leading to a conclusion which addresses the question, as follows:
- **1 mark** for the answer being presented in a structured way, with knowledge being organised in support of different factors.
- **1 mark** given for a conclusion with a valid judgement or overall summary.
- **1 mark** given for a reason being provided in support of the judgement.

28. *Candidates can be credited in a number of ways up to a maximum of 6 marks.*

Candidates must show a causal relationship between events.

Up to a **maximum of 6 marks in total**, **1 mark** should be given for each accurate, relevant reason, and a **second mark** should be given for reasons that are developed. Candidates

may achieve full marks by providing five straightforward reasons, three developed reasons, or a combination of these.

Possible reasons may include:
1. native populations were cleared from the islands/wiped out
2. fear of violent rebellion/Caribbean became more volatile
3. slave uprisings caused damage and destruction
4. small farms were replaced by large plantations
5. island economies stifled by slave trade (eg Jamaican economy became too reliant on sugar production)
6. natural beauty of island landscapes was damaged by the growth of plantations
7. slave trade brought racist attitudes to the Caribbean
8. new diseases were introduced to the islands

29. *Candidates can be credited in a number of ways up to a maximum of 6 marks.*

Candidates must make a judgement about the usefulness of the source and support this by making evaluative comments on identified aspects of the source.

1 mark should be given for each relevant comment made, up to a **maximum of 6 marks in total.**
- A maximum of **4 marks** can be given for evaluative comments relating to the author, type of source, purpose and timing.
- A maximum of **2 marks** may be given for comments relating to the content of the source.
- A maximum of **2 marks** may be given for comments relating to points of significant omission.

Examples of aspects of the source and relevant comments:

Aspect of the source	Possible comment
Author: William Wilberforce	Useful as it was from a well-known abolitionist who campaigned against slave trade
Type of Source: Speech	Useful as it was part of an official Parliamentary speech
Purpose: To persuade	Useful as it gives typical evidence/arguments used by abolitionists against slavery
Timing: 1789	Useful as it was delivered during the abolitionist campaign

Content	Possible comment
The right ankle of one is connected with the left ankle of another by a small iron fetter	Useful as it is accurate (slaves were chained together during the Middle Passage)
The slaves are so miserable at leaving their country, that they set sail at night	Useful as it is accurate (slave ships did leave at night due to fears held by slaves and fear of increased panic aboard slave ships)
For exercise, these miserable people, loaded down with chains and suffering from disease, are forced to dance by the terror of the whip	Useful as it is accurate (many slaves were punished if they refused to exercise on the deck/suffered from diseases)

Possible points of significant omission may include:
1. details of plantation conditions led to the boycott of sugar and slave produced goods
2. Equiano's eyewitness account of the Middle Passage in 'An Interesting Narrative' highlighted harsh conditions
3. Clarkson brought examples of slave equipment/plans of slave ships to show the public which caused outrage
4. other abolitionists used moral or religious arguments against slavery

Section 2, Context D, Changing Britain, 1760–1900

30. *Candidates can be credited in a number of ways up to a maximum of 8 marks.*

Candidates must use knowledge to present a balanced assessment of the influence of different possible factors and come to a reasoned conclusion. **Up to 5 marks** are allocated for relevant points of knowledge used to support factors (but one mark should be deducted if the process is not clear in at least **two** factors). **1 mark** should be given for each relevant, factual key point of knowledge used to support a factor. **If only one factor is presented, a maximum of 3 marks should be given for relevant points of knowledge.**

Possible factors may include:	Relevant, factual, key points of knowledge to support this factor may include:
Lack of clean water	1. contaminated/unclean drinking water led to diseases such as cholera 2. typhoid was also caused by contaminated drinking water
Lack of sanitation	3. open sewers allowed bacteria to multiply/ contaminated water supplies and led to the spread of disease
Lack of rubbish disposal	4. rubbish built up in the streets which attracted vermin/rats which caused disease (eg typhus)
Lack of adequate medical care/knowledge	5. poor families could not afford medical care, which meant that health problems were untreated/worsened 6. lack of knowledge/ treatment meant that some conditions that are treatable now were often fatal before 1900 (eg TB) 7. vaccinations for many diseases (eg measles/ polio) were not available/many of these diseases were often fatal
Overcrowding	8. overcrowding made it easier for disease to spread (eg cholera/TB)
Poor diet	9. poor diet/lack of vitamins led to conditions such as rickets 10. poor diet led to low immunity to disease/ meant that people took longer to/were less likely to recover from disease
Poor housing	11. poorly constructed houses were often damp/cold which made many medical conditions (eg TB/asthma) worse 12. lack of sunlight in cellar/ basement houses or cramped tenements/ closes led to conditions such as rickets

Up to 3 marks should be given for presenting the answer in a structured way, leading to a conclusion which addresses the question, as follows:
- **1 mark** for the answer being presented in a structured way, with knowledge being organised in support of different factors.
- **1 mark** given for a conclusion with a valid judgement or overall summary.
- **1 mark** given for a reason being provided in support of the judgement.

31. *Candidates can be credited in a number of ways up to a maximum of 6 marks.*

Candidates must make a judgement about the usefulness of the source and support this by making evaluative comments on identified aspects of the source.

1 mark should be given for each relevant comment made, up to a **maximum of 6 marks in total.**
- A **maximum of 4 marks** can be given for evaluative comments relating to the author, type of source, purpose and timing.
- A **maximum of 2 marks** may be given for comments relating to the content of the source.
- A **maximum of 2 marks** may be given for comments relating to points of significant omission.

Examples of aspects of the source and relevant comments:

Aspect of the source	Possible comment
Author: Government	Useful as the government will have first-hand knowledge of the steps taken to improve working conditions in factories
Type of Source: Act/Law	Useful as it gives a factual/ legal description of the new rules/official document
Purpose: To inform	Useful as it is intended to give a summary of the new laws that factory/mill owners have to abide by
Timing: 1833	Useful as it is from the time of improvements to working conditions in factories

Content	Possible comment
No children under the age of 9 should be employed in mills	Useful as it is accurate (the act did ban the employment of children under 9 in textile mills)
Limits to working hours (eg Children aged 9–13 must not work more than 8 hours each day/Children aged 14–18 must not work more than 12 hours each day/Children under 18 must not work at night)	Useful as it is accurate (the act did limit the working hours of children)
Government inspectors will be given the power to demand entry to textile mills and enforce these rules	Useful as it is accurate (the act did create government factory inspectors)

Possible points of significant omission may include:
1. 1844 act stated that women and children should no longer clean moving machinery/some machinery had to be fenced
2. 1847 act introduced a ten hour working day for women and children
3. 1878 act stated that no women should work more than 60 hours per week/no children under 10 should work in factories/introduced regulations for safety, ventilation and meals
4. new technology could make working conditions better

32. *Candidates can be credited in a number of ways* **up to a maximum of 6 marks.**

Candidates must show a causal relationship between events.

Up to **a maximum of 6 marks in total, 1 mark** should be given for each accurate, relevant reason, and a **second mark** should be given for reasons that are developed. Candidates may achieve full marks by providing five straightforward reasons, three developed reasons, or a combination of these.

Possible reasons may include:
1. their demands (eg …) were too radical for the time
2. the economy improved/jobs returned, so support for Chartism faded
3. the government refused to talk to the Chartists/rejected their petitions
4. many of the signatures on the petitions were false, so the Chartists lost respect
5. Chartists were ridiculed in the press, so lost respect
6. other movements offered more immediate and tangible benefits which attracted support away from Chartism
7. divisions amongst the Chartists (physical force/moral force) weakened the movement
8. Chartist demonstrations were broken up, so were not effective
9. the Chartists were poorly led (by Fergus O'Connor and William Lovett)

Section 2, Context E, The Making of Modern Britain, 1880–1951

33. *Candidates can be credited in a number of ways* **up to a maximum of 8 marks.**

Candidates must use knowledge to present a balanced assessment of the influence of different possible factors and come to a reasoned conclusion. **Up to 5 marks** are allocated for relevant points of knowledge used to support factors (but one mark should be deducted if the process is not clear

in at least **two** factors). **1 mark** should be given for each relevant, factual key point of knowledge used to support a factor. **If only one factor is presented, a maximum of 3 marks should be given for relevant points of knowledge.**

Possible factors may include:	Relevant, factual, key points of knowledge to support this factor may include:
Booth and Rowntree	1. Booth's report showed that 30.7% of the population of London were living in poverty. This shocked the public and government/provided evidence of poverty that could not be ignored 2. Booth's report showed that poverty was not always the poor person's own fault and helped to change laissez-faire/self-help attitudes 3. Rowntree's report showed that 27.8% of the population of York were living in poverty. This shocked the public and government/provided evidence of poverty that could not be ignored 4. Rowntree's report showed that poverty wasn't just in London/something had to be done to tackle poverty across Britain 5. Rowntree's report showed that there was a cycle of poverty, so helped convince people that the poor needed help at certain times of their lives
The Boer War/National Efficiency	6. during the Boer War 1/3 (as high as 2/3 in some areas) of recruits were unfit for service. This was often due to poor health caused by poverty – people were worried that if poverty was not tackled then Britain would not be able to defend herself in a war 7. people were concerned that Britain would not have a healthy productive workforce if poverty was not tackled
New Liberalism	8. new Liberals such as David Lloyd George and Winston Churchill wanted to pass reforms to help the poor and helped to change attitudes in the Liberal Party
The German example	9. the Germans had introduced welfare reforms already (pensions and national insurance) so the British wanted to keep up with Germany
Democracy/Trade Unions/The Threat of Labour	10. more men/the working classes could now vote so political parties had to change their policies on poverty to avoid losing votes 11. trade unions were becoming bigger/more influential/had helped to form the Labour Party and were pushing for reforms to help the poor 12. the Labour Party was formed in 1900 and supported reforms to help the poor/The other parties had to respond, or they would lose votes to the new Labour Party

Up to 3 marks should be given for presenting the answer in a structured way, leading to a conclusion which addresses the question, as follows:

1 mark for the answer being presented in a structured way, with knowledge being organised in support of different factors.

1 mark given for a conclusion with a valid judgement or overall summary.

1 mark given for a reason being provided in support of the judgement.

34. *Candidates can be credited in a number of ways up to a maximum of 6 marks.*

Candidates must show a causal relationship between events.

Up to **a maximum of 6 marks in total, 1 mark** should be given for each accurate, relevant reason, and a **second mark** should be given for reasons that are developed. Candidates may achieve full marks by providing six straightforward reasons, three developed reasons, or a combination of these.

Possible reasons may include:
1. free school meals made children healthier because this was the only meal that many children got in a day/parents could not afford to feed children at home
2. medical inspections at school made children healthier because they identified medical problems/later treatment was introduced
3. the Children Act/Children's Charter improved the lives of the young because they would no longer be sent to adult prisons/treated as adult criminals
4. the Children Act/Children's Charter improved the lives of the young because children could no longer be sentenced to death for committing a crime
5. pensions improved the lives of the elderly because they helped many of the elderly poor to stay out of the workhouse/gave the elderly poor enough extra money to get by
6. National Insurance helped to make workers healthier because free medical treatment was provided for insured workers
7. National Insurance improved the lives of families because maternity grants were given after the birth of children
8. National Insurance improved the lives of workers because they could now receive free specialist medical treatment for TB
9. National Insurance improved the lives of the unemployed because some workers received unemployment benefit, helping them to stay out of poverty
10. the Workmen's Compensation Act improved the lives of workers because now they could get compensation for illness or injury caused by work
11. labour exchanges improved the lives of the unemployed because they helped them to find a job and earn money

35. *Candidates can be credited in a number of ways up to a maximum of 6 marks.*

Candidates must make a judgement about the usefulness of the source and support this by making evaluative comments on identified aspects of the source.

1 mark should be given for each relevant comment made, up to a **maximum of 6 marks in total.**
- A maximum of **4 marks** can be given for evaluative comments relating to the author, type of source, purpose and timing.
- A maximum of **2 marks** may be given for comments relating to the content of the source.
- A maximum of **2 marks** may be given for comments relating to points of significant omission.

Examples of aspects of the source and relevant comments:

Aspect of the source	Possible comment
Author: Government	Useful as the government will have knowledge of the health service they are introducing
Type of Source: Advertisement	Useful as it will be informative/ easy to understand
Purpose: To inform	Useful as it is intended to give a summary of how the NHS will work
Timing: May 1948	Useful as it is a primary source from the time that the NHS was introduced

Content	Possible comment
The new NHS starts on the 5th July	Useful as it is accurate (the NHS was launched in the summer of 1948)
Anyone can use the NHS/men, women children/no age limits	Useful as this is accurate (the NHS was available to all)
Right to use NHS does not depend on weekly payments	Useful as this is accurate (access to the NHS did not depend on contributions)

Possible points of significant omission may include:
1. the NHS provided many services – GPs, hospital treatment, specialist treatment, opticians, dentists for example
2. the NHS was introduced by Aneurin Bevan
3. the NHS was recommended in the Beveridge Report/to tackle the 'giant' of disease
4. there was a huge demand for NHS services after it was introduced

Section 3, Context A, The Cross and the Crescent; the Crusades, 1071–1192

36. *Candidates can be credited in a number of ways up to a maximum of 4 marks.*

Candidates must make direct comparisons of the two sources, either or in detail. A simple comparison will indicate what points of detail or overall viewpoint they agree or disagree about and should be given **1 mark**. A developed comparison of the points of detail or overall viewpoint should be given **2 marks**. Candidates may achieve full marks by making four simple comparisons, two developed comparisons or by a combination of these.

Possible points of comparison may include:

Source A	Source B
Overall: Sources A and B agree that the Pope called the First Crusade in 1095	
The Pope said that Jerusalem must be recaptured	The Pope said Jerusalem was the most important city in the world and it must be taken back from the Muslims
The Pope warned that every Christian in the west must fight or the Muslims could advance into Europe	The Pope said a Christian army must be called to stop the Muslims before they captured every city they attacked
He appealed to the knights to stop their violent behaviour towards each other and instead use their military skills against God's enemy in the east	Pope Urban told the knights of Europe to stop fighting amongst each other and unite against the infidel

37. *Candidates can be credited in a number of ways up to a maximum of 6 marks.*

Candidates must make an overall judgement about how fully the source explains the events. **1 mark** may be given for each valid point interpreted from the source or each valid point of significant omission provided.

A maximum of 2 marks may be given for answers which refer only to the source.

Possible points which may be identified in the source include:
1. the Muslims were well prepared/had strengthened the wall around the city
2. the Muslims had collected the harvest early and had enough food to last for several months/expected a long siege
3. the Muslims fought back and forced the Crusaders to retreat
4. the Crusaders did not have scaling ladders or siege machines/required supplies from Europe

Possible points of significant omission may include:
5. the Muslims had poisoned/drained the local water wells and so the Crusaders had no water
6. Christians had been expelled from the city so the Crusaders did not have any allies inside Jerusalem
7. the city was built on slopes so could not be attacked from all angles
8. the city wall was strengthened by a large citadel/David's Tower which made an attack difficult

38. *Candidates can be credited in a number of ways up to a maximum of 5 marks.*

Candidates must show a causal relationship between events.

Up to a **maximum of 5 marks in total, 1 mark** should be given for each accurate, relevant reason, and a **second mark** should be given for reasons that are developed. Candidates may achieve full marks by providing five straightforward reasons, three developed reasons, or a combination of these.

Possible reasons may include:
1. the Crusader army was small (many Crusaders had returned to Europe) and so it was difficult to defend the Crusader states/Latin states
2. the Crusaders were constantly attacked by Muslims and so lost more soldiers/supplies
3. the Crusader states/Latin States were far apart and so were difficult to defend
4. the land was infertile so it was difficult to grow crops
5. there was a lack of peasants so there was no one to farm the land
6. the Crusaders did not have key supplies eg timber and so could not build siege machines
7. the Crusaders did not have enough boats needed to capture the coastal towns
8. the Crusaders fought among themselves and so were not united against the Muslims

39. *Candidates can be credited in a number of ways up to a maximum of 5 marks.*

They may take different perspectives on the events and may describe a variety of different aspects of the events.

1 mark should be given for each accurate relevant key point of knowledge. A **second mark** should be given for each point that is developed, up to a maximum of **5 marks**. Candidates may achieve full marks by providing five straightforward points, by making three developed points, or a combination of these.

Possible points of knowledge may include:
1. the Muslims attacked the Crusaders with darts and arrows
2. the Muslims attempted to draw the Crusaders from their defensive position
3. the Crusaders held their defensive line
4. the Muslim army grew tired
5. the Crusaders charged at the Muslims
6. many Muslims were killed/high number of casualties in the Muslim army
7. the Muslim army fled
8. the Crusaders won the battle

Section 3, Context B, 'Tea and Freedom': the American Revolution, 1774–1783

40. *Candidates can be credited in a number of ways up to a maximum of 5 marks.*

Candidates must show a causal relationship between events.

Up to a **maximum of 5 marks in total, 1 mark** should be given for each accurate, relevant reason, and a **second mark** should be given for reasons that are developed. Candidates may achieve full marks by providing five straightforward reasons, three developed reasons, or a combination of these.

Possible reasons may include:
1. Thomas Paine's pamphlet 'Common Sense' sold 150,000 copies and persuaded many British people the American cause was just
2. radicals in Britain opposed war and supported American demands for reform (eg no taxation without representation)
3. Edmund Burke thought that using force against the colonists would be counter-productive
4. Edmund Burke argued against taxation in America to raise funds for Britain
5. radicals in Britain supported the colonists demands for reform as they wanted political reform at home

41. *Candidates can be credited in a number of ways up to a maximum of 4 marks.*

Candidates must make direct comparisons of the two sources, either overall or in detail. A simple comparison will indicate what points of detail or overall viewpoint they agree or disagree about and should be given **1 mark**. A developed comparison of the points of detail or overall viewpoint should be given **2 marks**. Candidates may achieve full marks by making four simple comparisons, two developed comparisons or by a combination of these.

Possible points of comparison may include:

Source A	Source B
Overall: The sources agree about the capabilities of the Continental Army	
The troops themselves were usually inexperienced in battle	Many of the soldiers needed practice with their weapons
Many soldiers left to return home, leaving the army without enough men	The army needed troops even more than fortifications
Washington was always short of money to buy much needed supplies or to pay his soldiers	The Continental Army was always short of ammunition/Gunpowder was always in short supply but houses were stripped of lead for bullets

42. *Candidates can be credited in a number of ways **up to a maximum of 5 marks**.*

They may take different perspectives on the events and may describe a variety of different aspects of the events.

1 mark should be given for each accurate relevant key point of knowledge. A **second mark** should be given for each point that is developed, up to a maximum of **5 marks**. Candidates may achieve full marks by providing five straightforward points, by making three developed points, or a combination of these.

Possible points of knowledge may include:
1. British plan was to link their two armies to defeat the colonists
2. Burgoyne's army invaded from Canada
3. General Howe had taken the main British army to Philadelphia leaving General Clinton with a small army in New York
4. Americans cut down trees and blocked the British army's progress
5. colonists had destroyed crops and burned potential food supplies
6. some Indian troops deserted the British
7. St Leger's army was defeated/he retreated
8. British eventually outnumbered by colonists
9. Burgoyne's army surrounded and unable to break out, so surrendered

43. *Candidates can be credited in a number of ways **up to a maximum of 6 marks**.*

Candidates must make an overall judgement about how fully the source explains the events. **1 mark** may be given for each valid point interpreted from the source or each valid point of significant omission provided.

A maximum of 2 marks may be given for answers which refer only to the source.

Possible points which may be identified in the source include:
1. after the British defeat at Saratoga, many in Europe were keen to take advantage of British weakness
2. France wanted revenge for loss of colonies so offered financial support
3. France also gave military assistance in the form of soldiers and gunpowder to put more pressure on Britain
4. Spain saw an opportunity to try to retake Gibraltar to distract Britain

Possible points of significant omission may include:
5. foreign intervention challenged Britain's control of the seas
6. foreign intervention made it more difficult for Britain to reinforce and supply forces in America
7. the French attacked British colonies in the Caribbean which distracted them/Britain had to divert vital troops to Europe and the West Indies
8. foreign intervention affected British morale as they had no major allies
9. formal Franco-American alliance increased pressure on Britain

Section 3, Context C, USA 1850–1880

44. *Candidates can be credited in a number of ways **up to a maximum of 4 marks**.*

Candidates must make direct comparisons of the two sources, either overall or in detail. A simple comparison will indicate what points of detail or overall viewpoint they agree or disagree about and should be given **1 mark**. A developed comparison of the points of detail or overall

viewpoint should be given **2 marks**. Candidates may achieve full marks by making four simple comparisons, two developed comparisons or by a combination of these.

Possible points of comparison may include:

Source A	Source B
Overall: Both sources agree about the treatment of slaves on Southern Plantations	
Gave me meat and bread with the other slaves, which was not half enough for me to live upon	Slaves were given the absolute minimum amount of food to survive
He flogged me nearly every day/I got a severe flogging of one hundred lashes	The usual method of punishing slaves was using a system of floggings
He set me to work without any shirt in the cotton field, in a very hot sun	Some slaves were punished by being tied to trees on the plantation, often in the burning heat of the sun

45. *Candidates can be credited in a number of ways **up to a maximum of 6 marks**.*

Candidates must make an overall judgement about how fully the source explains the events. **1 mark** may be given for each valid point interpreted from the source or each valid point of significant omission provided.

A maximum of 2 marks may be given for answers which refer only to the source.

Possible points which may be identified in the source include:
1. southern States seceded in order to escape high taxes
2. southern States thought of themselves as a separate community
3. southern States disliked/despised/hated/feared their northern neighbours
4. there was also a feeling in the South that there would be more advantages to secession than staying in the union

Possible points of significant omission may include:
5. Lincoln's election alarmed pro-slavery Southerners/saw him as an abolitionist
6. southerners wanted to protect slavery for economic reasons/Southerners viewed slavery as essential to protecting their way of life
7. economic differences between the industrial North and agricultural South
8. secession down to a fear of losing states' rights

46. *Candidates can be credited in a number of ways **up to a maximum of 5 marks**.*

They may take different perspectives on the events and may describe a variety of different aspects of the events.

1 mark should be given for each accurate relevant key point of knowledge. A **second mark** should be given for each point that is developed, up to a maximum of **5 marks**. Candidates may achieve full marks by providing five straightforward points, by making three developed points, or a combination of these.

Possible points of knowledge may include:
1. the Bureau was set up to help newly freed black slaves
2. it helped to provide food for former slaves
3. helped former slaves to purchase land for farming
4. paid for the education of former slaves
5. set up hospitals for former slaves
6. helped former slaves find jobs
7. some Bureau agents were corrupt and incompetent

47. *Candidates can be credited in a number of ways up to a maximum of 5 marks.*

Candidates must show a causal relationship between events.

Up to **a maximum of 5 marks in total, 1 mark** should be given for each accurate, relevant reason, and a **second mark** should be given for reasons that are developed. Candidates may achieve full marks by providing five straightforward reasons, three developed reasons, or a combination of these.

Possible reasons may include:
1. clash of cultures – many white Americans saw Native Americans as savages/inferior (they thought westward expansion was their right)
2. Native Americans wanted freedom to roam/hunt; white Americans wanted to farm
3. treaties with the Native Americans broken – felt betrayed due to regularly broken promises
4. white settlers had a 'property attitude' towards land/ Native Americans did not/believed that Great Spirit had created land for their care
5. government grants to encourage gold prospecting alarmed Native Americans (Colorado & Montana in 1858/& the Black Hills in 1874)
6. many white Americans favoured setting up reservations/ Native Americans objected to reservation life – not enough government support
7. white/Native American tension led to atrocities/ massacres/wars (eg Fetterman massacre in 1866 Battle of Little Big Horn 1876)
8. hunting/sacred grounds disturbed by settlers/miners/ railroads crossing Native American territory on the way to California and Oregon
9. destruction of buffalo herds brought further conflict – took away Native American means of supporting life on the Plains

Section 3, Context D, Hitler and Nazi Germany, 1919–1939

48. *Candidates can be credited in a number of ways up to a maximum of 5 marks.*

They may take different perspectives on the events and may describe a variety of different aspects of the events.

1 mark should be given for each accurate relevant key point of knowledge. A **second mark** should be given for each point that is developed, up to a maximum of **5 marks**. Candidates may achieve full marks by providing five straightforward points, by making three developed points, or a combination of these.

Possible points of knowledge may include:
1. Hitler's oratory skills (his ability to put into words the frustrations of millions of Germans)
2. Hitler gave people somebody to blame for their problems: Communists, Jews, etc
3. Hitler promised something for everyone/claimed he was the only person who could create jobs and end Depression
4. to a worried middle-class Hitler looked like the only person willing to take on the Communists
5. the SA Brownshirts seemed well organised and disciplined/made Hitler look like a strong leader
6. Hitler's uncompromising stance against the Treaty of Versailles/the Weimar Republic
7. Hitler's genius at propaganda (eg uniforms, Swastika etc) made him and Nazis stand out from other political parties/clear simple message that appealed to many

49. *Candidates can be credited in a number of ways up to a maximum of 4 marks.*

Candidates must make direct comparisons of the two sources, either overall or in detail. A simple comparison will indicate what points of detail or overall viewpoint they agree or disagree about and should be given **1 mark**. A developed comparison of the points of detail or overall viewpoint should be given **2 marks**. Candidates may achieve full marks by making four simple comparisons, two developed comparisons or by a combination of these.

Possible points of comparison may include:

Source A	Source B
Overall: Sources A and B agree about the events of the Night of the Long Knives	
Units of the SS arrested the leaders of the SA	Members of the SS stormed a hotel where the SA had gathered, pulled Röhm and his henchmen from their beds and had them arrested
77 men were executed on charges of treason	Some were promptly executed
Röhm was shot	An SS officer shot Röhm at point blank range

50. *Candidates can be credited in a number of ways up to a maximum of 5 marks.*

Candidates must show a causal relationship between events.

Up to **a maximum of 5 marks in total, 1 mark** should be given for each accurate, relevant reason, and a **second mark** should be given for reasons that are developed. Candidates may achieve full marks by providing five straightforward reasons, three developed reasons, or a combination of these.

Possible reasons may include:
1. widespread fear of Nazi regime (eg Gestapo/informers/ concentration camps)
2. opposition leaders were arrested or killed/many leaders fled Germany
3. many Germans supported Hitler/many people who did not actively support the Nazis just kept their views quiet
4. opposition groups were often infiltrated by the Nazis/ the groups had to meet in secret
5. opposition faced difficulty in publicising their views/ strict censorship of anything critical of the regime
6. little co-operation between opposition groups/left wing opposition/Communists and Socialists refused to cooperate
7. opposition groups such as the Edelweiss Pirates, Texas Band and Navaho were disorganised
8. most church groups agreed to co-operate with the Nazis
9. outspoken individuals (Bonhoeffer, Neimoller) were rounded up/no protection from the courts, if arrested would be severely punished
10. overseas assistance was lacking

51. *Candidates can be credited in a number of ways up to a maximum of 6 marks.*

Candidates must make an overall judgement about how fully the source explains the events. **1 mark** may be given for each valid point interpreted from the source or each valid point of significant omission provided.

A maximum of 2 marks may be given for answers which refer only to the source.

154 ANSWERS FOR NATIONAL 5 HISTORY

Possible points which may be identified in the source include:

1. schools tried to develop a loyal following for Hitler
2. geography taught pupils about the land Germany had taken away from her in 1919 and the need for Germany to have living space
3. the science curriculum was changed so shooting had to be studied as well as bridge building and the impact of poisonous gases
4. girls had a different curriculum as they studied domestic science and racial studies (both of these were to prepare young girls to be the perfect wife and mother)

Possible points of significant omission may include:

5. in racial studies girls were taught about the characteristics to look out for in a perfect husband
6. all teachers had to be vetted by local Nazi officials (any teacher considered disloyal was sacked)
7. history was based on the glory of Germany – a nationalistic approach was compulsory
8. biology became a study of the different races to 'prove' the Nazi belief in racial superiority
9. teachers were expected to attack the life style of the Jews (Anti-Semitic textbooks even for young children to increase bad feeling towards Jews)
10. PE became a very important part of the curriculum to increase fitness/RE was removed as Nazis disliked Christianity
11. maths had a military slant (eg sums about the amount of bombs an aircraft could carry)
12. Hitler's photo/Swastika flag in classroom as a constant reminder of Nazism

Section 3, Context E, Red Flag: Lenin and the Russian Revolution, 1894–1921

52. *Candidates can be credited in a number of ways up to a maximum of 5 marks.*

They may take different perspectives on the events and may describe a variety of different aspects of the events.

1 mark should be given for each accurate relevant key point of knowledge. A **second mark** should be given for each point that is developed, up to a maximum of **5 marks**. Candidates may achieve full marks by providing five straightforward points, by making three developed points, or a combination of these.

Possible points of knowledge may include:

1. striking factory workers in St Petersburg marched to the Winter Palace
2. the Tsar was not there but the palace and the streets around it were guarded by troops
3. the march was led by Father Gapon
4. the police had asked the marchers to go home/not to march
5. the workers wanted to petition the Tsar about their working conditions/long hours and low pay
6. the crowd was large (200,000) but peaceful
7. the crowd included women and children
8. marchers wore their Sunday clothes, sang hymns and carried icons and pictures of the Tsar
9. mounted Cossacks at the front charged at the marchers
10. soldiers opened fire, killing and injuring many

53. *Candidates can be credited in a number of ways up to a maximum of 6 marks.*

Candidates must make an overall judgement about how fully the source explains the events. **1 mark** may be given for

each valid point interpreted from the source or each valid point of significant omission provided.

A maximum of 2 marks may be given for answers which refer only to the source.

Possible points which may be identified in the source include:

1. expansion of health services
2. system of health insurance for workers introduced
3. 50,000 additional primary schools established
4. expansion of secondary and higher educational institutions

Possible points of significant omission may include:

5. increased land available for peasants to purchase
6. creation of Kulaks
7. land organisation commissions set up to supervise these reforms
8. abolition of the Mir's communal land ownership
9. gave peasants full civil equality
10. improvement of working conditions in factories
11. trade unions legalised
12. some regulation of the justice system introduced

54. *Candidates can be credited in a number of ways up to a maximum of 5 marks.*

Candidates must show a causal relationship between events.

Up to **a maximum of 5 marks in total, 1 mark** should be given for each accurate, relevant reason, and a **second mark** should be given for reasons that are developed. Candidates may achieve full marks by providing five straightforward reasons, three developed reasons, or a combination of these.

Possible reasons may include:

1. Tsar decided to take personal control of the army during the First World War so was seen as responsible for defeats
2. Tsar went to the Front and left the Tsarina in charge – she was not competent to take charge/Tsarina allowed Rasputin to influence her decision making
3. Tsarina was German and many people thought she was not fully loyal/rumours she was a German spy which lost the Tsar further support
4. heavy losses demoralised the army and soldiers became reluctant to fight for the Tsar/rising numbers of deserters
5. shortage of weapons and ammunition during First World War further demoralised troops
6. generals lost faith in the Tsar and encouraged him to abdicate
7. peasants resented the loss of their sons in the fighting/loss of their animals to the army
8. war effort devastated the economy and the Tsar was blamed for this
9. workers demonstrated about shortages and working conditions/protest strikes began/shortages of food and fuel in cities led to great discontent
10. Tsar tried to return to Petrograd but the train was stopped and he had no choice but to abdicate

55. *Candidates can be credited in a number of ways up to a maximum of 4 marks.*

Candidates must make direct comparisons of the two sources, either overall or in detail. A simple comparison will indicate what points of detail or overall viewpoint they agree or disagree about and should be given **1 mark**. A developed comparison of the points of detail or overall viewpoint should be given **2 marks**. Candidates may achieve full marks by making four simple comparisons, two developed comparisons or by a combination of these.

Possible points of comparison may include:

Source B	Source C
Overall: Both sources agree about the reasons for the Bolshevik victory in the Civil War	
The territory held by the Bolsheviks was a great advantage to them/their control of central areas meant shorter lines of supply and communication	The Bolsheviks held better territory/had access to railways for their communication and supply lines
The Bolsheviks were better prepared to mobilise their troops and acquire resources	The Bolsheviks won the Civil War largely because they were well prepared and disciplined
The Whites were disorganised in battle	The Whites were disorganised, lacking in the ability to properly mobilise and lead their troops

Section 3, Context F, Mussolini and Fascist Italy, 1919–1939

56. *Candidates can be credited in a number of ways* **up to a maximum of 5 marks.**

They may take different perspectives on the events and may describe a variety of different aspects of the events.

1 mark should be given for each accurate relevant key point of knowledge. A **second mark** should be given for each point that is developed, up to a maximum of **5 marks.** Candidates may achieve full marks by providing five straightforward points, by making three developed points, or a combination of these.

Possible points of knowledge may include:
1. trade unions were outlawed
2. the currency was re-valued in the 'Battle for the Lira.'
3. high tariffs were placed on foreign imports
4. the Battle for Grain was established
5. Battle for Land to make marshland useable for farming eg the Pontine Marshes
6. the Ministry of Corporations was established, headed by Giuseppe Bottai
7. government investment to create employment and modernise industry eg electrification of railways, growth of car industry
8. paid national holidays were introduced in 1938

57. **Specific marking instructions for this question**

    Candidates can be credited in a number of ways **up to a maximum of 4 marks.**

Candidates must make direct comparisons of the two sources, either overall or in detail. A simple comparison will indicate what points of detail or overall viewpoint they agree or disagree about and should be given **1 mark.** A developed comparison of the points of detail or overall viewpoint should be given **2 marks.** Candidates may achieve full marks by making four simple comparisons, two developed comparisons or by a combination of these.

Possible points of comparison may include:

Source A	Source B
Overall: The sources disagree about the effectiveness of Fascist propaganda	
Mussolini was portrayed as athletic, strong and courageous and most Italians believed this	Few Italians believed the ridiculous claims that Mussolini was a brilliant athlete and musician
The Fascist regime was very successful in controlling the output of radio and cinema	While the Fascist regime did its best to control the media, in reality Italians watched American films which certainly did not support Fascist ideas
One admirer of him was the British Foreign Secretary, Austen Chamberlain, who was widely reported as saying that Mussolini was 'a wonderful man working for the greatness of his country'	Foreigners could see through the Fascists' crude propaganda attempts and in the European press Mussolini was often presented as a figure of fun

58. *Candidates can be credited in a number of ways* **up to a maximum of 6 marks.**

Candidates must make an overall judgement about how fully the source explains the events. **1 mark** may be given for each valid point interpreted from the source or each valid point of significant omission provided.

A maximum of 2 marks may be given for answers which refer only to the source.

Possible points which may be identified in the source include:
1. his main aim was to make Italy respected as a world power
2. to achieve this he wanted to build up the Italian armed forces to make Italy feared
3. Mussolini was determined that one day Italy would be the dominant power in the Mediterranean
4. he was particularly keen to extend Italian influence in the countries of the Balkans

Possible points of significant omission may include:
5. to increase Italian influence in Albania
6. to encourage the break-up of Yugoslavia
7. to encourage Fascism in Germany
8. to take over Ethiopia/to build an Italian Empire in Africa
9. to contain Hitler's influence in Austria

59. *Candidates can be credited in a number of ways* **up to a maximum of 5 marks.**

Candidates must show a causal relationship between events.

Up to a **maximum of 5 marks in total, 1 mark** should be given for each accurate, relevant reason, and a **second mark** should be given for reasons that are developed. Candidates may achieve full marks by providing five straightforward reasons, three developed reasons, or a combination of these.

Possible reasons may include:
1. opposition groups were weakened by their inability to unite on a common platform
2. opposition parties banned after 1926

3. opponents were afraid of imprisonment in concentration camps
4. Mussolini was popular amongst many people
5. opposition received relatively little publicity as loyal journalists received extra pay in the form of government grants
6. the regime was able to portray opposition as unpatriotic
7. people were afraid of the Blackshirts/secret police and this ensured Italians obeyed Mussolini
8. Lateran Treaty neutralised opposition from RC Church and its members

Section 3, Context G, Free at Last? Civil Rights in the USA, 1918—1968

60. *Candidates can be credited in a number of ways up to a maximum of 4 marks.*

Candidates must make direct comparisons of the two sources, either overall or in detail. A simple comparison will indicate what points of detail or overall viewpoint they agree or disagree about and should be given **1 mark**. A developed comparison of the points of detail or overall viewpoint should be given **2 marks**. Candidates may achieve full marks by making four simple comparisons, two developed comparisons or by a combination of these.

Possible points of comparison may include:

Source A	Source B
Overall: The sources agree about the activities of the Ku Klux Klan	
Dressed in their white hoods the Klan were very frightening – they looked like ghosts!	As far as I could see they were all disguised, with white sheets pulled over their heads
They sneaked around at night when us blacks were in our beds	The Klan came to my house about ten o'clock. I was in bed at that time fast asleep
The Klansmen tied up the blacks that they caught and beat them/They left their victims with their hands tied in the air and the blood streaming out of their wounds	They took me out into the yard they struck me three times over the head with a pistol

61. *Candidates can be credited in a number of ways up to a maximum of 6 marks.*

Candidates must make an overall judgement about how fully the source explains the events. **1 mark** may be given for each valid point interpreted from the source or each valid point of significant omission provided.

A maximum of 2 marks may be given for answers which refer only to the source.

Possible points which may be identified in the source include:
1. soldiers in World War II experienced life in a more equal society when abroad and were determined to fight against discrimination when they returned
2. black Americans were better educated than previous generations and therefore better equipped to challenge discrimination
3. the success of the Montgomery Bus Boycott encouraged others to become involved in the fight for civil rights

4. the leadership of civil rights campaigner Martin Luther King inspired others to join the civil rights campaign

Possible points of significant omission may include:
5. World War II had been fought against the racism of Nazi Germany for the supposed freedom of all Americans, leading to a growth in support for civil rights for black Americans
6. influence of 'Double-V' campaign encouraged greater demands for civil rights
7. organisations such as the NAACP were effective in highlighting the discrimination faced by black Americans and in attracting the support of black and white Americans in the movement for black civil rights
8. the support of federal government in ending segregation, such as at Central High School in Little Rock, encouraged black Americans to believe that their demands would not be ignored
9. civil rights campaigns, such as at the Marches on Birmingham and Washington, attracted great media publicity/further fuelled demands for change

62. *Candidates can be credited in a number of ways up to a maximum of 5 marks.*

They may take different perspectives on the events and may describe a variety of different aspects of the events.

1 mark should be given for each accurate relevant key point of knowledge. A **second mark** should be given for each point that is developed, up to a maximum of **5 marks**. Candidates may achieve full marks by providing five straightforward points, by making three developed points, or a combination of these.

Possible points of knowledge may include:
1. nine black students were encouraged to enrol at Central High School by the NAACP
2. the Governor of Arkansas, Orval Faubus, was strongly opposed to desegregation and sent State troopers to the school to prevent the black students from entering
3. a mob of white people also gathered outside awaiting the arrival of the black students
4. the first black student to attempt to enter the building was Elizabeth Eckford/she was faced with verbal abuse from white protestors outside the school
5. President Eisenhower ordered Governor Faubus to remove the State troopers
6. President Eisenhower sent in federal troops to protect the black students and ensure their safe entry to the school
7. the federal troops stayed for a year and even patrolled the corridors of Central High School
8. despite the presence of the troops the black students faced verbal and physical abuse from white students at Central High School

63. *Candidates can be credited in a number of ways up to a maximum of 5 marks.*

Candidates must show a causal relationship between events.

Up to a **maximum of 5 marks in total, 1 mark** should be given for each accurate, relevant reason, and a **second mark** should be given for reasons that are developed. Candidates may achieve full marks by providing five straightforward reasons, three developed reasons, or a combination of these.

Possible reasons may include:

1. predominantly white police forces led to resentment/ riots were sparked by police actions which were perceived by many black Americans to be unfair
2. discontent resulting from high levels of poverty/ unemployment in ghettos/those that did have work were frustrated that they earned so little
3. housing in the ghetto was overcrowded and of poor quality which further fuelled resentment amongst black Americans
4. black Americans were angry at the lack of health services in the ghetto
5. frustration at the lack of investment in ghetto schools/low educational standards which meant that black Americans saw no way out of the ghetto
6. high crime rates in the ghetto led to even greater feelings of despair
7. citizens of the ghettos were angry at a government which they believed to have ignored their needs for far too long
8. radical groups (eg the Black Panthers) encouraged direct action

Section 3, Context H, Appeasement and the Road to War, 1918–1939

64. *Candidates can be credited in a number of ways* **up to a maximum of 5 marks**.

Candidates must show a causal relationship between events.

Up to a **maximum of 5 marks in total**, **1 mark** should be given for each accurate, relevant reason, and a **second mark** should be given for reasons that are developed. Candidates may achieve full marks by providing five straightforward reasons, three developed reasons, or a combination of these.

Possible reasons may include:

1. many felt that the military terms of the Treaty of Versailles had been too harsh and Germany should be allowed to rearm
2. Hitler's claims that rearmament was merely required for security, helped soften opinion against German rearmament
3. Hitler's offer to disarm should other countries do so convinced others that military action was not required to halt German rearmament
4. cuts in defence spending and the weakness of the British armed forces restricted the opportunity for military action
5. given the horrors of World War One, there was little sign that British public opinion would have supported military action against Hitler
6. there was a thriving peace movement in Britain which further reduced support for military action
7. many within Britain saw a strong Germany as a useful barrier against the spread of communism and therefore supported German rearmament
8. the construction of the Maginot Line gave the French a defensive mentality and a sense of security that reduced fears of German rearmament

65. *Candidates can be credited in a number of ways* **up to a maximum of 5 marks**.

They may take different perspectives on the events and may describe a variety of different aspects of the events.

1 mark should be given for each accurate relevant key point of knowledge. A **second mark** should be given for each point that is developed, up to a maximum of **5 marks**. Candidates may achieve full marks by providing five straightforward points, by making three developed points, or a combination of these.

Possible points of knowledge may include:

1. the Austrian Nazi Party led by Seyss-Inquart had embarked on a series of activities which included mass demonstrations and bomb attacks
2. Chancellor Schuschnigg of Austria asked to meet Hitler to discuss the activities of the Austrian Nazis/Schuschnigg travelled to Berchtesgaden to meet Hitler
3. Schuschnigg expected to receive answers to his complaints about the Austrian Nazis but instead faced a display of temper, verbal aggression and threats from Hitler/Hitler demanded that Austrian Nazis be given important posts in the Austrian government and threatened to invade Austria if Schuschnigg did not agree
4. on his return to Austria, Schuschnigg decided to hold a plebiscite to ask the Austrian people if they wanted Austria to remain independent from Germany/Hitler was furious and plans were put in place for the invasion of Austria by Germany
5. Hitler demanded Schuschnigg's resignation and the cancellation of the plebiscite
6. Schuschnigg resigned and was replaced by Seyss-Inquart
7. Seyss-Inquart promptly invited the German Army in to Austria on the premise that they were required to help maintain law and order
8. on 12 March 1938, German soldiers crossed the border into Austria unopposed
9. German soldiers were greeted by crowds who cheered and threw flowers/Hitler himself received a rousing reception as he entered Linz in an open-topped Mercedes
10. the following day a new law was announced which incorporated Austria into the German Reich

66. *Candidates can be credited in a number of ways* **up to a maximum of 6 marks**.

Candidates must make an overall judgement about how fully the source explains the events. **1 mark** may be given for each valid point interpreted from the source or each valid point of significant omission provided.

A maximum of 2 marks may be given for answers which refer only to the source.

Possible points which may be identified in the source include:

1. the main reason was the invasion of Czechoslovakia which proved that Hitler was a liar and that he did not just want land where Germans lived
2. many were influenced by Churchill's speeches which meant appeasement was losing the support of the British people
3. Kristallnacht proved that the Nazi regime was evil and ought to be resisted
4. rearmament had strengthened Britain's armed forces too and gave Chamberlain the confidence to tackle Nazi aggression

Possible points of significant omission may include:

5. the Pact of Steel showed that appeasement had failed to satisfy Hitler and that he was planning for war
6. the Oxford by-election showed that there were many British people who did not agree with appeasing Hitler and who would support military action against Nazi aggression
7. fascists were growing in power across Europe – Franco came to power in Spain in February 1939 – and many felt that they had to be stopped
8. by March 1939, Britain was better prepared to protect its civilians against German attacks (eg a quarter of a million free air raid shelters are given to Londoners)

67. *Candidates can be credited in a number of ways up to a maximum of 4 marks.*

Candidates must make direct comparisons of the two sources, either overall or in detail. A simple comparison will indicate what points of detail or overall viewpoint they agree or disagree about and should be given **1 mark**. A developed comparison of the points of detail or overall viewpoint should be given **2 marks**. Candidates may achieve full marks by making four simple comparisons, two developed comparisons or by a combination of these.

Possible points of comparison may include:

Source B	Source C
Overall: The sources agree about the reasons why Stalin signed the Nazi-Soviet Non-Aggression Pact	
By signing the pact the Soviet Union gained time to prepare its defences against a future German attack	The pact gave the Soviet Union time to prepare for eventual German invasion
Stalin also gained the opportunity to take back lands Russia lost in the aftermath of the First World War	The chance to extend Soviet control over lands from which Russia had been excluded since the end of the First World War was another factor
The half-hearted attempt of the British to come to an agreement with the Soviet Union was another factor in Stalin's decision	The British were unenthusiastic about a possible Anglo-Soviet agreement, and this encouraged Stalin to sign the Nazi-Soviet Pact

Section 3, Context I, World War II, 1939–1945

68. *Candidates can be credited in a number of ways up to a maximum of 6 marks.*

Candidates must make an overall judgement about how fully the source explains the events. **1 mark** may be given for each valid point interpreted from the source or each valid point of significant omission provided.

A maximum of 2 marks may be given for answers which refer only to the source.

Possible points which may be identified in the source include:
1. Japan became increasingly angry with America for cutting off its oil supplies.
2. Japan was also determined to push American influence out of the Pacific
3. the attack was also intended to damage US military strength
4. Japan was confident of winning because the Japanese had rehearsed the attack for a year until they achieved an 80% hit rate

Possible points of significant omission may include:
1. Japan hoped to seize control in Asia and the Pacific and extend its Empire
2. the entire US Pacific fleet could be destroyed at Pearl Harbour giving Japan the upper hand
3. Japan hoped to crush US morale by destroying its prestigious naval fleet
4. Japan was angered after the First World War when the US placed immigration restrictions on it

69. *Candidates can be credited in a number of ways up to a maximum of 5 marks.*

They may take different perspectives on the events and may describe a variety of different aspects of the events.

1 mark should be given for each accurate relevant key point of knowledge. A **second mark** should be given for each point that is developed, up to a maximum of **5 marks**. Candidates may achieve full marks by providing five straightforward points, by making three developed points, or a combination of these.

Possible points of knowledge may include:
1. confiscation of Jewish property and businesses
2. Jews made to wear the Star of David
3. ghettos created for Jews in Poland and Eastern Europe
4. work camps, detention camps, transfer camps and concentration camps set up around Europe for the internment of Jews, gypsies, homosexuals, other religious minorities, asocials
5. in Eastern Europe mobile killing units were dispatched to eliminate Jews eg Lithuania, Latvia, Ukraine, Romania,
6. mobile gas chambers in vans appeared in Eastern occupied territories from late 1941 onwards
7. mass deportation of Jews and other prisoners from Western Europe to Eastern camps took place from 1942 onwards
8. liquidation of the ghettos
9. euthanasia of some minorities (eg the disabled)
10. used as slave labour

70. *Candidates can be credited in a number of ways up to a maximum of 4 marks.*

Candidates must make direct comparisons of the two sources, either overall or in detail. A simple comparison will indicate what points of detail or overall viewpoint they agree or disagree about and should be given **1 mark**. A developed comparison of the points of detail or overall viewpoint should be given **2 marks**. Candidates may achieve full marks by making four simple comparisons, two developed comparisons or by a combination of these.

Possible points of comparison may include:

Source B	Source C
Overall: The sources agree about collaboration in Nazi occupied Europe	
In many cases it was simply a way to survive such as doing the laundry of German soldiers to earn extra food for your family	Other examples of collaboration involved civilians working for the Germans in order to earn extra money or gain extra food rations
Others were more actively involved by informing the Germans of 'enemies' within the community	Collaboration on a large scale occurred in Vichy France where the authorities supplied information to help the Nazis round up 'undesirables'
Then there were those who supported the Nazi regime such as the local civilians and police who were recruited into the SS *death squads*	Over 33,000 Jews were slaughtered there in September 1941 by Nazi SS forces, assisted by the Ukrainian police

71. *Candidates can be credited in a number of ways up to a maximum of 5 marks.*

Candidates must show a causal relationship between events.

Up to a **maximum of 5 marks in total, 1 mark** should be given for each accurate, relevant reason, and a **second mark** should be given for reasons that are developed. Candidates may achieve full marks by providing five straightforward reasons, three developed reasons, or a combination of these.

Possible reasons may include:
1. the Allies had complete naval and air superiority of the area prior to the landings which allowed them to deliver supplies
2. Allied deception plans were successful because the German High command believed the attack would happen at Pas-de-Calais
3. strategic bombing of the area behind the lines prevented German Panzer forces being deployed to Normandy
4. the use of floating harbours (Mulberries) which were brought over from England by the Allies allowed more troops and supplies to be transported to the beach heads
5. Pluto, the undersea pipeline was able to deliver fuel to allow for the sustained attack on the beach heads and further into German occupied territory
6. the landing of airborne forces hindered a German counter-attack
7. the German Atlantic Wall was incomplete
8. assistance of French resistance (eg destroying German communications)

Section 3, Context J, The Cold War, 1945–1989

72. *Candidates can be credited in a number of ways up to a maximum of 5 marks.*

They may take different perspectives on the events and may describe a variety of different aspects of the events.

1 mark should be given for each accurate relevant key point of knowledge. A **second mark** should be given for each point that is developed, up to a maximum of **5 marks**. Candidates may achieve full marks by providing five straightforward points, by making three developed points, or a combination of these.

Possible points of knowledge may include:
1. the Soviets were disliked because they denied democratic freedoms
2. many hated Soviet control (eg the activities of the secret police)
3. many disliked Soviet control of education
4. many were angry at the suppression of religion (eg the Catholic Church)
5. many resented the Red Army as foreign occupiers
6. people were disappointed that Soviet central control had stifled economic growth/lowered living standards
7. some Hungarians supported the Soviets as they were committed Communists

73. *Candidates can be credited in a number of ways up to a maximum of 5 marks.*

Candidates must show a causal relationship between events.

Up to a **maximum of 5 marks in total, 1 mark** should be given for each accurate, relevant reason, and a **second mark** should be given for reasons that are developed. Candidates may achieve full marks by providing five straightforward reasons, three developed reasons, or a combination of these.

Possible reasons may include:
1. to prevent East Germans moving to the West
2. to reduce the possibility of flashpoints in Berlin which could cause war
3. to limit Western spying
4. to stop the embarrassment of people appearing to choose Capitalism over Communism
5. to shore up support for Communism elsewhere in Eastern Europe
6. to close the only gap in the Iron Curtain

74. *Candidates can be credited in a number of ways up to a maximum of 6 marks.*

Candidates must make an overall judgement about how fully the source explains the events. **1 mark** may be given for each valid point interpreted from the source or each valid point of significant omission provided.

A maximum of 2 marks may be given for answers which refer only to the source.

Possible points which may be identified in the source include:
1. they felt it was not America's job to fight a war thousands of miles from home
2. many remembered the Second World War and did not want a repeat of the casualties suffered in this conflict
3. by 1967, as many as 160 American soldiers were being killed every week
4. some Americans opposed the conflict as they felt its huge cost meant the government was unable to spend money on health and housing

Possible points of significant omission may include:
1. many thought America was trying to suppress the democratic wishes of the Vietnamese people
2. many were uncomfortable supporting the corrupt South Vietnamese regime
3. the revelation of US involvement in atrocities such as the My Lai massacre caused unease
4. people were uncomfortable with aerial bombing of civilians
5. many felt the Vietcong had the support of the Vietnamese public
6. US media contributed to changing attitudes to the conflict
7. many afraid that the war was spreading to Laos, Cambodia etc

75. *Candidates can be credited in a number of ways up to a maximum of 4 marks.*

Candidates must make direct comparisons of the two sources, either overall or in detail. A simple comparison will indicate what points of detail or overall viewpoint they agree or disagree about and should be given **1 mark**. A developed comparison of the points of detail or overall viewpoint should be given **2 marks**. Candidates may achieve full marks by making four simple comparisons, two developed comparisons or by a combination of these.

Possible points of comparison may include:

Source B	Source C
Overall: The sources agree about the aims of the policy of Glasnost	
His intention was to give a boost to the Soviet economy, which was performing badly	The hope was that Glasnost could help strengthen the Soviet economy
The aim of Glasnost was to allow open discussion of social and economic issues	He wanted to find new solutions to problems by allowing people to express their views freely
Gorbachev hoped this would strengthen the Communist system	Gorbachev remained a committed Communist and hoped that Glasnost would increase support for the system

NATIONAL 5 HISTORY
2017 SPECIMEN QUESTION PAPER

Section 1, Context A, The Wars of Independence, 1286–1328

1. *Candidates can be credited in a number of ways up to a maximum of 5 marks.*

Candidates must evaluate the extent to which a source is useful by commenting on evidence such as the author, type of source, purpose, timing, content or omission. For a mark to be awarded, the candidate must identify an aspect of the source <u>and</u> make a comment which shows why this aspect makes the source more or less useful.

A **maximum of 4 marks** can be awarded for evaluative comments relating to the author, type of source, purpose and timing. A **maximum of 2 marks** may be awarded for evaluative comments relating to the content of the source. A **maximum of 2 marks** may be awarded for evaluative comments relating to points of significant omission.

Examples of aspects of the source and relevant comments:

Aspect	Possible comment(s)
Author: Modern historian	Useful because he has expert knowledge/has studied a range of relevant sources
Type of Source: Textbook	Useful because it contains straightforward information without bias/well researched
Purpose: To inform	Useful because it provides detailed information
Timing: 2011	Useful because it has the benefit of hindsight

Content	Possible comment(s)
Balliol argued this because he was descended from the eldest daughter in the family of David, Earl of Huntingdon, brother of King William the Lion	Useful as this is accurate (as Balliol claimed being descended from David's eldest daughter he should be the next king)
According to Balliol it didn't matter that he was a generation younger than Bruce because the feudal law of primogeniture always supported the eldest line of a family	Useful as this is accurate (as Balliol argued that the feudal law of primogeniture meant he should be Scotland's next king)
Bruce argued the feudal law of primogeniture did not apply to kingdoms	Useful as this is accurate (as Bruce said the law of primogeniture didn't apply when determining Scotland's next king)

Possible points of significant omission may include:
1. Bruce said that Imperial Law supported him because he was one generation closer to the Earl of Huntingdon's family than Balliol
2. many nobles thought that they should be the next ruler of Scotland (eg thirteen competitors/factionalism amongst the Scottish nobility over the succession)
3. concerns that the succession problem could threaten law and order in Scotland
4. fears that a civil war could break out over the succession issue

Any other valid point of omission

2. *Candidates can be credited in a number of ways up to a maximum of 6 marks.*

Candidates must make a number of points that make the issue plain or clear, for example by showing connections between factors or causal relationships between events or ideas. These should be key reasons but there is no need for any evaluation or prioritising of these reasons.

Up to a maximum of 6 marks in total, **1 mark** should be awarded for each accurate, relevant reason, and a **second mark** should be awarded for reasons that are developed. Candidates may achieve full marks by providing six straightforward reasons, three developed reasons (or any combination of these).

Possible reasons may include:
1. Balliol had accepted Edward as his overlord, so weakening his authority
2. he was inexperienced in Scottish affairs as he was essentially an English noble
3. Balliol was unable to stop Edward interfering in the government of Scotland
4. Edward undermined him by summoning him to appear at court/before his parliament
5. Edward heard Scottish legal appeals which angered the Scots
6. Edward sent direct orders to the Scottish nobles which undermined Balliol as king
7. Edward forced him to appoint an Englishman as his Chancellor, further humiliating him
8. Balliol had been defeated by Edward at the Battle of Dunbar, which weakened his power
9. Edward had stripped John Balliol of his crown and title publicly, so humiliating him
10. Edward took Balliol away as a prisoner, leaving Scotland without a king
11. Bruce and other nobles had never supported Balliol, which weakened his authority
12. the Community of the Realm of Scotland made John Balliol share power with 12 Scottish Guardians, which showed little faith in him

Any other valid reason

3. *Candidates can be credited in a number of ways up to a maximum of 4 marks.*

They may take different perspectives on the events and may describe a variety of different aspects of the events. Candidates must make a number of relevant, factual points. These should be key points. These do not have to be in any particular order.

1 mark should be awarded for each accurate relevant key point of knowledge. A **second mark** should be awarded for each point that is developed, **up to a maximum of 4 marks**. Candidates may achieve full marks by providing four straightforward points, by making two developed points (or any combination of these).

Possible points of knowledge may include:
1. murdered Sheriff of Lanark which made him an outlaw and forced him into open rebellion
2. his use of guerrilla tactics was very successful against the English
3. he united people under his leadership as Guardian
4. he organised the army of Scotland
5. worked with Andrew Moray to defeat the English at the Battle of Stirling Bridge
6. tried to establish trade with the Low Countries
7. when he was defeated at the Battle of Falkirk he resigned the Guardianship
8. he continued to resist Edward till he was executed

Any other valid point of knowledge

4. *Candidates can be credited in a number of ways **up to a maximum of 6 marks**.*

Candidates must make a judgement about the extent to which the source provides a full description or explanation of a given event or development.

Up to a maximum of 6 marks in total, **1 mark** should be awarded for each valid point selected from the source or each valid point of significant omission provided.

Candidates should be awarded **up to 3 marks** for their identification of points from the source which support their judgement. Candidates should be awarded **up to 4 marks** for their identification of points of significant omission, based on their own knowledge, that support their judgement. A **maximum of 2 marks** may be awarded for answers in which no judgement has been made **or** which refer only to the source.

Possible points which may be identified from the source include:
1. gave the much larger English army no room to move because they were surrounded by marshes and streams
2. Bruce decided to take advantage of this mistake and to attack them
3. the English were so jammed together and so tangled up that their leaders struggled to organise any defence
4. they lost all confidence in Edward II for leading them into this trap

Possible points of significant omission may include:
5. Bruce organised the Scots into schiltrons which was an effective defensive formation
6. Bruce chose the higher ground which gave the Scots a positional advantage
7. Bruce trained his schiltrons to move which allowed them to respond to attacks
8. the death of de Bohun demoralised the English
9. the English had been arguing among themselves and could not agree on a plan
10. many English were trapped by the ditches by the Pelstream and Bannock burns and drowned

Any other valid point of significant omission

5. *Candidates can be credited in a number of ways **up to a maximum of 4 marks**.*

Candidates must interpret the evidence and make direct comparisons between sources. Candidates are expected to compare content directly on a point-by-point basis. They may compare the details in the sources and/or compare the viewpoints overall.

A **simple comparison** will indicate what points of detail or viewpoint the sources agree or disagree on and **should be awarded 1 mark**. A **developed comparison** of the points of detail or overall viewpoint **should be awarded a second mark**. Candidates may achieve full marks by making four simple comparisons, two developed comparisons (or by any combination of these).

Possible points of comparison may include:

Source C	Source D
Overall: The sources disagree about how much support Bruce had in 1320	
... all the Scots thought Robert Bruce was their rightful king	... some Scottish nobles were plotting against Robert Bruce
(... by saving Scotland from being taken over by England) he proved that he was worthy of being King of Scotland	(They felt he was a ruthless thug who had murdered his main rival in a church and) so he was unworthy of being King of Scots
They argued Bruce had royal blood	Other Scottish nobles claimed their blood ties meant they were more closely related to the Scottish royal family than Robert Bruce

Section 1, Context B, Mary Queen of Scots and the Scottish Reformation, 1542–1587

6. *Candidates can be credited in a number of ways **up to a maximum of 4 marks**.*

They may take different perspectives on the events and may describe a variety of different aspects of the events. Candidates must make a number of relevant, factual points. These should be key points. These do not have to be in any particular order.

1 mark should be awarded for each accurate relevant key point of knowledge. A **second mark** should be awarded for each point that is developed, **up to a maximum of 4 marks**. Candidates may achieve full marks by providing four straightforward points, by making two developed points (or any combination of these).

Possible points of knowledge may include:
1. the Scots broke the Treaty of Greenwich which stated that Mary would marry Edward, Henry VIII's son
2. Henry VIII ordered the Earl of Hertford to invade Scotland and burn Edinburgh
3. the English attacked Scotland and destroyed abbeys/ towns in the south of Scotland
4. Battle of Pinkie Cleugh 1547 – large Scottish army defeated
5. the Palace of Holyrood in Edinburgh was looted/large parts of Edinburgh were burned/the pier at Leith in Edinburgh was destroyed
6. Berwick upon Tweed was attacked and burned
7. Scots received help from the French who sent a force to Edinburgh in 1548
8. Treaty of Haddington was signed by the Scots and French which agreed Mary would marry the heir to the French throne and Mary was then sent to France for protection

Any other valid point of knowledge

7. *Candidates can be credited in a number of ways **up to a maximum of 6 marks**.*

Candidates must make a judgement about the extent to which the source provides a full description or explanation of a given event or development.

Up to a maximum of 6 marks in total, **1 mark** should be awarded for each valid point selected from the source or each valid point of significant omission provided.

Candidates should be awarded **up to 3 marks** for their identification of points from the source which support their judgement. Candidates should be awarded **up to 4 marks** for their identification of points of significant omission, based on their own knowledge, that support their judgement. A **maximum of 2 marks** may be awarded for answers in which no judgement has been made **or** which refer only to the source.

Possible points which may be identified from the source include:

1. some Scots began to criticise the teachings of the Catholic Church
2. the distribution of English translations of the Bible which helped the growth of Protestantism in Scotland
3. religious pamphlets, smuggled into Scotland from Europe, also spread Protestant ideas
4. the 'Good and Godly Ballads' encouraged the spread of Protestant ideas

Possible points of significant omission may include:

5. increasing criticism of the wealth of the Catholic Church/not using its wealth properly, eg to support the poor, sick etc
6. some Scots began to resent payments to the church claiming they were excessive
7. some churchmen lived scandalous lives which brought the Catholic Church into disrepute
8. John Knox returned to Scotland and helped spread Protestantism
9. anger at the way some Protestant preachers had been treated (eg Wishart)
10. resentment of French/Catholic influence over Scotland

Any other valid point of significant omission

8. *Candidates can be credited in a number of ways **up to a maximum of 4 marks**.*

Candidates must interpret the evidence and make direct comparisons between sources. Candidates are expected to compare content directly on a point-by-point basis. They may compare the details in the sources and/or compare the viewpoints overall.

A **simple comparison** will indicate what points of detail or viewpoint the sources agree or disagree on and **should be awarded 1 mark**. A **developed comparison** of the points of detail or overall viewpoint **should be awarded a second mark**. Candidates may achieve full marks by making four simple comparisons, two developed comparisons (or by any combination of these).

Possible points of comparison may include:

Source B	Source C
Overall: The sources disagree about how well Mary, Queen of Scots ruled Scotland	
... she neglected the government of Scotland	... to begin with, Mary had been a successful ruler in Scotland/had established a successful government
... Mary was happy to leave the running of the country to a group of Protestant nobles	... she had defeated the Protestant nobles who challenged her authority
... she showed little interest in the issue of religion in Scotland	... she decided that she would tolerate Scotland's new Protestant church

9. *Candidates can be credited in a number of ways **up to a maximum of 5 marks**.*

Candidates must evaluate the extent to which a source is useful by commenting on evidence such as the author, type of source, purpose, timing, content or omission. For a mark to be awarded, the candidate must identify an aspect of the source and make a comment which shows why this aspect makes the source more or less useful.

A **maximum of 4 marks** can be awarded for evaluative comments relating to the author, type of source, purpose

and timing. A **maximum of 2 marks** may be awarded for evaluative comments relating to the content of the source. A **maximum of 2 marks** may be awarded for evaluative comments relating to points of significant omission

Examples of aspects of the source and relevant comments:

Aspect	Possible comment(s)
Author: Modern historian	Useful because has expert knowledge/ has studied a range of relevant sources
Type of Source: Textbook	Useful because it contains straightforward information without bias/well researched
Purpose: To inform	Useful because it provides detailed information
Timing: 2007	Useful because it has the benefit of hindsight

Content	Possible comment(s)
Some Scots simply did not want to be ruled by a woman, as they believed that only men should be in positions of power	Useful as this is accurate (as many Scots believed that a woman was too weak to rule a country properly)
Others were suspicious of Mary's religion ...	Useful as this is accurate (as Mary was a Catholic while most Scots were Protestant)
... the Earl of Moray, forced her into giving up her power ...	Useful as this is accurate (as Mary's brother, the Earl of Moray, made her give up the throne)

Possible points of significant omission may include:

1. many Scots blamed her for the murder of Darnley/people would not accept being ruled by a murderess
2. she had caused a scandal by marrying Bothwell shortly after the murder of Darnley
3. Mary's Protestant critics disapproved of her frivolity (criticised Mary for dancing)
4. Scottish nobles, mainly Protestant, rebelled against Mary

Any other valid point of significant omission

10. *Candidates can be credited in a number of ways **up to a maximum of 6 marks**.*

Candidates must make a number of points that make the issue plain or clear, for example by showing connections between factors or causal relationships between events or ideas. These should be key reasons but there is no need for any evaluation or prioritising of these reasons.

Up to a maximum of 6 marks in total, **1 mark** should be awarded for each accurate, relevant reason, and a **second mark** should be awarded for reasons that are developed. Candidates may achieve full marks by providing six straightforward reasons, three developed reasons (or any combination of these).

Possible reasons may include:

1. Catholics plotted to kill Elizabeth and to make Mary Queen of England, which convinced English Protestants Mary was a menace
2. Mary claimed that she was the true, Catholic Queen of England, which worried English Protestants
3. Mary was Elizabeth's heir and she didn't trust Mary/saw Mary as a threat
4. Elizabeth was afraid if Mary got free she would return to Scotland where she could cause trouble for Elizabeth by making it a base for French and Roman Catholic activities

5. Mary's son, who was next in line to the English crown, was a Protestant, so Mary's death would ensure England remained Protestant
6. 1580: the Pope's policy of encouraging plots against Elizabeth persuaded many Protestants that Mary was a threat
7. 1585: after several plots, the English government passed a law stating that Mary would be executed if she was actively involved in any plot against Elizabeth
8. Mary had not been involved in any of these plots but the law was changed to make beneficiaries of plots liable to the death penalty
9. 1586: Babington contacted Mary to inform her of his plans to kill Elizabeth and help Mary to escape and Mary replied agreeing to Elizabeth's death
10. the incriminating letter was intercepted by Elizabeth's spies which proved she was plotting against Elizabeth
11. Elizabeth hesitated to execute her cousin but the death warrant was concealed amongst a pile of letters all of which Elizabeth signed

Any other valid reason

Section 1, Context C, The Treaty of Union, 1689–1715

11. *Candidates can be credited in a number of ways up to a maximum of 6 marks.*

Candidates must make a number of points that make the issue plain or clear, for example by showing connections between factors or causal relationships between events or ideas. These should be key reasons but there is no need for any evaluation or prioritising of these reasons.

Up to a maximum of 6 marks in total, **1 mark** should be awarded for each accurate, relevant reason, and a **second mark** should be awarded for reasons that are developed. Candidates may achieve full marks by providing six straightforward reasons, three developed reasons (or any combination of these).

Possible reasons may include:

1. Scots were excluded from trading with England's colonies which offered great wealth
2. the monarch was in England but was out of touch with the wishes of the Scots
3. many Scots, loyal to the House of Stewart, felt that King James was their rightful king
4. the wars between England and France had damaged Scottish trade with France
5. Scotland gained nothing from peace treaties at the end of these wars
6. the Scots blamed the English for the failure of the Darien Scheme as they offered no financial, military or political support
7. Queen Anne found it difficult to govern Scotland from Westminster
8. Scots accused Queen Anne of policies which were damaging to Scotland
9. the Worcester Affair turned ordinary Scots against what they regarded as English pirates
10. England feared a French threat in the future if the discontented Scots ever wanted to revive the Auld Alliance
11. the English were angry that the Scots were intruding into their colonies/markets
12. the religious differences between Scotland and England caused mistrust

Any other valid reason

12. *Candidates can be credited in a number of ways up to a maximum of 4 marks.*

Candidates must interpret the evidence and make direct comparisons between sources. Candidates are expected to compare content directly on a point-by-point basis. They may compare the details in the sources and/or compare the viewpoints overall.

A **simple comparison** will indicate what points of detail or viewpoint the sources agree or disagree on and **should be awarded 1 mark**. A **developed comparison** of the points of detail or overall viewpoint **should be awarded a second mark**.

Candidates may achieve full marks by making four simple comparisons, two developed comparisons (or by any combination of these).

Possible points of comparison may include:

Source A	Source B
Overall: The sources disagree about Scottish attitudes to a possible Union of the Parliaments	
Supporters of the Union saw it as a way of settling the Protestant Succession and closing the door to the Jacobite claimant to the throne	The Jacobites encouraged opposition to the Union in the hope of restoring their king to his throne
Other Scots saw the economic benefits of gaining access to England's colonies	They feared that Scotland's economy would be ruined by cheap goods flooding up from England
They weren't worried about wanting a closer relationship with England	Many Scots disliked the idea of entering a Union with 'the Auld Enemy'

13. *Candidates can be credited in a number of ways up to a maximum of 4 marks.*

They may take different perspectives on the events and may describe a variety of different aspects of the events. Candidates must make a number of relevant, factual points. These should be key points. These do not have to be in any particular order.

1 mark should be awarded for each accurate relevant key point of knowledge. A **second mark** should be awarded for each point that is developed, **up to a maximum of 4 marks**. Candidates may achieve full marks by providing four straightforward points, by making two developed points (or any combination of these).

Possible points of knowledge may include:

1. when the draft of the treaty was made public there were riots on the streets of Scottish towns and cities
2. violent demonstrations took place outside Parliament House in Edinburgh
3. the Edinburgh mob threatened and insulted judges and Members of the Scottish Parliament
4. serious riots took place in Glasgow
5. in Glasgow, Dumfries and Lanark people had taken up arms
6. there were protests and demonstrations against the Union in many Scottish burghs
7. in Edinburgh a huge crowd marched up the High Street shouting, 'No Union, No Union'
8. the Edinburgh mob threw stones at house windows which showed a light

Any other valid point of knowledge

14. *Candidates can be credited in a number of ways up to a maximum of 6 marks.*

Candidates must make a judgement about the extent to which the source provides a full description or explanation of a given event or development.

Up to a maximum of 6 marks in total, **1 mark** should be awarded for each valid point selected from the source or each valid point of significant omission provided.

Candidates should be awarded **up to 3 marks** for their identification of points from the source which support their judgement. Candidates should be awarded **up to 4 marks** for their identification of points of significant omission, based on their own knowledge, that support their judgement. A **maximum of 2 marks** may be awarded for answers in which no judgement has been made **or** which refer only to the source.

Possible points which may be identified from the source include:

1. Hamilton however was indecisive and unreliable/he suddenly changed sides
2. there was widespread belief that, like many, Hamilton had been bribed to support the Union
3. Hamilton's activities kept the opponents of the Union disorganised
4. opponents of the Union were unable to overcome the ruthless methods used by supporters of the Union

Possible points of significant omission may include:

5. the government had sent Argyll and then Queensberry/ secret agents, to organise and promote support for the Union
6. the government threatened Scottish trade if the Union was not passed
7. government officials in Scotland were warned they would not be paid wage arrears unless they supported the Union
8. the Church of Scotland was won over to the Union by guaranteeing its position
9. the Equivalent, which made money available to Scotland, won over many people
10. people were offered titles and jobs in return for supporting the Union

Any other valid point of significant omission

15. *Candidates can be credited in a number of ways up to a maximum of 5 marks.*

Candidates must evaluate the extent to which a source is useful by commenting on evidence such as the author, type of source, purpose, timing, content or omission. For a mark to be awarded, the candidate must identify an aspect of the source and make a comment which shows why this aspect makes the source more or less useful.

A **maximum of 4 marks** can be awarded for evaluative comments relating to the author, type of source, purpose and timing. A **maximum of 2 marks** may be awarded for evaluative comments relating to the content of the source. A **maximum of 2 marks** may be awarded for evaluative comments relating to points of significant omission.

Examples of aspects of the source and relevant comments:

Aspect	Possible comment(s)
Author: Modern historian	Useful because has expert knowledge/has studied a range of relevant sources
Type of Source: Textbook	Useful because it contains straightforward information without bias/well researched
Purpose: To inform	Useful because it provides detailed information
Timing: 1994	Useful because it has the benefit of hindsight

Content	Possible comment(s)
The Church of Scotland was outraged when patronage was reintroduced into the church and Episcopalians were to be tolerated	Useful as this is accurate (because the reintroduction of church patronage angered the Church of Scotland)
Many Scots thought these changes also broke the terms of the Treaty of Union	Useful as this is accurate (because Scots were disappointed with the results of the Treaty of Union and believed they'd been cheated)
They were unhappy with the introduction of the Malt Tax ...	Useful as this is accurate (because Scots opposed having to pay tax on malt)

Possible points of significant omission may include

1. were soon disillusioned because the Union did not bring immediate prosperity
2. they disliked the changes in Scotland's weights, measures, money, etc
3. nobles and important politicians had left Edinburgh for London
4. some believed that English imports were ruining Scottish businesses

Any other valid point of omission

Section 1, Context D, Migration and Empire, 1830–1939

16. *Candidates can be credited in a number of ways up to a maximum of 6 marks.*

Candidates must make a judgement about the extent to which the source provides a full description or explanation of a given event or development.

Up to a maximum of 6 marks in total, **1 mark** should be awarded for each valid point selected from the source or each valid point of significant omission provided.

Candidates should be awarded **up to 3 marks** for their identification of points from the source which support their judgement. Candidates should be awarded **up to 4 marks** for their identification of points of significant omission, based on their own knowledge, that support their judgement. A **maximum of 2 marks** may be awarded for answers in which no judgement has been made **or** which refer only to the source.

Possible points which may be identified from the source include:

1. the Irish potato famine of the mid-1840s led to a sharp increase in numbers moving to Scotland
2. others left for Scotland as some landlords evicted those who could not pay their rent
3. transport costs were cheap making it easy to travel to Scotland
4. The Irish were attracted to the west of Scotland as wages were higher than those in Ireland

Possible points of significant omission may include:

5. some Irish already had family in Scotland who helped them with the cost of emigrating/encouraged them to come to Scotland

6. poverty of Irish tenants encouraged them to leave home
7. work was available for unskilled workers in factories eg jute mills and cotton mills
8. building railways and canals/work in the coal and iron ore mines provided employment for many Irish
9. seasonal labour on farms also provided a lot of jobs for the Irish
10. housing was available/often better (not 'good') in Scotland's growing towns and cities

Any other valid point of significant omission

17. *Candidates can be credited in a number of ways up to a maximum of 4 marks.*

They may take different perspectives on the events and may describe a variety of different aspects of the events. Candidates must make a number of relevant, factual points. These should be key points. These do not have to be in any particular order.

1 mark should be awarded for each accurate relevant key point of knowledge. A **second mark** should be awarded for each point that is developed, **up to a maximum of 4 marks.** Candidates may achieve full marks by providing four straightforward points, by making two developed points (or any combination of these).

Possible points of knowledge may include:
1. Empire cultures and religions brought to Scotland
2. provided raw materials for factories, such as cotton, jute and sugar
3. many jobs were created in manufacturing industries to produce goods for export to the Empire eg locomotives and ships
4. trade with the Empire increased the wealth/population of cities such as Glasgow
5. profits from the Empire led to impressive new public buildings and mansions being built
6. provided jobs for Scots in the Empire (such as in the armed forces and civil service)
7. immigrant workers provided a cheap labour force which kept wages down
8. later the Empire became a source of competition to Scottish economy: farm produce from Australia, Jute mill development in India, etc

Any other valid point of knowledge

18. *Candidates can be credited in a number of ways up to a maximum of 4 marks.*

Candidates must interpret the evidence and make direct comparisons between sources. Candidates are expected to compare content directly on a point-by-point basis. They may compare the details in the sources and/or compare the viewpoints overall.

A **simple comparison** will indicate what points of detail or viewpoint the sources agree or disagree on and **should be awarded 1 mark**. A **developed comparison** of the points of detail or overall viewpoint **should be awarded a second mark**. Candidates may achieve full marks by making four simple comparisons, two developed comparisons (or by any combination of these).

Possible points of comparison may include:

Source B	Source C
Overall: The sources disagree about Scottish attitudes to Irish immigration	
Newspapers were eager to describe the violent activities of groups of Irish men	... the Irish are of good character and behave very well
They were also blamed for being dirty and responsible for spreading disease.	When they first came over they were, in general, very clean
... Irish however were accused of being too lazy to work (and for relying on charity)	... the Irish are always ready to work hard for their pay

19. *Candidates can be credited in a number of ways up to a maximum of 5 marks.*

Candidates must evaluate the extent to which a source is useful by commenting on evidence such as the author, type of source, purpose, timing, content or omission. For a mark to be awarded, the candidate must identify an aspect of the source <u>and</u> make a comment which shows why this aspect makes the source more or less useful.

A **maximum of 4 marks** can be awarded for evaluative comments relating to the author, type of source, purpose and timing. A **maximum of 2 marks** may be awarded for evaluative comments relating to the content of the source. A **maximum of 2 marks** may be awarded for evaluative comments relating to points of significant omission.

Examples of aspects of the source and relevant comments:

Aspect	Possible comment(s)
Author: Modern historian	Useful because has expert knowledge/ has studied a range of relevant sources
Type of Source: Textbook	Useful because it contains straightforward information without bias/well researched
Purpose: To inform	Useful because it provides detailed information
Timing: 1992	Useful because it has the benefit of hindsight

Content	Possible comment(s)
Many Scots had farms which they could sell to raise funds for emigration	Useful as this is accurate (many Scots farmers sold their land to pay for the cost of emigrating)
... many emigrants were happy to help pay for relatives to come and join them	Useful as this is accurate (as Scots who had prospered were willing to help pay for other family members to emigrate)
The journey became much easier and cheaper with the development of faster and more efficient steam ships	Useful as this is accurate (as improvements in steam ships made the journey more affordable for Scots)

Possible points of significant omission may include
1. landowners, especially in Highlands, were willing to help pay for their tenants to emigrate/landlords wrote off rent arrears so that emigrants had money to emigrate
2. various Scottish societies provided support for poorer Scots to emigrate
3. the government gave help after the First World War to those who wanted to emigrate/1922 Empire Settlement Act – money for travel, trading and land purchase
4. charities such as Barnardos, Quarriers and the YMCA assisted with passages

Any other valid point of significant omission

20. *Candidates can be credited in a number of ways up to a maximum of 6 marks.*

Candidates must make a number of points that make the issue plain or clear, for example by showing connections between factors or causal relationships between events or ideas. These should be key reasons but there is no need for any evaluation or prioritising of these reasons.

Up to a maximum of 6 marks in total, **1 mark** should be awarded for each accurate, relevant reason, and a **second mark** should be awarded for reasons that are developed. Candidates may achieve full marks by providing six straightforward reasons, three developed reasons (or any combination of these).

Possible reasons may include:

1. Scottish emigrants usually had a good level of education which helped them succeed
2. most Scots spoke English which helped them settle in the USA and countries of the Empire
3. some Scots had great financial and business skills which they used to develop a variety of industries
4. many Scots brought capital with them to start farms and businesses
5. they made their fortune from developing businesses, banks and trading companies
6. Scottish farmers were successful as they were skilled at working more difficult land/developed sheep farming in Australia
7. Scots were entrepreneurial and had a reputation for hard work which helped them succeed
8. Scots were imaginative and came up with new ideas eg William Davidson organised the first shipment of frozen meat from New Zealand to Britain
9. Scots founded many industries eg paper-making in New Zealand (credit examples such as wool/brewing/steel) which made them rich
10. money from Scottish banks was skilfully invested in business and industry
11. Scottish emigrants helped each other by providing work and housing
12. tradesmen such as stonemasons were in demand to work in the building industry in USA

Any other valid reason

Section 1, Context E, The Era of the Great War, 1900–1928

21. *Candidates can be credited in a number of ways up to a maximum of 4 marks.*

They may take different perspectives on the events and may describe a variety of different aspects of the events. Candidates must make a number of relevant, factual points. These should be key points. These do not have to be in any particular order.

1 mark should be awarded for each accurate relevant key point of knowledge. A **second mark** should be awarded for each point that is developed, **up to a maximum of 4 marks**. Candidates may achieve full marks by providing four straightforward points, by making two developed points (or any combination of these).

Possible points of knowledge may include:

1. poison gas was used to cause confusion/disable enemy during an attack
2. gas was unreliable as a change in wind direction could blow it back
3. chlorine gas caused choking, while mustard gas caused burns and blindness
4. the development of gas masks helped protect soldiers from poison gas

5. tanks crushed barbed wire/provided cover for advancing soldiers
6. tanks frequently broke down, ran out of fuel or got stuck in the mud
7. range and speed of machine guns meant they could kill large numbers of attacking soldiers
8. aircraft could spot enemy activity/take aerial photographs to help plan more effective attacks/drop bombs on enemy trenches

Any other valid point of knowledge

22. *Candidates can be credited in a number of ways up to a maximum of 5 marks.*

Candidates must evaluate the extent to which a source is useful by commenting on evidence such as the author, type of source, purpose, timing, content or omission. For a mark to be awarded, the candidate must identify an aspect of the source <u>and</u> make a comment which shows why this aspect makes the source more or less useful.

A **maximum of 4 marks** can be awarded for evaluative comments relating to the author, type of source, purpose and timing. A **maximum of 2 marks** may be awarded for evaluative comments relating to the content of the source. A **maximum of 2 marks** may be awarded for evaluative comments relating to points of significant omission.

Examples of aspects of the source and relevant comments:

Aspect	Possible comment(s)
Author: Modern historian	Useful because has expert knowledge/ has studied a range of relevant sources
Type of Source: Textbook	Useful because it contains straightforward information without bias/well researched
Purpose: To inform	Useful because it provides detailed information
Timing: 1984	Useful because it has the benefit of hindsight

Content	Possible comment(s)
British Summer Time was introduced to give more daylight working hours	Useful as this is accurate (the government did this to increase daylight working hours and so increase food production)
Pub opening hours were limited to prevent drunkenness	Useful as this is accurate (as the government restricted drinking hours to try and reduce drunkenness damaging war production)
(High casualties on the Western Front) led to conscription, forcing unmarried men between 18 and 41 to join the armed forces	Useful as this is accurate (the government made it compulsory for single men between 18–41 to fight for their country)

Possible points of significant omission may include:

1. the government censored newspapers to keep morale high
2. restrictions were imposed on aliens (foreign citizens) to protect Britain from spies
3. rationing was introduced to ensure everyone got a fair share of the food
4. government took greater control over essential industries to ensure strikes didn't damage essential war production

Any other valid point of significant omission

23. *Candidates can be credited in a number of ways up to a maximum of 4 marks.*

Candidates must interpret the evidence and make direct comparisons between sources. Candidates are expected to compare content directly on a point-by-point basis. They may compare the details in the sources and/or compare the viewpoints overall.

A **simple comparison** will indicate what points of detail or viewpoint the sources agree or disagree on and **should be awarded 1 mark.** A **developed comparison** of the points of detail or overall viewpoint **should be awarded a second mark.** Candidates may achieve full marks by making four simple comparisons, two developed comparisons (or by any combination of these).

Possible points of comparison may include:

Source B	Source C
Overall: The sources disagree about the impact of the First World War on employment opportunities for women	
From the outbreak of war there was a steady increase in the female workforce ...	At the beginning of the war, thousands of women were unemployed
The vital role they played in the war helped change many people's attitude to women	Despite women's contribution to the war effort, it didn't change deep-seated beliefs many people had about the role of women
When the war ended, many women voluntarily gave up their jobs to men returning from the fighting	Many women wanted to keep their jobs but when the fighting ended, large numbers of women were sacked

24. *Candidates can be credited in a number of ways up to a maximum of 6 marks.*

Candidates must make a judgement about the extent to which the source provides a full description or explanation of a given event or development.

Up to a maximum of 6 marks in total, **1 mark** should be awarded for each valid point selected from the source or each valid point of significant omission provided.

Candidates should be awarded **up to 3 marks** for their identification of points from the source which support their judgement. Candidates should be awarded **up to 4 marks** for their identification of points of significant omission, based on their own knowledge, that support their judgement. A **maximum of 2 marks** may be awarded for answers in which no judgement has been made **or** which refer only to the source.

Possible points which may be identified from the source include:
1. when the war ended, there was a sharp drop in demand for Clyde-built warships
2. this decline of shipbuilding in the 1920s had a damaging effect on the iron and steel industries
3. Scotland's manufacturers failed to invest in new technology
4. overseas markets lost during the war often preferred to stay with their new suppliers

Possible points of significant omission may include:
5. pre-war lack of investment left Scottish shipyards using outdated methods/facilities/bad management

6. the slump of the 1920s had led to a drop in demand for merchant ships
7. industrial unrest (strikes) damaged the reputation of Scottish industries
8. overseas competitors continued to produce quality goods more cheaply than Scottish industries could after the war
9. increased use of electricity and oil cut demand for coal
10. new textiles such as rayon and nylon cut demand for traditional textiles such as cotton and wool

Any other valid point of significant omission

25. *Candidates can be credited in a number of ways up to a maximum of 6 marks.*

Candidates must make a number of points that make the issue plain or clear, for example by showing connections between factors or causal relationships between events or ideas. These should be key reasons but there is no need for any evaluation or prioritising of these reasons.

Up to a maximum of 6 marks in total, **1 mark** should be awarded for each accurate, relevant reason, and a **second mark** should be awarded for reasons that are developed. Candidates may achieve full marks by providing six straightforward reasons, three developed reasons (or any combination of these).

Possible reasons may include:
1. the women's campaigns for the vote had gradually gained momentum before the War
2. suffragist peaceful campaign of persuasion gained support from across the social spectrum including men as well as women
3. women had gained voting rights in local elections and showed they could use it sensibly
4. there was a gradual widening of the franchise to men and a sense that it was only a matter of time before women were given the vote
5. the Suffragette militant campaigns kept the issue in the public eye/gained a lot of publicity
6. hunger strikes/force feeding in prison won public sympathy for votes for women
7. by calling off their campaign during the war, the women's groups gained a lot of respect and support for them being given the vote
8. women's work during the war was recognised as significant and persuaded many men that women deserved the vote
9. militant actions such as the Glasgow Rent Strikes reminded the government that women could resume their pre-war campaigning if ignored
10. voting laws had to be changed to allow returning soldiers the vote, which created the opportunity to give the vote to some women in 1918

Any other valid reason

Section 2, Context A, The Creation of the Medieval Kingdoms, 1066–1406

26. *Candidates can be credited in a number of ways up to a maximum of 5 marks.*

Candidates must evaluate the extent to which a source is useful by commenting on evidence such as the author, type of source, purpose, timing, content or omission. For a mark to be awarded, the candidate must identify an aspect of the source <u>and</u> make a comment which shows why this aspect makes the source more or less useful.

A **maximum of 4 marks** can be awarded for evaluative comments relating to the author, type of source, purpose and timing. A **maximum of 2 marks** may be awarded for evaluative comments relating to the content of the source. A **maximum of 2 marks** may be awarded for evaluative comments relating to points of significant omission.

Examples of aspects of the source and relevant comments:

Aspect	Possible comment(s)
Author: William's priest	Useful because he would have been an eyewitness/well placed to see what William was doing
Type of Source: Chronicle	Useful because it was a detailed record of events
Purpose: To inform	Useful because it was written to inform about William's role in trying to control England/perhaps less useful because he would have been biased in favour of William
Timing: 1077	Useful because it is a primary source written from the time William was attempting to bring England under his control

Content	Possible comment(s)
The remaining English Earls were confirmed in their lands and titles	Useful because it is accurate (William allowed the other English Earls to keep their land and titles)
... his loyal Norman lords undertook a programme of castle building to maintain their hold on the kingdom	Useful because it is accurate (Norman lords built castles to strengthen their control of England)
He gave rich fiefs to the men he had brought over from France ...	Useful because it is accurate (William did reward his loyal supporters who came over from France)

Possible points of significant omission may include:

1. no mention of William's cruelty/military campaigns against the Saxons/'Harrying of the North' following rebellion there
2. severe taxation was applied
3. replacing Saxon lords killed at Hastings with Norman barons
4. Tower of London built to intimidate the capital

Any other valid point of significant omission

27. *Candidates can be credited in a number of ways up to a maximum of 9 marks.*

Candidates must make a judgement about the extent to which different factors contributed to an event or development, or its impact. They are required to provide a balanced account of the influence of different factors and come to a reasoned conclusion based on the evidence presented.

Up to 5 marks can be awarded for relevant, factual, key points of knowledge used to support factors, with **1 mark** awarded for each point (but **one mark should be deducted** if the correct process is not clear in at least two factors). If **only one factor is presented, a maximum of 3 marks should be awarded** for relevant points of knowledge. A **further 4 marks** can be awarded for providing the answer in a structured way and coming to a reasoned conclusion.

Possible factors	Key points of knowledge to support this factor may include:
Corruption in the legal system	1. there was no uniform law in the kingdom/sheriffs decided the law in their local area 2. Sheriffs were corrupt/could not be trusted by the king 3. Barons held the office of sheriff and abused their position/had set up their own law courts 4. Barons were keeping the fines collected from criminals, instead of giving them to the king
Barons had become too powerful during the civil war	5. castles had been built without the king's permission which increased the Barons' power/king's authority had been reduced 6. some Barons openly challenged Henry eg Earl of York, Scarborough Castle 7. Barons had private armies/hired mercenaries 8. Barons were stealing land from their weaker neighbours and increasing their power
Henry ruled over a wide area	9. Henry ruled from the Pyrenees to the Scottish border a huge area which was difficult to control effectively 10. there was no common language or traditions in Henry's empire to help hold it together
Authority of the Church increased	11. the Church had gained more power and its clergy were not tried in the king's court if they were suspected of a crime 12. Church courts had become powerful/were using their own laws instead of the kings

Up to **4 marks** should be awarded for presenting the answer in a structured way, leading to a conclusion which addresses the question, as follows:

1 mark for an introduction (which places the question in its historical context or outlines relevant factors).

1 mark for the answer being presented in a structured way (with knowledge being organised in support of different factors).

1 mark for a conclusion with a valid judgement (or overall summary).

1 mark for a reason in support of the judgement (a summary cannot be supported).

Any other valid factor

28. *Candidates can be credited in a number of ways up to a maximum of 6 marks.*

Candidates must make a number of points that make the issue plain or clear, for example by showing connections between factors or causal relationships between events or ideas. These should be key reasons but there is no need for any evaluation or prioritising of these reasons.

Up to a maximum of 6 marks in total, **1 mark** should be awarded for each accurate, relevant reason, and a **second mark** should be awarded for reasons that are developed. Candidates may achieve full marks by providing six straightforward reasons, three developed reasons (or any combination of these).

Possible reasons may include:

1. provided centres of worship for communities
2. offered support and comfort in difficult times/ encouraged people not to give up/hope that life after death would be better
3. offered spiritual guidance on how to be a good Christian
4. provided guidelines/controlled how people should live their lives
5. carried out important rituals eg baptism, marriage, last rites
6. the Church was a place of education and was used to train boys who wished to become priests
7. kept one third of its tithe/crops to give to the parish in times of need
8. canon law had a major impact on people's lives eg whom you could marry, holidays, no red meat on Fridays
9. had political power – it could excommunicate a king or place a country under interdict
10. had great economic importance; it owned land and made a profit from this
11. held its own court and enforced Canon Law
12. employed large number of people from the local community

Any other valid reason

29. *Candidates can be credited in a number of ways up to a maximum of 6 marks.*

Candidates must make a judgement about the extent to which the source provides a full description or explanation of a given event or development.

Up to a maximum of 6 marks in total, **1 mark** should be awarded for each valid point selected from the source or each valid point of significant omission provided.

Candidates should be awarded **up to 3 marks** for their identification of points from the source which support their judgement. Candidates should be awarded **up to 4 marks** for their identification of points of significant omission, based on their own knowledge, that support their judgement. A **maximum of 2 marks** may be awarded for answers in which no judgement has been made **or** which refer only to the source.

Possible points which may be identified from the source include:

1. one in three of the population of England died
2. Lords, who relied on their peasants to farm their land, became desperate to retain them
3. Lords were forced to pay more to keep each peasant on their land
4. some peasants left their own Lord's land in search of higher pay elsewhere

Possible points of significant omission may include:

5. Black Death led to a lack of shepherds/farm workers/ labourers
6. some villages became derelict
7. disastrous effects on agriculture eg animals died, crops rotted in the fields
8. trade was seriously interrupted
9. affected the attitudes of survivors eg less deferential towards the church
10. led to worsening relations between peasants and landowners

Any other valid point of significant omission

Section 2, Context B, War of the Three Kingdoms, 1603–1651

30. *Candidates can be credited in a number of ways up to a maximum of 9 marks.*

Candidates must make a judgement about the extent to which different factors contributed to an event or development, or its impact. They are required to provide a balanced account of the influence of different factors and come to a reasoned conclusion based on the evidence presented.

Up to 5 marks can be awarded for relevant, factual, key points of knowledge used to support factors, with **1 mark** awarded for each point (but **one mark should be deducted** if the correct process is not clear in at least two factors). If **only one factor is presented, a maximum of 3 marks should be awarded** for relevant points of knowledge. A **further 4 marks** can be awarded for providing the answer in a structured way and coming to a reasoned conclusion.

Possible factors	Key points of knowledge to support this factor may include:
Financial grievances	1. James was viewed as extravagant by Parliament/by some as overgenerous to his favourites
	2. Parliament was dismissed in 1610 because of arguments over finances and the failure of the Great Contract
	3. the 'Addled Parliament' was dismissed in 1614 due to arguments over impositions (extra customs tax) and subsidies
	4. Crown and Parliament quarrelled over the sale of monopolies
Religious differences	5. the Millenary Petition of 1603 requested changes to be made to practices in the Church of England; James rejected most of the changes
	6. James licensed Archbishop Bancroft's Canons which stated that the clergy had to follow 39 articles and the Prayer Book, which annoyed the clergy
	7. James gave bishops more control in the Church (Direction of Preachers, 1622) which worried Puritans
	8. Parliament was suspicious of James' perceived Catholic sympathies
Political disputes	9. James' belief in the Divine Rights of Kings offended many in Parliament
	10. James was criticised for neglecting Parliament in favour of leisure pursuits
	11. quarrels over the King's choice of leading ministers eg Duke of Buckingham
	12. James rules without Parliament from 1614 to 1621

Up to 4 marks should be awarded for presenting the answer in a structured way, leading to a conclusion which addresses the question, as follows:

1 mark for an introduction (which places the question in its historical context or outlines relevant factors).

1 mark for the answer being presented in a structured way (with knowledge being organised in support of different factors).

1 mark for a conclusion with a valid judgement (or overall summary).

1 mark for a reason in support of the judgement (a summary cannot be supported).

Any other valid interpretation

31. *Candidates can be credited in a number of ways **up to a maximum of 6 marks**.*

Candidates must make a number of points that make the issue plain or clear, for example by showing connections between factors or causal relationships between events or ideas. These should be key reasons but there is no need for any evaluation or prioritising of these reasons.

Up to a maximum of 6 marks in total, **1 mark** should be awarded for each accurate, relevant reason, and a **second mark** should be awarded for reasons that are developed. Candidates may achieve full marks by providing six straightforward reasons, three developed reasons (or any combination of these).

Possible reasons may include:

1. resentment of Charles as an absentee monarch
2. many Scots were suspicious that Charles wanted to be an absolute monarch
3. the General Assembly was not allowed to meet which caused resentment
4. resentment at Charles' money raising methods (eg Ship Money)
5. Scottish nobles resented Charles' Act of Revocation whereby church lands which had been alienated since 1540 had to be returned to the Crown
6. Charles' coronation in Edinburgh was a High Church ceremony based on Anglican forms and Scottish Presbyterians were suspicious of Anglican ideas
7. Charles demanded that Scottish Ministers accept and use the new English Prayer Book which caused a great deal of resentment and some riots in Edinburgh
8. Scottish clergy opposed Laud's Canons and their requirement to wear gowns and surplices because it seemed too Catholic
9. Bishops were to be introduced into the Scottish Church which was resented by the Scots
10. rejection of the Canons was included in the National Covenant for the Defence of True Religion in 1638 and was signed by thousands because they wanted to protect Scottish religious practices

Any other valid reason

32. *Candidates can be credited in a number of ways **up to a maximum of 5 marks**.*

Candidates must evaluate the extent to which a source is useful by commenting on evidence such as the author, type of source, purpose, timing, content or omission. For a mark to be awarded, the candidate must identify an aspect of the source <u>and</u> make a comment which shows why this aspect makes the source more or less useful.

A **maximum of 4 marks** can be awarded for evaluative comments relating to the author, type of source, purpose and timing. A **maximum of 2 marks** may be awarded for evaluative comments relating to the content of the source. A **maximum of 2 marks** may be awarded for evaluative comments relating to points of significant omission.

Examples of aspects of the source and relevant comments:

Aspect	Possible comment(s)
Author: Sir John Eliot, a Member of Parliament	Useful as it is from an eyewitness/had first-hand experience of the dispute with the king
Type of Source: A letter	Useful as it is likely to give an honest/accurate description of the growing opposition to the reign of King Charles I
Purpose: To inform	Useful as it provides a detailed account of the growing opposition/less useful as it may be biased as Eliot was an outspoken critic of Charles
Timing: 1630s	Useful because it is a primary source from the time when there was growing opposition to the reign of King Charles I

Content	Possible comment(s)
Members of Parliament complained that the terms of Charles' marriage contract included unacceptable concessions to English Catholics	Useful because it is accurate (Parliament was suspicious of any concessions given to Catholics)
In addition we were suspicious of Charles' foreign policy which meant Parliament was reluctant to grant him funds	Useful because it is accurate (Parliament didn't trust Charles' foreign policy and was unwilling to fund it)
... launching a fierce criticism of Charles' favourite, Buckingham's mismanagement of the Cadiz expedition	Useful because it is accurate (many MPs criticised Buckingham's disastrous Cadiz campaign)

Possible points of significant omission may include:

1. growing opposition to Charles' belief in the Divine Right of Kings
2. anger at Charles' refusal to let Parliament meet in 1629/ MPs arrived to find the doors locked
3. Protestants were upset at his marriage to Henrietta Maria – a Catholic
4. criticised for his spending habits eg paintings and expensive clothes

Any other valid point of significant omission

33. *Candidates can be credited in a number of ways **up to a maximum of 6 marks**.*

Candidates must make a judgement about the extent to which the source provides a full description or explanation of a given event or development.

Up to a maximum of 6 marks in total, **1 mark** should be awarded for each valid point selected from the source or each valid point of significant omission provided.

Candidates should be awarded **up to 3 marks** for their identification of points from the source which support their judgement. Candidates should be awarded **up to 4 marks** for their identification of points of significant omission, based on their own knowledge, that support their judgement. A **maximum of 2 marks** may be awarded for answers in which no judgement has been made **or** which refer only to the source.

Possible points which may be identified from the source include:

1. Parliament was dismissed in 1640 because MPs would not give Charles what he wanted/He still didn't get the money he wanted
2. Charles faced growing criticism in Parliament from Pym and other Puritan MPs regarding his religious policies
3. Parliament accused the king's chief minister, Strafford, of treason and executed him
4. many MPs were unhappy with the way Pym twisted the laws to get Strafford executed, which led to further disputes in Parliament

Possible points of significant omission may include:

5. activities of the Long Parliament angered the King eg arrest and imprisonment of Archbishop Laud
6. the Grand Remonstrance in November 1641 divided the House of Commons in support for the King
7. attempted arrest of 5 Members of Parliament in January 1642 angered Parliament
8. Parliament's decision to throw bishops out of the House of Lords in February 1642 divided the House of Commons
9. Parliament took control of the army in March 1642 without the King's assent
10. the Nineteen Propositions of June 1642 were rejected by Charles, this divided Parliament and the King's supporters left London

Any other valid point of significant omission

Section 2, Context C, The Atlantic Slave Trade, 1770–1807

34. *Candidates can be credited in a number of ways up to a maximum of 5 marks.*

Candidates must evaluate the extent to which a source is useful by commenting on evidence such as the author, type of source, purpose, timing, content or omission. For a mark to be awarded, the candidate must identify an aspect of the source and make a comment which shows why this aspect makes the source more or less useful.

A **maximum of 4 marks** can be awarded for evaluative comments relating to the author, type of source, purpose and timing. A **maximum of 2 marks** may be awarded for evaluative comments relating to the content of the source. A **maximum of 2 marks** may be awarded for evaluative comments relating to points of significant omission.

Examples of aspects of the source and relevant comments:

Aspect	Possible comment(s)
Author: Slave ship doctor	Useful as he is an eyewitness/has first-hand experience
Type of Source: Diary	Useful as it is an honest personal account
Purpose: To record	Useful as it is a private record and is likely to tell the truth
Timing: 1788	Useful as it was written during the period of the slave trade

Content	Possible comment(s)
… led to diarrhoea and fevers among the slaves	Useful because it is accurate (the terrible conditions meant disease was common on ships and it spread very quickly below deck)
… the apartments became so extremely hot (as to be only bearable for a very short time)	Useful because it is accurate (conditions in the hold of the ship were often very hot and stuffy with little or no fresh air)
The floor of the place where the slaves lay was covered in blood and diarrhoea (which had come from them because of their sickness)	Useful because it is accurate (as the floor of the hold where the slaves were kept was covered in human waste which was seldom cleaned)

Possible points of significant omission may include:

1. slaves were held on board using tight pack/loose pack system
2. crew were often cruel towards slaves/female slaves often suffered sexual abuse
3. food was limited and bland/unfamiliar to slaves – some had to be force fed
4. slaves taken above deck and whipped to make them exercise

Any other valid point of omission

35. *Candidates can be credited in a number of ways up to a maximum of 6 marks.*

Candidates must make a judgement about the extent to which the source provides a full description or explanation of a given event or development.

Up to a **maximum of 6 marks** in total, **1 mark** should be awarded for each valid point selected from the source or each valid point of significant omission provided.

Candidates should be awarded **up to 3 marks** for their identification of points from the source which support their judgement. Candidates should be awarded **up to 4 marks** for their identification of points of significant omission, based on their own knowledge, that support their judgement. A **maximum of 2 marks** may be awarded for answers in which no judgement has been made **or** which refer only to the source.

Possible points which may be identified from the source include:

1. (the slaves outnumbered the white population about 20 to 1 which) created a fear of rebellion among the white population
2. fear of a slave uprising led to the introduction of a legal system which supported slavery
3. slave laws were introduced which allowed slave owners to brutally punish or even execute slaves
4. the concentration on sugar production did lasting damage to the Jamaican economy

Possible points of significant omission may include:

5. many of the native people, the Arawaks, were killed or cleared off their land by white settlers
6. new diseases were introduced to the islands by the slaves
7. small farms were replaced by large plantations
8. slave uprisings caused damage and destruction to the Caribbean
9. natural beauty, vegetation and wildlife damaged by the growth of plantations
10. slave trade brought racist attitudes to the Caribbean
11. island economies stifled by slave trade

Any other valid point of significant omission

36. *Candidates can be credited in a number of ways up to a maximum of 6 marks.*

Candidates must make a number of points that make the issue plain or clear, for example by showing connections between factors or causal relationships between events or ideas. These should be key reasons but there is no need for any evaluation or prioritising of these reasons.

Up to a maximum of 6 marks in total, **1 mark** should be awarded for each accurate, relevant reason, and a **second mark** should be awarded for reasons that are developed. Candidates may achieve full marks by providing six straightforward reasons, three developed reasons (or any combination of these).

Possible reasons may include:
1. slaves were controlled by strict laws or codes which scared them from resisting
2. slave risings lacked effective leadership making planning resistance difficult
3. slave resistance was crushed by the better armed and organised whites/the slaves had no weapons
4. plantation owners often used black overseers to help them maintain control
5. captured slaves were subjected to brutal torture or even put to death and this acted as a powerful warning to other slaves
6. slaves lived in fear of being sold off/separated from their families if they broke the rules
7. slaves had little or no education and could be brainwashed into accepting plantation life/the slaves didn't think they could succeed
8. many islands were small and it was difficult for slaves to evade capture
9. plantation owners offered large rewards for the capture of escaped slaves
10. escaped slaves could easily be identified by brandings or lack of legal papers
11. plantation owners used bounty hunters/bloodhounds to track down runaway slaves

Any other valid reason

37. *Candidates can be credited in a number of ways up to a maximum of 9 marks.*

Candidates must make a judgement about the extent to which different factors contributed to an event or development, or its impact. They are required to provide a balanced account of the influence of different factors and come to a reasoned conclusion based on the evidence presented.

Up to 5 marks can be awarded for relevant, factual, key points of knowledge used to support factors, with **1 mark** awarded for each point (but **one mark should be deducted** if the correct process is not clear in at least two factors). If **only one factor is presented, a maximum of 3 marks should be awarded** for relevant points of knowledge. A **further 4 marks** can be awarded for providing the answer in a structured way and coming to a reasoned conclusion.

Possible factors	Key points of knowledge to support this factor may include:
Role of Olaudah Equiano	1. Equiano was a freed slave who travelled throughout the country speaking against slavery 2. his first-hand account of his experiences as a slave persuaded many people about the evils of slavery 3. his was the only book to be written by an African telling about his experiences as a slave and it persuaded many people to support the abolition of the slave trade
Wilberforce	4. Wilberforce used evidence gathered by abolitionists to try to persuade Parliament to abolish the African slave trade 5. Wilberforce regularly introduced anti-slavery bills in Parliament 6. Wilberforce made speeches which brought great publicity to the cause of the abolition of the slave trade
Clarkson	7. Thomas Clarkson collected information about the terrible conditions on slave ships/displayed equipment used on the slave ships, such as iron handcuffs and branding irons, to demonstrate the barbarity of the slave trade
Newton	8. John Newton had been a slave ship captain who campaigned against the slave trade/his book provided an eyewitness account of the slave trade/wrote the song Amazing Grace
Anti-slave trade groups	9. the Society for the Abolition of the Slave Trade had campaigned, with growing support for many years 10. women played an important role in persuading grocers to stop selling sugar produced by slaves and campaigned to get people to stop eating it
Changing attitudes	11. people had begun to think of Africans as fellow human beings making them regard the slave trade as unacceptable 12. Christian teaching led people to change their attitude to the slave trade

Up to **4 marks** should be awarded for presenting the answer in a structured way, leading to a conclusion which addresses the question, as follows:

1 mark for an introduction (which places the question in its historical context or outlines relevant factors).

1 mark for the answer being presented in a structured way (with knowledge being organised in support of different factors).

1 mark for a conclusion with a valid judgement (or overall summary).

1 mark for a reason in support of the judgement (a summary cannot be supported).

Any other relevant factor

Section 2, Context D, Changing Britain, 1760–1914

38. *Candidates can be credited in a number of ways up to a maximum of 9 marks.*

Candidates must make a judgement about the extent to which different factors contributed to an event or development, or its impact. They are required to provide a balanced account of the influence of different factors and come to a reasoned conclusion based on the evidence presented.

Up to 5 marks can be awarded for relevant, factual, key points of knowledge used to support factors, with **1 mark** awarded for each point (but **one mark should be deducted** if the correct process is not clear in at least two factors). If **only one factor is presented, a maximum of 3 marks should be awarded** for relevant points of knowledge. A **further 4 marks** can be awarded for providing the answer in a structured way and coming to a reasoned conclusion.

Up to **4 marks** should be awarded for presenting the answer in a structured way, leading to a conclusion which addresses the question, as follows:

1 mark for an introduction (which places the question in its historical context or outlines relevant factors).

1 mark for the answer being presented in a structured way (with knowledge being organised in support of different factors).

1 mark for a conclusion with a valid judgement (or overall summary).

1 mark for a reason in support of the judgement (a summary cannot be supported).

Possible factors	Key points of knowledge to support this factor may include:
Medical advances	1. after 1858 all doctors had to be fully qualified/improved standard of nursing/midwifery 2. building of more hospitals/cleaner hospitals reduced infection 3. vaccination against killer diseases such as smallpox/antiseptics/anaesthetics
Better diet	4. farming improvements led to better, more varied, nutritious diet eg fresh vegetables and fruit, meat, dairy products 5. railways transported fresh food and milk to towns 6. improved food standards reduced illness caused by adulterated food
Improvements in public health	7. Public Health Acts gave councils power to improve conditions 8. improved sewerage systems/proper drainage reduced spread of germs/diseases 9. provision of fresh, clean water reduced the threat of disease
Improvements in hygiene	10. cheaper soap kept people cleaner/reduced risk of disease 11. wash houses and public baths introduced in 1878 which helped improve hygiene

Any other relevant factor

39. *Candidates can be credited in a number of ways up to a maximum of 6 marks.*

Candidates must make a judgement about the extent to which the source provides a full description or explanation of a given event or development.

Up to a maximum of 6 marks in total, **1 mark** should be awarded for each valid point selected from the source or each valid point of significant omission provided.

Candidates should be awarded **up to 3 marks** for their identification of points from the source which support their judgement. Candidates should be awarded **up to 4 marks** for their identification of points of significant omission, based on their own knowledge, that support their judgement. A **maximum of 2 marks** may be awarded for answers in which no judgement has been made **or** which refer only to the source.

Possible points which may be identified from the source include:
1. powered machines went on hour after hour and many workers struggled to keep up with them
2. owners had very strict rules and workers had to do what they were told to do
3. wages were usually better than farm work
4. if business became slow then workers were laid off, with no income at all

Possible points of significant omission may include:
5. poor ventilation/air was full of harmful dust particles which damaged lungs/caused TB
6. bending over all day led to children becoming deformed
7. working long hours led to tiredness and accidents
8. children pulled into machines and seriously injured/machines were dangerous as they were unfenced
9. new machinery made work easier/machines easy to operate
10. changing rooms provided in some mills/water was available for workers/there was decent sanitation in some mills

Any other valid point of significant omission

40. *Candidates can be credited in a number of ways up to a maximum of 5 marks.*

Candidates must evaluate the extent to which a source is useful by commenting on evidence such as the author, type of source, purpose, timing, content or omission. For a mark to be awarded, the candidate must identify an aspect of the source <u>and</u> make a comment which shows why this aspect makes the source more or less useful.

A **maximum of 4 marks** can be awarded for evaluative comments relating to the author, type of source, purpose and timing. A **maximum of 2 marks** may be awarded for evaluative comments relating to the content of the source. A **maximum of 2 marks** may be awarded for evaluative comments relating to points of significant omission.

Examples of aspects of the source and relevant comments:

Aspect	Possible comment(s)
Author: Railway engineer	Useful as it was written by an eyewitness to the events
Type of Source: Diary	Useful as it's an honest personal account
Purpose: To record	Useful as it's a private record/less likely to tell lies
Timing: 1840s	Useful as it was written during the early period of railway expansion

Content	Possible comment(s)
Lady Seafield very decidedly told us that she hated railways/'Cheap travel brought together such an objectionable variety of people'	Useful because it is accurate (many landowners objected to railways/they would bring industrial workers out to the countryside)
The railway would frighten away the grouse from his moors	Useful because it is accurate (there was concern that railways would spoil hunting on estates)
What would become of the men employed who float timber down the river Spey to the sea?	Useful because it is accurate (many people were worried railways would take away people's jobs)

Possible points of significant omission may include:

1. factory owners saw the advantages of cheaper transport for their goods
2. farmers were happy they could sell their goods further afield
3. working class pleased about the job opportunities on the railways/could go away on day trips to seaside or the countryside
4. workers in other forms of transport such as stage coaches and canals saw railways as a threat to their jobs

Any other valid point of significant omission

41. *Candidates can be credited in a number of ways up to a maximum of 6 marks.*

Candidates must make a number of points that make the issue plain or clear, for example by showing connections between factors or causal relationships between events or ideas. These should be key reasons but there is no need for any evaluation or prioritising of these reasons.

Up to a maximum of 6 marks in total, **1 mark** should be awarded for each accurate, relevant reason, and a **second mark** should be awarded for reasons that are developed. Candidates may achieve full marks by providing six straightforward reasons, three developed reasons (or any combination of these).

Possible reasons may include:

1. need to include middle classes in government because they were key to generating the country's wealth
2. political reform was no longer seen as a threat to the country's stability
3. campaigns by groups such as the National Reform League put pressure on the government to give more people the vote
4. fear of revolution helped convince many politicians it would be dangerous to deny giving the vote to some of the working class
5. increasingly obvious skilled workers were vital to Britain's economic success/many of whom were better educated and respectable therefore deserved the vote
6. better education in towns made it more reasonable to extend the franchise
7. development of railways and growth of cheap popular newspapers raised political awareness of the working class
8. spread of radical ideas and moral arguments; equality became more of an issue
9. political benefits at Westminster for parties; they saw potential voters
10. population growth in the towns made politicians more politically sensitive

11. Hyde Park riots put more pressure on the government
12. Chartist movement provided organised political pressure for change

Section 2, Context E, The Making of Modern Britain, 1880–1951

42. *Candidates can be credited in a number of ways up to a maximum of 5 marks.*

Candidates must evaluate the extent to which a source is useful by commenting on evidence such as the author, type of source, purpose, timing, content or omission. For a mark to be awarded, the candidate must identify an aspect of the source and make a comment which shows why this aspect makes the source more or less useful.

A **maximum of 4 marks** can be awarded for evaluative comments relating to the author, type of source, purpose and timing. A **maximum of 2 marks** may be awarded for evaluative comments relating to the content of the source. A **maximum of 2 marks** may be awarded for evaluative comments relating to points of significant omission.

Examples of aspects of the source and relevant comments:

Aspect	Possible comment(s)
Author: Social investigator	Useful as would be an eyewitness/ has expertise
Type of Source: Report	Useful because reports are usually well researched
Purpose: Inform/persuade	Useful because it provides a detailed description of the effects of poverty/less useful as could exaggerate to try to bring about improvements
Timing: 1892	Useful because it was from a time of widespread poverty in Britain

Content	Possible comment(s)
The two room apartment on the ground floor is occupied by Fletcher, a pedlar, his wife and six of his children	Useful as it is accurate (because many people lived in very overcrowded conditions)
In most of the apartments the walls and ceilings are black with filth	Useful as it is accurate (because in many rooms the wall and ceilings were very dirty)
In these buildings it is a common occurrence to find sewage running down the walls	Useful as it is accurate (because it wasn't unusual to find sewage seeping through the walls)

Possible points of significant omission may include:

1. many people lived in poor quality housing which was often damp/lacked good ventilation/little sunlight
2. lack of fresh, clean water made it difficult to keep themselves/houses clean
3. poor sanitation led to frequent outbreaks of disease
4. poor diet/children often malnourished which contributed to poor health

Any other valid point of significant omission

43. *Candidates can be credited in a number of ways up to a maximum of 6 marks.*

Candidates must make a judgement about the extent to which the source provides a full description or explanation of a given event or development.

Up to a maximum of 6 marks in total, 1 mark should be awarded for each valid point selected from the source or each valid point of significant omission provided.

Candidates should be awarded up to 3 marks for their identification of points from the source which support their judgement. Candidates should be awarded up to 4 marks for their identification of points of significant omission, based on their own knowledge, that support their judgement. A maximum of 2 marks may be awarded for answers in which no judgement has been made or which refer only to the source.

Possible points which may be identified from the source include:
1. medical care was only provided for the worker, it did not cover his wife or children
2. other benefits were only to last for a short period of time
3. the amounts paid as benefits were not enough to live on
4. as the pension only applied to people over 70, many elderly still received no help

Possible points of significant omission may include:
5. not compulsory for local authorities to introduce free school meals
6. school medical inspections did not provide treatment (until school clinics in 1912)
7. amount of old age pensions was not enough to prevent poverty
8. health insurance lasted only 13 weeks at 10s, 5s weekly for next 13 weeks
9. unemployment insurance only covered certain/seasonal industries
10. no attempts were made to tackle poor housing

Any other valid point of significant omission

44. *Candidates can be credited in a number of ways up to a maximum of 6 marks.*

Candidates must make a number of points that make the issue plain or clear, for example by showing connections between factors or causal relationships between events or ideas. These should be key reasons but there is no need for any evaluation or prioritising of these reasons.

Up to a maximum of 6 marks in total, 1 mark should be awarded for each accurate, relevant reason, and a second mark should be awarded for reasons that are developed. Candidates may achieve full marks by providing six straightforward reasons, three developed reasons (or any combination of these).

Possible reasons may include:
1. bombing broke down barriers between middle and working classes eg bomb shelters, war work and people began to have more sympathy for each other
2. during the war, classes were mixing in society who previously had little in common which led to greater sympathy towards helping those in need/a greater sense of "community" was created
3. evacuation exposed continuing poverty in cities and created desire for Government action to improve things
4. in wartime the Government took more responsibility for the nation's health eg free milk and vitamins/free medical care for those who were victims of war and people saw the benefit of this
5. rationing during the war helped encourage the idea of universal sharing of the nation's food supply and people wanted this to continue
6. during the war the Government interfered more in people's lives eg conscription, direction of labour and many wanted this to continue
7. as a result of people's experience during the war, Government assistance was no longer seen as shameful

8. suffering of war caused a determination to create a better society once the war was over/the public expected the Government to do more for them since they had worked together to achieve victory during the war
9. Beveridge Report produced in 1942 was well received by the public and encouraged Government involvement in solving the problems of society
10. Beveridge Report showed the true nature of poverty and had widespread support
11. changing expectations of Government involvement in easing the problems of society since everyone was suffering hardship
12. Labour Party's socialist ideology said there should be redistribution of wealth

Any other valid reason

45. *Candidates can be credited in a number of ways up to a maximum of 9 marks.*

Candidates must make a judgement about the extent to which different factors contributed to an event or development, or its impact. They are required to provide a balanced account of the influence of different factors and come to a reasoned conclusion based on the evidence presented.

Up to 5 marks can be awarded for relevant, factual, key points of knowledge used to support factors, with 1 mark awarded for each point (but one mark should be deducted if the correct process is not clear in at least two factors). If only one factor is presented, a maximum of 3 marks should be awarded for relevant points of knowledge. A further 4 marks can be awarded for providing the answer in a structured way and coming to a reasoned conclusion.

Possible factors	Key points of knowledge to support this factor may include:
National Health Service	1. National Health Service Act provided free medical treatment for everyone 2. National Health Service offered many services eg hospitals, dentistry, opticians, prescriptions, vaccinations
National Insurance	3. National Insurance Act provided comprehensive insurance for all workers eg sickness and unemployment benefit, pensions 4. National Assistance Act provided benefits for those not covered by the National Insurance Act 5. maternity and widows' benefits ensured that families were also covered 6. Family Allowance Act provided extra financial help to families with more than one child
Housing	7. 200,000 homes built a year between 1948 and 1951 8. New Towns Act laid plans for 14 new towns in Britain which helped ease overcrowding in cities and create healthier living conditions
Education	9. Education Act made secondary education compulsory up to the age of 15 which improved education opportunities/made secondary education a reality for all 10. massive school building programme was started which improved access to education
Employment	11. the government promoted a policy of full employment 12. nationalisation of key industries eg electricity, gas, iron and steel, kept unemployment levels down to 2.5%

Up to **4 marks** should be awarded for presenting the answer in a structured way, leading to a conclusion which addresses the question, as follows:

1 mark for an introduction (which places the question in its historical context or outlines relevant factors).

1 mark for the answer being presented in a structured way (with knowledge being organised in support of different factors).

1 mark for a conclusion with a valid judgement (or overall summary).

1 mark for a reason in support of the judgement (a summary cannot be supported).

Any other relevant factor

Section 2, Context A, The Cross and the Crescent: the Crusades, 1071–1192

46. *Candidates can be credited in a number of ways **up to a maximum of 6 marks**.*

Candidates must make a judgement about the extent to which the source provides a full description or explanation of a given event or development.

Up to a maximum of 6 marks in total, **1 mark** should be awarded for each valid point selected from the source or each valid point of significant omission provided.

Candidates should be awarded **up to 3 marks** for their identification of points from the source which support their judgement. Candidates should be awarded **up to 4 marks** for their identification of points of significant omission, based on their own knowledge, that support their judgement. A **maximum of 2 marks** may be awarded for answers in which no judgement has been made **or** which refer only to the source.

Possible points which may be identified from the source include:

1. castles became a key symbol of power
2. were also the administrative centres of each town
3. an ideal base for the local garrison carrying out guard duty
4. during times of attack when food, drink and other supplies could be stored there

Possible points of significant omission may include:

5. castles were used as a court where local law was enforced
6. castles were used to defend and protect the lord's lands and the people who lived on them
7. used as a home for the lord's family
8. centre of entertainment eg feasts and banquets
9. peasants' taxes would be paid in produce and this was often stored in the grounds of the castle
10. castles were used as a place to keep criminals/prisoners

Any other valid point of significant omission

47. *Candidates can be credited in a number of ways **up to a maximum of 4 marks**.*

Candidates must interpret the evidence and make direct comparisons between sources. Candidates are expected to compare content directly on a point-by-point basis. They may compare the details in the sources and/or compare the viewpoints overall.

A **simple comparison** will indicate what points of detail or viewpoint the sources agree or disagree on and **should be awarded 1 mark**. A **developed comparison** of the points of detail or overall viewpoint **should be awarded a second mark**. Candidates may achieve full marks by making four simple comparisons, two developed comparisons (or by any combination of these).

Possible points of comparison may include:

Source B	Source C
Overall: The sources agree about what happened to Jews during the First Crusade	
Many Crusaders were poor and hungry so they began stealing food and possessions from the Jews	(In the riot that followed) Jewish houses were robbed and valuables stolen
Some forced the Jews to change religion and become Christian	Those Jews who survived the massacre were forced to give up their faith and become Christians
Others, against the orders of Peter the Hermit, slaughtered the Jews	Immediately Peter the Hermit's army began attacking and killing Jewish men, women and children

48. *Candidates can be credited in a number of ways **up to a maximum of 9 marks**.*

Candidates must make a judgement about the extent to which different factors contributed to an event or development, or its impact. They are required to provide a balanced account of the influence of different factors and come to a reasoned conclusion based on the evidence presented.

Up to 5 marks can be awarded for relevant, factual, key points of knowledge used to support factors, with **1 mark** awarded for each point (but **one mark should be deducted** if the correct process is not clear in at least two factors). If **only one factor is presented, a maximum of 3 marks should be awarded** for relevant points of knowledge. A **further 4 marks** can be awarded for providing the answer in a structured way and coming to a reasoned conclusion.

Possible factors	Key points of knowledge to support this factor may include:
Muslim divisions	1. Muslims refused to join together and only thought of their own land 2. Muslims frequently fought against each other so weakening their cause 3. a Muslim was bribed to let the Crusaders into Antioch 4. Muslim communities didn't attack the Crusaders/gave them money to keep the peace
Crusaders' military advantages	5. Crusaders had effective leaders in Bohemond of Taranto and Raymond of Toulouse who were experienced knights/both men were involved in key victories eg Antioch/Jerusalem 6. Crusaders used effective tactics to defeat the Muslims eg siege towers used at Jerusalem 7. the knights were militarily superior to the Muslim forces eg the knights' tactics of charging at Dorylaeum/Antioch secured victory
Crusading ideals	8. many Christians believed that it was their duty to recapture Jerusalem/believed they were doing God's work 9. Crusaders were inspired by the promise that all their sins would be forgiven if they took part in the Crusade
Support for Crusaders	10. the Crusaders received help from Italian ports eg cities such as Pisa/Genoa/Venice supplied timber for siege machines 11. the Crusaders received help from Emperor Alexius eg provided Crusaders with additional soldiers/supplies at Constantinople etc 12. secured important trade routes ensuring Crusaders had access to vital supplies

Up to **4 marks** should be awarded for presenting the answer in a structured way, leading to a conclusion which addresses the question, as follows:

1 mark for an introduction (which places the question in its historical context or outlines relevant factors).

1 mark for the answer being presented in a structured way (with knowledge being organised in support of different factors).

1 mark for a conclusion with a valid judgement (or overall summary).

1 mark for a reason in support of the judgement (a summary cannot be supported).

Any other relevant factor

49. *Candidates can be credited in a number of ways **up to a maximum of 6 marks**.*

Candidates must make a number of points that make the issue plain or clear, for example by showing connections between factors or causal relationships between events or ideas. These should be key reasons but there is no need for any evaluation or prioritising of these reasons.

Up to a maximum of 6 marks in total, **1 mark** should be awarded for each accurate, relevant reason, and a **second mark** should be awarded for reasons that are developed. Candidates may achieve full marks by providing six straightforward reasons, three developed reasons (or any combination of these).

Possible reasons may include:
1. Crusaders were divided eg Guy de Lusignan and Reynald of Chatillon hated each other
2. Crusaders had different ideologies towards the Muslims eg the Hawks and the Doves
3. death of Baldwin IV meant that Jerusalem did not have a strong ruler
4. King Guy made a tactical error by leaving Jerusalem with the Crusader army
5. Crusaders were defeated at the Battle of Hattin where most of the nobility were taken prisoner, including King Guy
6. Crusaders lacked resources to defend Jerusalem once the army was defeated
7. when a portion of the wall was mined, it collapsed and the Crusaders were unable to push Saladin's troops back from the breach
8. by the end of September there were only a few dozen knights and a handful of remaining men-at-arms capable of bearing arms and defending the wall
9. Muslims were united under Saladin's leadership making them stronger
10. Saladin's army outnumbered the Crusaders

Any other valid reason

50. *Candidates can be credited in a number of ways **up to a maximum of 4 marks**.*

They may take different perspectives on the events and may describe a variety of different aspects of the events. Candidates must make a number of relevant, factual points. These should be key points. These do not have to be in any particular order.

1 mark should be awarded for each accurate relevant key point of knowledge. A **second mark** should be awarded for each point that is developed, **up to a maximum of 4 marks**. Candidates may achieve full marks by providing four straightforward points, by making two developed points (or any combination of these).

Possible points of knowledge may include:
1. in July 1192 Saladin laid siege to the town of Jaffa
2. Saladin's soldiers successfully stormed the walls after three days of bloody clashes
3. the Crusaders however held out in Jaffa's citadel
4. Richard gathered a small army (of knights, a few hundred infantrymen, and about 2,000 crossbowmen) and led them into battle
5. the Muslim army panicked at the sudden attack/fled the city in disarray
6. Saladin launched a counter attack on Jaffa
7. Richard ordered the infantry and knights to form a defensive hedge of spears, with the crossbowmen behind
8. Saladin's cavalry repeatedly charged but suffered heavy casualties so he ordered it to withdraw

Any other valid point of knowledge

Section 3, Context B, 'Tea and Freedom': the American Revolution, 1774–1783

51. *Candidates can be credited in a number of ways **up to a maximum of 9 marks**.*

Candidates must make a judgement about the extent to which different factors contributed to an event or development, or its impact. They are required to provide a balanced account of the influence of different factors and come to a reasoned conclusion based on the evidence presented.

Up to 5 marks can be awarded for relevant, factual, key points of knowledge used to support factors, with **1 mark** awarded for each point (but **one mark should be deducted** if the correct process is not clear in at least two factors). If **only one factor is presented, a maximum of 3 marks should be awarded** for relevant points of knowledge. A **further 4 marks** can be awarded for providing the answer in a structured way and coming to a reasoned conclusion.

Up to **4 marks** should be awarded for presenting the answer in a structured way, leading to a conclusion which addresses the question, as follows:

1 mark for an introduction (which places the question in its historical context or outlines relevant factors).

1 mark for the answer being presented in a structured way (with knowledge being organised in support of different factors).

1 mark for a conclusion with a valid judgement (or overall summary).

1 mark for a reason in support of the judgement (a summary cannot be supported).

Possible factors	Key points of knowledge to support this factor may include:
Raising revenue	1. the Revenue Act (the Sugar Act) – cut duty on molasses but it was now more strictly enforced 2. the Stamp Act – all legal documents, commercial papers, newspapers and pamphlets had to be officially stamped 3. Townshend Duties – taxes on tea, lead, glass, paper and paint 4. colonists resented being taxed without representation
George III	5. colonists were angry at George III's desire to exert greater control over colonies/was accused of becoming a tyrant 6. George III was blamed for refusing to introduce sensible laws/a fair justice system in the colonies
British troops	7. colonists were unhappy with the continuing presence of British soldiers in the colonies following the defeat of the French in 1763 8. colonists were further angered by the passing of the Quartering Act
British restrictions	9. some colonists were frustrated that the British were stopping them from moving west 10. some colonists felt that the policies of the British government were damaging trade
Outbreaks of violence	11. the Boston Massacre increased tension between Britain and the colonists 12. fighting at Lexington and Concord in April 1775 led to formation of Continental Army

Any other relevant factor

52. *Candidates can be credited in a number of ways up to a maximum of 6 marks.*

Candidates must make a number of points that make the issue plain or clear, for example by showing connections between factors or causal relationships between events or ideas. These should be key reasons but there is no need for any evaluation or prioritising of these reasons.

Up to a maximum of 6 marks in total, **1 mark** should be awarded for each accurate, relevant reason, and a **second mark** should be awarded for reasons that are developed. Candidates may achieve full marks by providing six straightforward reasons, three developed reasons (or any combination of these).

Possible reasons may include:
1. many colonists had become wealthy through trade with Britain/merchants feared damage to their trade if the colonists won
2. King George III still commanded some respect among many colonists/some colonists had a great loyalty to the King/saw the monarchy as important
3. some colonists feared law and order would break down if British rule was overthrown
4. some loyalists felt their power and influence had increased under British rule

5. some colonists greatly feared the spread of revolutionary ideas if the colonists won
6. loyalists were mainly conservative and feared change if the British lost
7. many loyalists believed in the importance of the Empire and opposed any threat to it
8. individuals like Flora McDonald encouraged Scots colonists to remain loyal to Britain
9. some hoped to win favour with the British Government by remaining loyal
10. most colonists were of British descent and were proud of being British
11. some loyalists felt that the conflict was the colonists' fault and had no sympathy for them

Any other valid reason

53. *Candidates can be credited in a number of ways up to a maximum of 6 marks.*

Candidates must make a judgement about the extent to which the source provides a full description or explanation of a given event or development.

Up to a maximum of 6 marks in total, **1 mark** should be awarded for each valid point selected from the source or each valid point of significant omission provided.

Candidates should be awarded **up to 3 marks** for their identification of points from the source which support their judgement. Candidates should be awarded **up to 4 marks** for their identification of points of significant omission, based on their own knowledge, that support their judgement. A **maximum of 2 marks** may be awarded for answers in which no judgement has been made **or** which refer only to the source.

Possible points which may be identified from the source include:
1. the American forces were often led by inefficient, even incompetent, commanders who fought muddled campaigns
2. the men gathering in Boston were very enthusiastic
3. they were however badly armed and lacking supplies
4. most men were part-time and served for only a few months at a time

Possible points of significant omission may include:
5. many American officers lacked proper military training/training in the different types of warfare
6. American forces were short of artillery and cavalry
7. many soldiers lacked experience in battle/needed practice with their weapons
8. many soldiers didn't even have a uniform
9. troops grew exhausted and sick as the campaign went on
10. troops suffered from poor food/shortages of food and cold weather during winter campaigns

Any other valid point of significant omission

54. *Candidates can be credited in a number of ways up to a maximum of 4 marks.*

They may take different perspectives on the events and may describe a variety of different aspects of the events. Candidates must make a number of relevant, factual points. These should be key points. These do not have to be in any particular order.

1 mark should be awarded for each accurate relevant key point of knowledge. A **second mark** should be awarded for each point that is developed, **up to a maximum of 4 marks.** Candidates may achieve full marks by providing four straightforward points, by making two developed points (or any combination of these).

Possible points of knowledge may include:
1. British plan was to link their two armies to defeat the colonists
2. Burgoyne's army invaded from Canada
3. colonists cut down trees and blocked British army's progress
4. colonists destroyed crops and other potential food supplies
5. Native Americans deserted the British
6. St Leger's British army was defeated/he retreated
7. British at Saratoga outnumbered and surrounded by colonists
8. Burgoyne's army unable to break out so he surrendered (6,000 men and 30 cannon) to colonists

Any other valid point of knowledge

55. *Candidates can be credited in a number of ways* **up to a maximum of 4 marks.**

Candidates must interpret the evidence and make direct comparisons between sources. Candidates are expected to compare content directly on a point-by-point basis. They may compare the details in the sources and/or compare the viewpoints overall.

A **simple comparison** will indicate what points of detail or viewpoint the sources agree or disagree on and **should be awarded 1 mark**. A **developed comparison** of the points of detail or overall viewpoint **should be awarded a second mark**. Candidates may achieve full marks by making four simple comparisons, two developed comparisons (or by any combination of these).

Possible points of comparison may include:

Source B	Source C
Overall: The sources agree about the events of the Battle of Yorktown	
Cornwallis moved into Virginia and began to build a base at Yorktown	... Cornwallis's British forces set up camp at Yorktown.
By late summer, Cornwallis's position at Yorktown was deteriorating fast	Yorktown however turned out to be a poor position and his situation became more serious
... American forces prevented him from moving inland ...	... American troops moved quickly into the area to surround him and keep him there

Section 3, Context C, USA 1850–1880

56. *Candidates can be credited in a number of ways* **up to a maximum of 6 marks.**

Candidates must make a number of points that make the issue plain or clear, for example by showing connections between factors or causal relationships between events or ideas. These should be key reasons but there is no need for any evaluation or prioritising of these reasons.

Up to a maximum of 6 marks in total, **1 mark** should be awarded for each accurate, relevant reason, and a **second mark** should be awarded for reasons that are developed. Candidates may achieve full marks by providing six straightforward reasons, three developed reasons (or any combination of these).

Possible reasons may include:
1. desire for good farmland/thought the land would be more fertile in the West

2. ranch owners realised the Great Plains could feed their huge herds of cattle
3. government publicity encouraged people to move West with promises of a better life
4. Government Acts eg Homestead Act, offered cheap/free land to settlers
5. to fulfil Manifest Destiny as many Americans saw it as their duty to spread their way of life
6. searching for gold/'California gold rush' attracted many hoping to become rich
7. railways encouraged many settlers to move West by providing quick transport
8. railway companies sold land cheaply to settlers which encouraged settlers to move
9. some settlers were attracted West by a sense of adventure
10. to be able to enjoy religious freedom away from other people eg Mormons
11. freed slaves headed West after 1865 to escape persecution

Any other valid reason

57. *Candidates can be credited in a number of ways* **up to a maximum of 6 marks.**

Candidates must make a judgement about the extent to which the source provides a full description or explanation of a given event or development.

Up to a maximum of 6 marks in total, **1 mark** should be awarded for each valid point selected from the source or each valid point of significant omission provided. Candidates should be awarded **up to 3 marks** for their identification of points from the source which support their judgement. Candidates should be awarded **up to 4 marks** for their identification of points of significant omission, based on their own knowledge, that support their judgement. A **maximum of 2 marks** may be awarded for answers in which no judgement has been made **or** which refer only to the source.

Possible points which may be identified from the source include:
1. the Compromise of 1850 was created by Henry Clay and others to deal with the balance between slave and free states
2. the Kansas-Nebraska Act of 1854, however, increased tensions
3. pro-slavery people of Missouri began to pour into Kansas to help force it to be a slave state
4. the fight over slavery even erupted on the floor of the Senate/Anti-slavery campaigner Charles Sumner was beat over the head by South Carolina's pro-slavery Senator Preston Brooks

Possible points of significant omission may include:
5. Dred Scott case caused unhappiness among abolitionists and Northern States
6. attack on Harper's Ferry by John Brown heightened tension
7. South was alarmed by election of Lincoln who wanted to halt spread of slavery
8. Lincoln's election was seen as the last straw by Southern States
9. South Carolina seceded and other Southern States followed
10. Fort Sumter was besieged by Confederate troops/food supplies cut off
11. the Confederates opened fire on the fort which led to an outburst of patriotic fever in the North

Any other valid point of significant omission

58. *Candidates can be credited in a number of ways up to a maximum of 4 marks.*

They may take different perspectives on the events and may describe a variety of different aspects of the events. Candidates must make a number of relevant, factual points. These should be key points. These do not have to be in any particular order.

1 mark should be awarded for each accurate relevant key point of knowledge. A **second mark** should be awarded for each point that is developed, **up to a maximum of 4 marks**. Candidates may achieve full marks by providing four straightforward points, by making two developed points (or any combination of these).

Possible points of knowledge may include:
1. was set up to help newly freed slaves
2. it helped provide food for poor freed slaves
3. helped former slaves buy land for farming
4. paid for schools/helped former slaves learn to read and write
5. set up/paid for hospitals for former slaves
6. provided temporary shelter for former slaves
7. helped former slaves find employment

Any other valid point of knowledge

59. *Candidates can be credited in a number of ways up to a maximum of 4 marks.*

Candidates must interpret the evidence and make direct comparisons between sources. Candidates are expected to compare content directly on a point-by-point basis. They may compare the details in the sources and/or compare the viewpoints overall.

A **simple comparison** will indicate what points of detail or viewpoint the sources agree or disagree on and **should be awarded 1 mark**. A **developed comparison** of the points of detail or overall viewpoint **should be awarded a second mark**. Candidates may achieve full marks by making four simple comparisons, two developed comparisons (or by any combination of these).

Possible points of comparison may include:

Source B	Source C
Overall: The sources agree about what happened during Reconstruction	
Hostility was shown to the school teachers like me who taught in schools for blacks	Teachers in schools for black Americans became key figures so they were frequently intimidated
They came at night and gave these warnings	These attacks usually took place at night …
… they were whipping me …	… they whipped, mutilated and murdered black people

60. *Candidates can be credited in a number of ways up to a maximum of 9 marks.*

Candidates must make a judgement about the extent to which different factors contributed to an event or development, or its impact. They are required to provide a balanced account of the influence of different factors and come to a reasoned conclusion based on the evidence presented.

Up to 5 marks can be awarded for relevant, factual, key points of knowledge used to support factors, with **1 mark** awarded for each point (but **one mark should be deducted** if the correct process is not clear in at least two factors).

If **only one factor is presented, a maximum of 3 marks should be awarded** for relevant points of knowledge. A **further 4 marks** can be awarded for providing the answer in a structured way and coming to a reasoned conclusion.

Possible factors	Key points of knowledge to support this factor may include:
Discovery of gold	1. Bozeman Trail was cause of conflict/ triggered war: Native Americans opposed white men building road to gold mines 2. Trail passed through Yellowstone River/ heart of Sioux hunting grounds 3. Custer's discovery of gold in Black Hills brought thousands of miners/Black Hills were sacred Sioux territory 4. grants to encourage gold prospecting alarmed Native Americans (Colorado and Montana in 1858 and the Black Hills in 1874)
Railways	5. railroads caused tension with Native Americans: opened up West/encouraged white settlers to buy prairie lands 6. building railways across the Plains disturbed the Native American hunting grounds/migration of the buffalo
Buffalo	7. Native Americans feared destruction of bison/buffalo herds: reliance on buffalo for all their needs 8. railroad companies sent in hunters to kill buffalo
Beliefs	9. Native Americans believed Great Spirit created land for their care; whites had a 'property attitude' 10. white settlers believed in Manifest Destiny that they had the right to settle where they wanted
Treaties	11. treaties with the Native Americans were broken/Native Americans felt betrayed due to broken promises
Reservations	12. many white Americans favoured setting up reservations to keep Native Americans out of their way/Native American feared reservations would mean the destruction of their way of life

Any other relevant information

Section 3, Context D, Hitler and Nazi Germany, 1919–1939

61. *Candidates can be credited in a number of ways up to a maximum of 4 marks.*

They may take different perspectives on the events and may describe a variety of different aspects of the events. Candidates must make a number of relevant, factual points. These should be key points. These do not have to be in any particular order.

1 mark should be awarded for each accurate relevant key point of knowledge. A **second mark** should be awarded for each point that is developed, **up to a maximum of 4 marks**. Candidates may achieve full marks by providing four straightforward points, by making two developed points (or any combination of these).

Possible points of knowledge may include:
1. Von Kahr, Governor of Bavaria, was making a speech at a meeting in a Munich beer hall
2. Nazi SA men surrounded the building

3. Hitler burst into the hall and ordered three Bavarian leaders, Von Kahr, Von Seisser and Von Lossow into a private/side room
4. Hitler claimed they had agreed to support him/announced a national revolution had begun
5. Ludendorff let the Bavarian leaders go once they had promised their support
6. once free the Bavarian leaders withdrew their support and ordered the putsch to be crushed
7. next day Hitler marched in centre of Munich with several thousand Nazis
8. police blocked their way and shooting broke out and a number of Nazis and policemen were killed

Any other valid point of knowledge

62. *Candidates can be credited in a number of ways **up to a maximum of 9 marks.***

Candidates must make a judgement about the extent to which different factors contributed to an event or development, or its impact. They are required to provide a balanced account of the influence of different factors and come to a reasoned conclusion based on the evidence presented.

Up to 5 marks can be awarded for relevant, factual, key points of knowledge used to support factors, with **1 mark** awarded for each point (but **one mark should be deducted** if the correct process is not clear in at least two factors). If **only one factor is presented, a maximum of 3 marks should be awarded** for relevant points of knowledge. A **further 4 marks** can be awarded for providing the answer in a structured way and coming to a reasoned conclusion.

Possible factors	Key points of knowledge to support this factor may include:
Weimar Republic	1. blamed for signing the hated Treaty of Versailles (November Criminals) and its harsh terms 2. criticised for the voting system, proportional representation, which produced weak coalition governments 3. unpopular as coalition governments lacked authority/seemed unable to solve problems facing Germany 4. blamed for economic hardships such as hyperinflation, the Wall Street Crash and mass unemployment
Appeal of Hitler	5. Hitler appeared to offer strong, decisive leadership 6. Hitler was an outstanding orator who inspired people 7. had a clear, simple message which appealed to many people
Nazi Policies	8. Nazis seemed to offer something to most groups/classes in Germany, such as jobs for the unemployed, crush Communism, remilitarisation, destroy Treaty of Versailles 9. promised to restore order to Germany after chaos of the Weimar period
Nazi propaganda	10. Nazi use of propaganda eg posters, Nazi newspapers gained widespread support 11. held large public meetings, parades, rallies, eg Nuremberg, which excited and impressed people 12. use of SA to impress people/well-disciplined in times of chaos

Up to **4 marks** should be awarded for presenting the answer in a structured way, leading to a conclusion which addresses the question, as follows:

1 mark for an introduction (which places the question in its historical context or outlines relevant factors).

1 mark for the answer being presented in a structured way (with knowledge being organised in support of different factors).

1 mark for a conclusion with a valid judgement (or overall summary).

1 mark for a reason in support of the judgement (a summary cannot be supported).

Any other relevant point

63. *Candidates can be credited in a number of ways **up to a maximum of 4 marks.***

Candidates must interpret the evidence and make direct comparisons between sources. Candidates are expected to compare content directly on a point-by-point basis. They may compare the details in the sources and/or compare the viewpoints overall.

A **simple comparison** will indicate what points of detail or viewpoint the sources agree or disagree on and **should be awarded 1 mark**. A **developed comparison** of the points of detail or overall viewpoint **should be awarded a second mark**. Candidates may achieve full marks by making four simple comparisons, two developed comparisons (or by any combination of these).

Possible points of comparison may include:

Source A	Source B
Overall: The sources agree about the Nazi ideas on race	
… differences between the races was a matter of scientific fact	… biological research had shown that there was a distinction between races
… Aryan people of northern Europe were superior in every way	… Aryans of Germany and Scandinavia were the Master Race
It was logical that superior people like this should be in control of all other races	This gave these superior races the authority to rule over the peoples of the world

64. *Candidates can be credited in a number of ways **up to a maximum of 6 marks.***

Candidates must make a number of points that make the issue plain or clear, for example by showing connections between factors or causal relationships between events or ideas. These should be key reasons but there is no need for any evaluation or prioritising of these reasons.

Up to a maximum of 6 marks in total, **1 mark** should be awarded for each accurate, relevant reason, and a **second mark** should be awarded for reasons that are developed. Candidates may achieve full marks by providing six straightforward reasons, three developed reasons (or any combination of these).

Possible reasons may include:
1. fear of the Nazi regime/intimidation by the SS deterred opposition
2. opposition groups often infiltrated by Gestapo/spies leading to their arrest
3. opponents scared by brutal treatment/hanging of opponents
4. opposition leaders were arrested and sent to concentration camps/outspoken individuals eg Bonhoeffer, Niemoller were arrested and sent to camps which weakened opposition groups

5. many opponents of the Nazis fearful for their lives fled abroad
6. opposition groups had to meet in secret, making meetings difficult/dangerous
7. all other political parties/trade unions were banned
8. little cooperation between the opposition groups as they didn't trust each other
9. Nazi control of the media made it difficult for opponents to publicise their views
10. Nazi propaganda brainwashed people into supporting the Nazis
11. there was widespread support for the Nazis and most Germans were impressed as Hitler was a strong leader/ solving Germany's problems
12. Nazi control of the courts meant opponents were harshly punished

Any other valid reason

65. *Candidates can be credited in a number of ways up to a maximum of 6 marks.*

Candidates must make a judgement about the extent to which the source provides a full description or explanation of a given event or development.

Up to a maximum of 6 marks in total, **1 mark** should be awarded for each valid point selected from the source or each valid point of significant omission provided.

Candidates should be awarded **up to 3 marks** for their identification of points from the source which support their judgement. Candidates should be awarded **up to 4 marks** for their identification of points of significant omission, based on their own knowledge, that support their judgement. A **maximum of 2 marks** may be awarded for answers in which no judgement has been made **or** which refer only to the source.

Possible points which may be identified from the source include:
1. the introduction of new Nazi textbooks
2. the number of PE periods was increased at the expense of religious education
3. competitive field games were added to curriculum
4. at the start of class, we had to raise our arms in the "Heil Hitler!" salute

Possible points of significant omission may include:
5. indoctrination of Nazi ideas eg anti-Semitism/militarism
6. biology was used to 'prove' the Nazi belief in racial superiority/introduction of new subjects such as Racial Science/Eugenics
7. for girls emphasis on 'female' subjects (Kinder, Kirche, Kuche)
8. all teachers had to join the Nazi Teachers' League/teachers suspected of being disloyal to the Party were arrested/ pictures of Hitler/Swastika flag in classrooms
9. Jewish children were humiliated/from 1938 only allowed to attend Jewish schools

Any other valid point of significant omission

Section 3, Context E, Red Flag: Lenin and the Russian Revolution, 1894–1921

66. *Candidates can be credited in a number of ways up to a maximum of 4 marks.*

They may take different perspectives on the events and may describe a variety of different aspects of the events. Candidates must make a number of relevant, factual points. These should be key points. These do not have to be in any particular order.

1 mark should be awarded for each accurate relevant key point of knowledge. A **second mark** should be awarded

for each point that is developed, **up to a maximum of 4 marks.** Candidates may achieve full marks by providing four straightforward points, by making two developed points (or any combination of these).

Possible points of knowledge may include:
1. Tsar was an autocrat/not answerable to anyone
2. Orthodox Church preached that his rule was the will of God
3. the army was loyal and was used to put down any uprisings
4. secret police, Okhrana, kept watch on any suspected opponents
5. execution/prison/exile to Siberia extensively used as a deterrent
6. the press was censored
7. government ran the trades unions to maintain control of the workers
8. policy of Russification used to keep control of national minorities

Any other valid point of knowledge

67. *Candidates can be credited in a number of ways up to a maximum of 6 marks.*

Candidates must make a number of points that make the issue plain or clear, for example by showing connections between factors or causal relationships between events or ideas. These should be key reasons but there is no need for any evaluation or prioritising of these reasons.

Up to a maximum of 6 marks in total, **1 mark** should be awarded for each accurate, relevant reason, and a **second mark** should be awarded for reasons that are developed. Candidates may achieve full marks by providing six straightforward reasons, three developed reasons (or any combination of these).

Possible reasons may include:
1. people hated the repressive policies of the Tsar and his government
2. most groups felt that their problems were being ignored by the government
3. peasants struggled to make a living off the land/high taxes/redemption debt
4. factory workers in the industrial cities faced terrible hardship, with long hours, low wages, dangerous working conditions, and terrible living conditions
5. the policy of Russification caused anger and discontent among national minorities
6. the economic problems people faced grew worse during the war with Japan
7. defeat by Japan led to unrest/strengthened the revolutionary movement
8. shortages of food, fuel and high unemployment in industrial cities made people desperate and angry
9. impact of Bloody Sunday angered people and led to discontent and strikes
10. workers and liberal middle classes united against Tsar
11. revolutionary groups became more organised eg formation of St Petersburg Soviet
12. discontent in the armed forces increased during the war

Any other valid reason

68. *Candidates can be credited in a number of ways up to a maximum of 6 marks.*

Candidates must make a judgement about the extent to which the source provides a full description or explanation of a given event or development.

Up to a maximum of 6 marks in total, **1 mark** should be awarded for each valid point selected from the source or each valid point of significant omission provided.

Candidates should be awarded **up to 3 marks** for their identification of points from the source which support their judgement. Candidates should be awarded **up to 4 marks** for their identification of points of significant omission, based on their own knowledge, that support their judgement. A **maximum of 2 marks** may be awarded for answers in which no judgement has been made **or** which refer only to the source.

Possible points which may be identified from the source include:

1. the October Manifesto established a parliament or Duma elected by the people
2. it also allowed the Russian people basic rights, such as freedom of speech
3. his land reforms allowed peasants to become owners of their own land
4. he set up a peasants' bank to provide loans to help them buy the land

Possible points of significant omission may include:

5. political parties were legalised
6. peasants no longer had to pay the redemption debt
7. peasants could consolidate the size of their land holdings
8. a system of health insurance introduced for industrial workers
9. introduced some improvements to working conditions in factories
10. thousands more primary schools established

Any other valid point of significant omission

69. *Candidates can be credited in a number of ways up to a maximum of 4 marks.*

Candidates must interpret the evidence and make direct comparisons between sources. Candidates are expected to compare content directly on a point-by-point basis. They may compare the details in the sources and/or compare the viewpoints overall.

A **simple comparison** will indicate what points of detail or viewpoint the sources agree or disagree on and **should be awarded 1 mark**. A **developed comparison** of the points of detail or overall viewpoint **should be awarded a second mark**. Candidates may achieve full marks by making four simple comparisons, two developed comparisons (or by any combination of these).

Possible points of comparison may include:

Source B	Source C
Overall: The sources agree about the effects of the First World War on the Russian people	
Prices have gone up …	The shortages meant that food prices went up …
Food is hard to get	… Russian cities suffered from a shortage of food
They blame the Tsar and say 'he does not care we might starve'	… urban workers faced terrible starvation …

70. *Candidates can be credited in a number of ways up to a maximum of 9 marks.*

Candidates must make a judgement about the extent to which different factors contributed to an event or development, or its impact. They are required to provide a balanced account of the influence of different factors and come to a reasoned conclusion based on the evidence presented.

Up to 5 marks can be awarded for relevant, factual, key points of knowledge used to support factors, with **1 mark**

awarded for each point (but **one mark should be deducted** if the correct process is not clear in at least two factors). If **only one factor is presented, a maximum of 3 marks should be awarded** for relevant points of knowledge. A **further 4 marks** can be awarded for providing the answer in a structured way and coming to a reasoned conclusion.

Possible factors	Key points of knowledge to support this factor may include:
Trotsky	1. Trotsky was a skilled commander of the Red Army who was decisive and ruthless 2. Trotsky disciplined the Red Army to be an effective fighting force/conscripted men to raise 5 million by 1920/raised the Red Cavalry to counter the Cossacks 3. Trotsky used experienced Tsarist officers, supervised by political commissars/used Cheka to discourage desertions
Red Army	4. by the end of 1919 the Red soldiers outnumbered the Whites by ten to one 5. soldiers were well supplied (boots, food, tobacco) 6. energetic propaganda campaign boosted soldiers' morale
Territorial advantage	7. Reds controlled a compact area in the centre of Russia (easier to defend) 8. Reds had control of the industrial centres/factories 9. Reds controlled the railways/had good communication/able to transport of munitions, etc
Weaknesses of Whites	10. Whites had weak leadership, many generals were corrupt/incompetent 11. White forces were split/never united their full strength/White generals did not co-ordinate their attacks/strategy 12. Whites held peripheral areas/did not control the industrial centre or rail networks making it difficult to supply troops

Up to **4 marks** should be awarded for presenting the answer in a structured way, leading to a conclusion which addresses the question, as follows:

1 mark for an introduction (which places the question in its historical context or outlines relevant factors).

1 mark for the answer being presented in a structured way (with knowledge being organised in support of different factors).

1 mark for a conclusion with a valid judgement (or overall summary).

1 mark for a reason in support of the judgement (a summary cannot be supported).

Any other relevant point

Section 3, Context F, Mussolini and Fascist Italy, 1919–1939

71. *Candidates can be credited in a number of ways up to a maximum of 4 marks.*

Candidates must interpret the evidence and make direct comparisons between sources. Candidates are expected to compare content directly on a point-by-point basis. They may compare the details in the sources and/or compare the viewpoints overall.

A **simple comparison** will indicate what points of detail or viewpoint the sources agree or disagree on and **should be** awarded **1 mark**. A **developed comparison** of the points of detail or overall viewpoint **should be awarded a second mark**. Candidates may achieve full marks by making four simple comparisons, two developed comparisons (or by any combination of these).

Possible points of comparison may include:

Source A	Source B
Overall: The sources agree about the events which led to Mussolini's seizure of power in Italy in 1922	
This put Mussolini in the position to challenge the government, which he did in what became known as the famous 'March on Rome'	... Mussolini decided to seize the government when he and his followers marched on the capital, Rome
The government decided to send in the army to try and stop Mussolini.	... the prime minister called out the army when the Fascists surrounded Rome
The king, Victor Emmanuel III, however decided instead of using the army, to give in to Mussolini's demands	...the pressure proved too much for the Italian King who refused to use the military to squash Mussolini's 'march'

72. *Candidates can be credited in a number of ways **up to a maximum of 6 marks.***

Candidates must make a judgement about the extent to which the source provides a full description or explanation of a given event or development.

Up to a maximum of 6 marks in total, **1 mark** should be awarded for each valid point selected from the source or each valid point of significant omission provided.

Candidates should be awarded **up to 3 marks** for their identification of points from the source which support their judgement. Candidates should be awarded **up to 4 marks** for their identification of points of significant omission, based on their own knowledge, that support their judgement. A **maximum of 2 marks** may be awarded for answers in which no judgement has been made **or** which refer only to the source.

Possible points which may be identified from the source include:
1. the leadership cult in Fascist Italy started almost as soon as Mussolini came to power in 1922
2. his role as Duce of Fascism and Head of the Government had been secured by changes to the law
3. Mussolini had undoubted charisma and political intelligence (with which to maintain his power over Fascism and the Italian people)
4. his main talents lay chiefly in the areas of acting and propaganda

Possible points of significant omission may include:
5. the cult was intended to build popular support for the dictator and to secure support for the government
6. the media played an important role in establishing the cult of 'Il Duce'
7. Mussolini was shown as a man chosen by destiny to save Italy and its people from Communism and Socialism
8. he was portrayed as the new Caesar/a man of genius/a man of action
9. he established 'holy days' such as 23 March, to remind Italians of the advent of Fascism
10. newspapers were forbidden to mention any signs of illness and even his birthdays were to be ignored as this would reveal his age

Any other valid point of significant omission

73. *Candidates can be credited in a number of ways **up to a maximum of 6 marks.***

Candidates must make a number of points that make the issue plain or clear, for example by showing connections between factors or causal relationships between events or ideas. These should be key reasons but there is no need for any evaluation or prioritising of these reasons.

Up to a maximum of 6 marks in total, **1 mark** should be awarded for each accurate, relevant reason, and a **second mark** should be awarded for reasons that are developed. Candidates may achieve full marks by providing six straightforward reasons, three developed reasons (or any combination of these).

Possible reasons may include:
1. revaluation of the lira in 1927 led to decline in exports, causing discontent
2. increase in unemployment 1926–28. By 1933 unemployment had reached 2 million, causing unpopularity
3. high tariffs restricted imports, so people unhappy
4. real wages fell, so people were angry
5. many workers were unhappy when trade unions were outlawed
6. sick pay and paid holidays were not introduced until 1938, which disappointed people
7. the failure to make Italy self-sufficient contributed to growing unpopularity
8. as part of the Battle for Grain, land in central and southern regions was turned over to wheat production despite being unsuitable (traditional agricultural exports declined), unpopular in these areas
9. increasing government control of industry was resented

Any other valid reason

74. *Candidates can be credited in a number of ways **up to a maximum of 4 marks.***

They may take different perspectives on the events and may describe a variety of different aspects of the events. Candidates must make a number of relevant, factual points. These should be key points. These do not have to be in any particular order.

1 mark should be awarded for each accurate relevant key point of knowledge. A **second mark** should be awarded for each point that is developed, **up to a maximum of 4 marks**. Candidates may achieve full marks by providing four straightforward points, by making two developed points (or any combination of these).

Possible points of knowledge may include:
1. to make Italy a great world power/the dominant power in the Mediterranean
2. to expand Italy's colonial empire in Africa/take over Ethiopia
3. to increase Italian influence in the Balkans
4. to build up Italy's armed forces to make Italy feared
5. to make Albania into an Italian satellite state
6. to encourage the break-up of Yugoslavia
7. to improve relations with Britain
8. to contain Germany's influence in Austria

Any other valid point of knowledge

75. *Candidates can be credited in a number of ways **up to a maximum of 9 marks.***

Candidates must make a judgement about the extent to which different factors contributed to an event or development, or its impact. They are required to provide a balanced account of the influence of different factors and come to a reasoned conclusion based on the evidence presented.

Up to **5 marks** can be awarded for relevant, factual, key points of knowledge used to support factors, with **1 mark** awarded for each point (but **one mark should be deducted** if the correct process is not clear in at least two factors). If **only one factor is presented, a maximum of 3 marks should be awarded** for relevant points of knowledge. A **further 4 marks** can be awarded for providing the answer in a structured way and coming to a reasoned conclusion.

Possible factors	Key points of knowledge to support this factor may include:
Fear/use of violence	1. a secret police force was set up, the OVRA, which spied on opponents 2. many opponents of the regime were murdered/sent to concentration camps, which scared people 3. people were afraid of the Blackshirts and this ensured Italians didn't challenge Mussolini
Mussolini	4. he seemed to provide the strong leadership which Italians longed for and who would restore Italy's greatness 5. he was the new Caesar/a man of genius/a man of action
Weakness of opposition	6. after 1926, all rival political parties were declared illegal 7. opposition newspapers were banned in Italy making it difficult for them to get publicity 8. opposition groups were weakened by the inability to unite on a common platform
Propaganda	9. radio and the cinema were also used to broadcast Fascist propaganda 10. censorship made it difficult to oppose Mussolini
Popular support	11. he bought off key groups: the workers were promised an eight-hour day/the rich benefited from a reduction in death duties 12. got the support of the Roman Catholic Church by making religious education compulsory in all elementary schools/entering into the Lateran Treaty

Up to **4 marks** should be awarded for presenting the answer in a structured way, leading to a conclusion which addresses the question, as follows:

1 mark for an introduction (which places the question in its historical context or outlines relevant factors).

1 mark for the answer being presented in a structured way (with knowledge being organised in support of different factors).

1 mark for a conclusion with a valid judgement (or overall summary).

1 mark for a reason in support of the judgement (a summary cannot be supported).

Any other relevant factor

Section 3, Context G, Free at Last? Civil Rights in the USA, 1918–1968

76. *Candidates can be credited in a number of ways **up to a maximum of 9 marks**.*

Candidates must make a judgement about the extent to which different factors contributed to an event or development, or its impact. They are required to provide a balanced account

of the influence of different factors and come to a reasoned conclusion based on the evidence presented.

Up to **5 marks** can be awarded for relevant, factual, key points of knowledge used to support factors, with **1 mark** awarded for each point (but **one mark should be deducted** if the correct process is not clear in at least two factors). If **only one factor is presented, a maximum of 3 marks should be awarded** for relevant points of knowledge. A **further 4 marks** can be awarded for providing the answer in a structured way and coming to a reasoned conclusion.

Possible factors	Key points of knowledge to support this factor may include:
Fear of revolution	1. 'Red Scare' – many Americans were afraid that immigrants from Eastern Europe would bring in dangerous new ideas such as communism 2. growing fear of social unrest/violent revolution in America in the aftermath of Russian Revolution 3. 1919 huge wave of strikes in USA which Americans claimed were caused by revolutionary workers from Eastern Europe
Self-interest	4. concern that immigrants would take jobs/depress wages/break strikes 5. concern that immigrants would create pressure on scarce housing 6. American workers saw immigrants as a threat to their standard of living
Racism	7. old immigrants, especially the WASPs, had lived in USA for several generations and many thought the new immigrants were inferior 8. WASPs saw the new immigrants as a threat to the American way of life 9. immigrants were often blamed for crime, disease, alcoholism and other social problems in cities 10. WASPs argued America must not be turned into a second rate power by second rate people (new immigrants)
Social factors	11. there were religious differences – older immigrants mainly Protestant, new immigrants Catholic/Jewish 12. new immigrants often settled amongst people from their own countries leading to a perception that they were unwilling to mix with other Americans

Up to **4 marks** should be awarded for presenting the answer in a structured way, leading to a conclusion which addresses the question, as follows:

1 mark for an introduction (which places the question in its historical context or outlines relevant factors).

1 mark for the answer being presented in a structured way (with knowledge being organised in support of different factors).

1 mark for a conclusion with a valid judgement (or overall summary).

1 mark for a reason in support of the judgement (a summary cannot be supported).

Any other relevant factor

77. *Candidates can be credited in a number of ways **up to a maximum of 4 marks**.*

Candidates must interpret the evidence and make direct comparisons between sources. Candidates are expected to compare content directly on a point-by-point basis. They may compare the details in the sources and/or compare the viewpoints overall.

A **simple comparison** will indicate what points of detail or viewpoint the sources agree or disagree on and **should be awarded 1 mark**. A **developed comparison** of the points of detail or overall viewpoint **should be awarded a second mark**. Candidates may achieve full marks by making four simple comparisons, two developed comparisons (or by any combination of these).

Possible points of comparison may include:

Source A	Source B
Overall: The sources agree about the experience of immigrants in the USA during the 1920s	
They headed for the great cities (where there was a far better prospect of finding employment)	My family lived in the city of Chicago
Few planned to stay in America for long, but wanted to return to Italy some day	My father came from Monfalcone in Italy and always hoped to return there.
Italian Americans succeeded in jobs requiring little formal education	(When I was 14 years old I started dodging school) and so didn't get much formal education

78. *Candidates can be credited in a number of ways **up to a maximum of 4 marks.***

They may take different perspectives on the events and may describe a variety of different aspects of the events. Candidates must make a number of relevant, factual points. These should be key points. These do not have to be in any particular order.

1 mark should be awarded for each accurate relevant key point of knowledge. A **second mark** should be awarded for each point that is developed, **up to a maximum of 4 marks.** Candidates may achieve full marks by providing four straightforward points, by making two developed points (or any combination of these).

Possible points of knowledge may include:
1. created a segregated society/enforced segregation between black and white people
2. some states made relationships/marriage between races illegal
3. separate schooling was enforced
4. separate toilets, washrooms and canteens
5. separate drinking fountains/hospital wards
6. transport facilities – trains and buses – were segregated
7. separate leisure and sporting facilities
8. black Americans were humiliated/made to feel inferior

Any other valid point of knowledge

79. *Candidates can be credited in a number of ways **up to a maximum of 6 marks.***

Candidates must make a number of points that make the issue plain or clear, for example by showing connections between factors or causal relationships between events or ideas. These should be key reasons but there is no need for any evaluation or prioritising of these reasons.

Up to a maximum of 6 marks in total, **1 mark** should be awarded for each accurate, relevant reason, and a **second mark** should be awarded for reasons that are developed. Candidates may achieve full marks by providing six straightforward reasons, three developed reasons (or any combination of these).

Possible reasons may include:
1. the groundwork for a Civil rights movement had been laid by early reformers such as du Bois, Garvey and Washington who inspired others to join the cause
2. the experience of black American servicemen during WW2 had made them aware of non-segregated societies and more determined to fight against discrimination
3. during WW2 all Americans were called upon to fight for freedom and democracy but black Americans felt that they were denied their basic rights in their own country leading to growing support for civil rights for black Americans
4. success of Philip Randolph and the 'Double-V' campaign encouraged greater demands for civil rights
5. NAACP and other organisations effectively highlighted discrimination faced by black Americans and gained support of both black and white Americans in support of civil rights
6. black people in the South living under a system of segregation/were subjected to violent persecution, such as lynching, and demanded reform
7. concern at other inequalities faced by black Americans eg low wages, poor housing and growing demands for improvements
8. success of non-violent protests – eg Montgomery Bus Boycott, Birmingham march encouraged others to become involved
9. leadership of black leaders such as Martin Luther King/ Malcolm X inspired others to join the civil rights campaign
10. successes of non-violent movement encouraged black Americans to demand more
11. impact of more radical protests such as Nation of Islam attracted those who didn't believe peaceful methods were working
12. media coverage especially television heightened awareness and motivated many to support the campaign

Any other valid reason

80. *Candidates can be credited in a number of ways **up to a maximum of 6 marks.***

Candidates must make a judgement about the extent to which the source provides a full description or explanation of a given event or development.

Up to a maximum of 6 marks in total, **1 mark** should be awarded for each valid point selected from the source or each valid point of significant omission provided.

Candidates should be awarded **up to 3 marks** for their identification of points from the source which support their judgement. Candidates should be awarded **up to 4 marks** for their identification of points of significant omission, based on their own knowledge, that support their judgement. A **maximum of 2 marks** may be awarded for answers in which no judgement has been made **or** which refer only to the source.

Possible points which may be identified from the source include:
1. urged that it was now time to defend black Americans against this white aggression
2. (Huey Newton) he voiced the distrust many black Americans felt towards the police
3. self-help programmes organised by the Black Panthers
4. they also had a ten-point programme which included demands for better housing and education

Possible points of significant omission may include:
5. Black Panthers condoned use of violence and this appealed to many blacks who were frustrated by the non-violent methods of the Civil Rights Movement

6. Black Panthers had charismatic leaders who gained attention and popularity
7. they demanded the release of black prisoners which had widespread support
8. Black Panthers gained support due to their efforts to give practical help to poor blacks such as breakfast clubs in schools and providing free health clinics
9. The Black Panthers encouraged blacks to be proud of the colour of their skin and their African American culture which appealed to many
10. Black Panthers gained much publicity from the support of athletes at the 1968 Olympic Games eg Black Power salute was a political demonstration conducted by African-American athletes, which inspired many other black Americans

Any other valid point of significant omission

Section 3, Context H, Appeasement and the Road to War, 1918–1939

81. *Candidates can be credited in a number of ways up to a maximum of 6 marks.*

Candidates must make a number of points that make the issue plain or clear, for example by showing connections between factors or causal relationships between events or ideas. These should be key reasons but there is no need for any evaluation or prioritising of these reasons.

Up to a maximum of 6 marks in total, **1 mark** should be awarded for each accurate, relevant reason, and a **second mark** should be awarded for reasons that are developed. Candidates may achieve full marks by providing six straightforward reasons, three developed reasons (or any combination of these).

Possible reasons may include:
1. furious as it was far harsher than expected and would cripple Germany
2. expected a peace treaty based on Wilson's Fourteen Points and angry it wasn't
3. criticised it as a diktat/dictated peace as Germany had been denied any say in it
4. hated the shame of the War Guilt clause which Germany claimed was unfair
5. accused the Treaty of being based on Allies' desire for revenge
6. angry at having to pay reparations which Germany claimed it couldn't afford
7. resented the loss of German colonies which it said was unfair
8. angry at the loss of land containing many Germans, especially land lost to Poland
9. furious at the reduction in Germany's armed forces which it claimed left Germany defenceless
10. angry that Germans were denied self-determination
11. argued Germany did not deserve to be punished so severely since the Kaiser and generals were gone
12. new German Government was angry because it felt it had little chance of success after the terms were imposed

Any other valid reason

82. *Candidates can be credited in a number of ways up to a maximum of 4 marks.*

Candidates must interpret the evidence and make direct comparisons between sources. Candidates are expected to compare content directly on a point-by-point basis. They may compare the details in the sources and/or compare the viewpoints overall.

A **simple comparison** will indicate what points of detail or viewpoint the sources agree or disagree on and **should be awarded 1 mark**. A **developed comparison** of the points of detail or overall viewpoint **should be awarded a second mark**. Candidates may achieve full marks by making four simple comparisons, two developed comparisons (or by any combination of these).

Possible points of comparison may include:

Source A	Source B
Overall: The sources agree about the work of League of Nations	
The refusal of the USA to join the League however greatly weakened its ability to succeed	The failure of several big powers, including the USA, to join the League badly damaged its effectiveness
The League did manage to settle disputes between smaller nations who could be leaned on	The League however did achieve some success in solving arguments between lesser countries
When disputes involved larger countries, the League however often failed to act	Actions against larger nations who challenged the League were inadequate and frequently half-hearted

83. *Candidates can be credited in a number of ways up to a maximum of 4 marks.*

They may take different perspectives on the events and may describe a variety of different aspects of the events. Candidates must make a number of relevant, factual points. These should be key points. These do not have to be in any particular order.

1 mark should be awarded for each accurate relevant key point of knowledge. A **second mark** should be awarded for each point that is developed, **up to a maximum of 4 marks**. Candidates may achieve full marks by providing four straightforward points, by making two developed points (or any combination of these).

Possible points of knowledge may include:
1. to restore German power by breaking the Treaty of Versailles
2. to build up the German army/create a German air force
3. to remilitarise the Rhineland
4. to regain the territory that Germany had lost after World War One
5. to achieve Anschluss with Austria
6. to create a Greater Germany for all Germans
7. to gain Lebensraum/'living space' in Eastern Europe for the German people
8. to defeat communism

Any other valid point of knowledge

84. *Candidates can be credited in a number of ways up to a maximum of 9 marks.*

Candidates must make a judgement about the extent to which different factors contributed to an event or development, or its impact. They are required to provide a balanced account of the influence of different factors and come to a reasoned conclusion based on the evidence presented.

Up to 5 marks can be awarded for relevant, factual, key points of knowledge used to support factors, with **1 mark** awarded for each point (but **one mark should be deducted** if the correct process is not clear in at least two factors). If **only one factor is presented, a maximum of 3 marks should be awarded** for relevant points of knowledge. A

further 4 marks can be awarded for providing the answer in a structured way and coming to a reasoned conclusion.

Up to **4 marks** should be awarded for presenting the answer in a structured way, leading to a conclusion which addresses the question, as follows:

Possible factors	Key points of knowledge to support this factor may include:
Military concerns	1. chiefs of the armed forces advised that the British military was unprepared for war/ Britain had failed to modernise her armed forces 2. Britain was concerned about Germany's powerful army and air force 3. Britain's air preparations were inadequate, with insufficient fighter planes, radar systems or anti-aircraft artillery 4. there was fear of bombing from the air – 'The Bomber will always get through', according to the government
Public opinion	5. majority of the public were still fearful of war after the huge losses suffered during World War One 6. public concerns over the cost of rearmament (welfare vs warfare) 7. there was a significant pacifist movement in the 1930s which was strongly against war eg the 'Peace Ballot'
Relations with Hitler	8. Chamberlain believed that Hitler had a genuine grievance over the Sudetenland/ Versailles was unjust and Germans should have some form of self-determination 9. Chamberlain felt Hitler had only limited demands/was a man he could do business with
Lack of allies	10. France was unwilling to support conflict over the Sudetenland 11. USA was following an isolationist policy 12. Empire was unwilling to fight eg disturbances in India

1 mark for an introduction (which places the question in its historical context or outlines relevant factors).

1 mark for the answer being presented in a structured way (with knowledge being organised in support of different factors).

1 mark for a conclusion with a valid judgement (or overall summary).

1 mark for a reason in support of the judgement (a summary cannot be supported).

Any other relevant factor

85. *Candidates can be credited in a number of ways **up to a maximum of 6 marks**.*

Candidates must make a judgement about the extent to which the source provides a full description or explanation of a given event or development.

Up to a maximum of 6 marks in total, **1 mark** should be awarded for each valid point selected from the source or each valid point of significant omission provided.

Candidates should be awarded **up to 3 marks** for their identification of points from the source which support their judgement. Candidates should be awarded **up to 4 marks** for their identification of points of significant omission, based on their own knowledge, that support their judgement. A **maximum of 2 marks** may be awarded for

answers in which no judgement has been made **or** which refer only to the source.

Possible points which may be identified from the source include:
1. in March 1939, German troops marched into Czechoslovakia
2. Slovakia broke away and became a pro-German 'puppet state'
3. Bohemia and Moravia became a German protectorate
4. Germany's aggression led to Great Britain and France abandoning the policy of appeasement

Possible points of significant omission may include:
5. German demands to Poland eg return of Danzig/permission to build a road and railway line through Poland
6. Britain and France promise to defend Poland if she was attacked by Germany
7. Germany and Italy sign the 'Pact of Steel' which required them to help each other in time of war
8. August 1939, Germany and Russia sign the Nazi-Soviet Non-Aggression Pact, agreeing not to go to war with each other so Germany was safe in the east
9. September 1st, Germany invades Poland/didn't respond to Britain and France's ultimatum to withdraw German forces from Poland or face war
10. September 3rd, Britain and France declare war on Germany

Any other valid point of significant omission

Section 3, Context I, World War II, 1939–1945

86. *Candidates can be credited in a number of ways **up to a maximum of 6 marks**.*

Candidates must make a number of points that make the issue plain or clear, for example by showing connections between factors or causal relationships between events or ideas. These should be key reasons but there is no need for any evaluation or prioritising of these reasons.

Up to a maximum of 6 marks in total, **1 mark** should be awarded for each accurate, relevant reason, and a **second mark** should be awarded for reasons that are developed. Candidates may achieve full marks by providing six straightforward reasons, three developed reasons (or any combination of these).

Possible reasons may include:
1. Hitler hated the Communist ideals of the USSR/thought Communism was a threat to Germany
2. Hitler believed in the expansion rights of the Master Race and wanted Russian land as Lebensraum (living space)/ declared plans to invade in Mein Kampf
3. Hitler believed the Russian army would be easily defeated due to Russia's failure in the Finnish war/as well as the purge of Red Army
4. he believed USSR would be an easy target and would fall in 6 to 8 weeks
5. Hitler wanted to enslave the Russian people (untermenschen) to work for the German Master Race
6. Hitler wanted the valuable resources contained in Russia eg grain, oil, iron ore/Germany was running short of vital raw materials by 1940
7. Hitler believed Russia to be a threat to Germany's interests in the Balkans and Scandinavia
8. Stalin had resisted joining Germany, Italy and Japan in the Tripartite Pact of 1940
9. Nazi-Soviet Pact of 1939 was only an alliance of convenience so that Hitler could successfully invade Poland/Hitler did not really trust Stalin
10. Hitler believed the conquest of Russia would force Britain to surrender

Any other valid reason

87. *Candidates can be credited in a number of ways up to a maximum of 4 marks.*

They may take different perspectives on the events and may describe a variety of different aspects of the events. Candidates must make a number of relevant, factual points. These should be key points. These do not have to be in any particular order.

1 mark should be awarded for each accurate relevant key point of knowledge. A **second mark** should be awarded for each point that is developed, **up to a maximum of 4 marks.** Candidates may achieve full marks by providing four straightforward points, by making two developed points (or any combination of these).

Possible points of knowledge may include:
1. as the last part of their plan to conquer a Pacific Empire, the Japanese decided to attack the American airbase on the Island of Midway
2. Japanese fighter aircraft launched repeated attacks on American aircraft on Midway
3. American torpedo bombers launched a fierce attack and fatally damaged two Japanese aircraft carriers
4. bombers from the Yorktown were then bombed and destroyed another Japanese carrier
5. Japanese dive bombers attacked the Yorktown resulting in the carrier having to be abandoned
6. the Americans counter-attacked and dive bombers from Enterprise mortally wounded the Japanese carrier Hiryu
7. this forced Admiral Yamamoto to abandon the Japanese Midway invasion plans
8. Battle of Midway resulted in the US Navy inflicting a huge defeat on the Japanese navy/Japanese Imperial Navy lost four large aircraft carriers, Americans only lost one

Any other valid point of knowledge

88. *Candidates can be credited in a number of ways up to a maximum of 4 marks.*

Candidates must interpret the evidence and make direct comparisons between sources. Candidates are expected to compare content directly on a point-by-point basis. They may compare the details in the sources and/or compare the viewpoints overall.

A **simple comparison** will indicate what points of detail or viewpoint the sources agree or disagree on and **should be awarded 1 mark.** A **developed comparison** of the points of detail or overall viewpoint **should be awarded a second mark.** Candidates may achieve full marks by making four simple comparisons, two developed comparisons (or by any combination of these).

Possible points of comparison may include:

Source A	Source B
Overall: The sources agree about the work of the French Resistance	
Their methods included sabotage of the German rail network	They destroyed trains carrying German troops and military equipment
The help they gave the Allies was extremely important	… the French Resistance scored key victories against the German occupation forces
If members of the Resistance were caught they would almost certainly be tortured and executed	These accomplishments carried a heavy price as many members of the Resistance paid for their bravery with their lives

89. *Candidates can be credited in a number of ways up to a maximum of 9 marks.*

Candidates must make a judgement about the extent to which different factors contributed to an event or development, or its impact. They are required to provide a balanced account of the influence of different factors and come to a reasoned conclusion based on the evidence presented.

Up to 5 marks can be awarded for relevant, factual, key points of knowledge used to support factors, with **1 mark** awarded for each point (but **one mark should be deducted** if the correct process is not clear in at least two factors). If **only one factor is presented, a maximum of 3 marks should be awarded** for relevant points of knowledge. A **further 4 marks** can be awarded for providing the answer in a structured way and coming to a reasoned conclusion.

Up to 4 marks should be awarded for presenting the answer in a structured way, leading to a conclusion which addresses the question, as follows:

1 mark for an introduction (which places the question in its historical context or outlines relevant factors).

1 mark for the answer being presented in a structured way (with knowledge being organised in support of different factors).

1 mark for a conclusion with a valid judgement (or overall summary).

1 mark for a reason in support of the judgement (a summary cannot be supported).

Possible factors	Key points of knowledge to support this factor may include:
German mistakes	1. German High Command remained fixated on the Calais area even after the attack on Normandy had started 2. a number of key German commanders were absent from their posts during the critical first hours of June 6, including Rommel who was in Germany 3. communication problems caused German commanders to fail to react quickly enough to the assault 4. many of the German coastal units were made up of conscripts from Nazi-conquered lands who did not wish to die for Hitler and surrendered the first chance they had 5. the Luftwaffe's last remaining fighter squadrons in France had been moved far out of range from the Normandy beaches, thus missing the chance to spot the Allied build-up and being able to disrupt or destroy it
Effective allied planning	6. deception plans led German intelligence to believe an attack would target Calais/use of dummy staging areas in Dover fooled the Germans 7. Allies took advantage of bad weather to surprise the Germans
Allied resources	8. use of Mulberry harbours allowed more troops and supplies to be brought to the beach heads 9. use of Pluto – pipeline transporting fuel across the Channel to allow a sustained attack by the allies
Allied military advantages	10. allied superiority in men and equipment 11. paratroopers landed the night before to secure bridges and roads near the Normandy landing sites and hindered German counter attack 12. members of the French Resistance and the British Special Operations Executive (SOE) provided intelligence and helped weaken German defences through sabotage

Any other relevant point

90. *Candidates can be credited in a number of ways up to a maximum of 6 marks.*

Candidates must make a judgement about the extent to which the source provides a full description or explanation of a given event or development.

Up to **a maximum of 6 marks** in total, **1 mark** should be awarded for each valid point selected from the source or each valid point of significant omission provided. Candidates should be awarded **up to 3 marks** for their identification of points from the source which support their judgement. Candidates should be awarded **up to 4 marks** for their identification of points of significant omission, based on their own knowledge, that support their judgement. A **maximum of 2 marks** may be awarded for answers in which no judgement has been made **or** which refer only to the source.

Possible points which may be identified from the source include:
1. the Soviets sent him a birthday present in the form of an artillery barrage right into the heart of the Berlin
2. the Western Allies launched a massive air raid
3. young boys who had 'volunteered' to join the SS and die for their Führer in defence of Berlin
4. boys who were found hiding were hanged as traitors by the SS

Possible points of significant omission may include:
5. before the main battle in Berlin commenced, the Russian army was able to encircle the city by mid-April due to their success in previous battles
6. the Russians advanced easily against poor German defences at the Oder River
7. the defence of the city of Berlin relied upon disorganised/poorly armed units from the German army and Hitler Youth members/elderly men
8. within a few days, the Soviets rapidly advanced through the city and reached the city centre where close combat raged
9. before the battle was over, Hitler and a number of his followers committed suicide
10. faced with overwhelming odds, the city's defenders finally surrendered on 2 May

Any other valid point of significant omission

Section 3, Context J, The Cold War, 1945–1989

91. *Candidates can be credited in a number of ways up to a maximum of 4 marks.*

Candidates must interpret the evidence and make direct comparisons between sources. Candidates are expected to compare content directly on a point-by-point basis. They may compare the details in the sources and/or compare the viewpoints overall.

A **simple comparison** will indicate what points of detail or viewpoint the sources agree or disagree on and **should be awarded 1 mark**. A **developed comparison** of the points of detail or overall viewpoint **should be awarded a second mark**. Candidates may achieve full marks by making four simple comparisons, two developed comparisons (or by any combination of these).

Possible points of comparison may include:

Source A	Source B
Overall: The sources agree about the reasons why a Cold War broke out between the Soviet Union and the USA	
(Once World War Two was over) relations between the two allies deteriorated, to be replaced by a climate of suspicion between America and the Soviet Union	As soon as the war ended the Soviet Union and the Americans developed open hostility towards each other
Soviet and American leaders held opposing ideological views …	(The new American President Truman and Soviet leader Stalin seemed hostile to one another and) this emphasised their ideological divisions
America's decision to develop and use the atomic bomb against the Japanese without consulting the Soviets placed further strain on relations	The tension at Potsdam was increased by America's use of the atomic bomb against Japan

92. *Candidates can be credited in a number of ways up to a maximum of 6 marks.*

Candidates must make a judgement about the extent to which the source provides a full description or explanation of a given event or development.

Up to a maximum of 6 marks in total, **1 mark** should be awarded for each valid point selected from the source or each valid point of significant omission provided.

Candidates should be awarded **up to 3 marks** for their identification of points from the source which support their judgement. Candidates should be awarded **up to 4 marks** for their identification of points of significant omission, based on their own knowledge, that support their judgement. A **maximum of 2 marks** may be awarded for answers in which no judgement has been made **or** which refer only to the source.

Possible points which may be identified from the source include:
1. a new East German labour law, which stopped workers from going on strike, had led to growing unrest in the factories
2. agriculture reforms had led to higher prices and food shortages
3. all of this led to a massive increase in the numbers of refugees fleeing to the West
4. in the six months up to June 1961, 103,000 East Germans had fled through Berlin

Possible points of significant omission may include:
5. in June 1961 the Soviet Premier Khrushchev raised tensions by threatening to end the existing four-power agreements guaranteeing American, British, and French rights to access West Berlin
6. President Kennedy asked Congress for an additional $3 billion to increase America's armed forces
7. the Soviets accused the West of using Berlin as a centre of operations against East Germany and the Soviet Union

8. in August 1961 the East German government took the decision to close the border between East and West Berlin
9. East German troops and workers had begun to tear up streets running alongside the barrier to make them impassable to most vehicles, and to install barbed wire entanglements and fences around the three western sectors
10. East Germans then started building a wall to separate the east and west of the city

Any other valid point of significant omission

93. *Candidates can be credited in a number of ways **up to a maximum of 6 marks.***

Candidates must make a number of points that make the issue plain or clear, for example by showing connections between factors or causal relationships between events or ideas. These should be key reasons but there is no need for any evaluation or prioritising of these reasons.

Up to a maximum of 6 marks in total, **1 mark** should be awarded for each accurate, relevant reason, and a **second mark** should be awarded for reasons that are developed. Candidates may achieve full marks by providing six straightforward reasons, three developed reasons (or any combination of these).

Possible reasons may include:
1. Cuban leader Castro had formed a close alliance with the Soviet Union which alarmed the USA
2. Castro had angered American businesses by nationalising key Cuban industries
3. there were fears that Castro would turn Cuba into a communist stronghold
4. Kennedy was looking for an opportunity to take revenge against Castro after the failure of the Bay of Pigs incident
5. Castro agreed to site Soviet missiles on Cuba which USA saw as a threat to US cities
6. US spy planes took photographs of missile bases being constructed on Cuba
7. Cuba was only a short distance from the American mainland so caused great concern in the USA
8. an American U2 spy plane was shot down over Cuba further increasing tension
9. America was furious at Soviets as they refused to remove their missiles from Cuba
10. Soviet ships sailing towards the American blockade around Cuba with additional missiles increased the tension
11. President Kennedy was under huge pressure to stand up to communist aggression
12. American public opinion would not accept the presence of Soviet missiles on Cuba

Any other valid reason

94. *Candidates can be credited in a number of ways **up to a maximum of 9 marks.***

Candidates must make a judgement about the extent to which different factors contributed to an event or development, or its impact. They are required to provide a balanced account of the influence of different factors and come to a reasoned conclusion based on the evidence presented.

Up to 5 marks can be awarded for relevant, factual, key points of knowledge used to support factors, with **1 mark** awarded for each point (but **one mark should be deducted** if the correct process is not clear in at least two factors). If **only one factor is presented**, a maximum of 3 marks

should be awarded for relevant points of knowledge. A **further 4 marks** can be awarded for providing the answer in a structured way and coming to a reasoned conclusion.

Up to **4 marks** should be awarded for presenting the answer in a structured way, leading to a conclusion which addresses the question, as follows:

1 mark for an introduction (which places the question in its historical context or outlines relevant factors).

1 mark for the answer being presented in a structured way (with knowledge being organised in support of different factors).

1 mark for a conclusion with a valid judgement (or overall summary).

1 mark for a reason in support of the judgement (a summary cannot be supported).

Possible factors	Key points of knowledge to support this factor may include:
Vietcong tactics	1. Vietcong were expert in conducting guerrilla warfare 2. Vietcong made full use of local knowledge/knowledge of the terrain 3. Vietcong generally avoided large scale attacks/when they attacked it was with fanatical determination 4. Vietcong travelled light carrying few supplies and basic weapons
American soldiers	5. American soldiers were poorly trained and ill-equipped for jungle warfare/did not cope with the guerrilla tactics 6. the draft system meant that there was a lack of experience among American forces 7. American soldiers had low morale and lacked respect for their officers – reduced their combat effectiveness
Opposition in USA	8. increasingly people in the USA were tired of the war/the war was wasting young American lives 9. the media presented evidence of cruelty by American soldiers, war crimes such as the My Lai massacre, tactics of defoliation 10. welfare programmes in America were being dropped because of the cost of the war in Vietnam
US military problems	11. failure of American tactics – strategic hamlets, carpet bombing, use of defoliants (Agent Orange) 12. the US was trying to supply a war 8000 miles from America which made it very difficult for them

Any other relevant factor

95. *Candidates can be credited in a number of ways **up to a maximum of 4 marks.***

They may take different perspectives on the events and may describe a variety of different aspects of the events. Candidates must make a number of relevant, factual points. These should be key points. These do not have to be in any particular order.

1 mark should be awarded for each accurate relevant key point of knowledge. A **second mark** should be awarded for each point that is developed, **up to a maximum of 4 marks.**

Candidates may achieve full marks by providing four straightforward points, by making two developed points (or any combination of these).

Possible points of knowledge may include:
1. a hotline between the Soviet and American leaders was established following the Cuban Missile Crisis
2. the Non-Proliferation Treaty, which aimed to prevent the spread of nuclear weapons, was signed in 1968
3. in 1971 Brezhnev announced the 'programme for peace' to improve relations between East and West
4. war in Vietnam was scaled down and then ended in the early 1970s and this had a positive influence on superpower relations
5. President Nixon's visit to Moscow in 1973 helped to reduce tension
6. USA and USSR signed Helsinki Accords in 1975 to improve relations between the Communist bloc and the West
7. both sides reached agreement to limit or reduce nuclear weapons – SALT II
8. trade agreements between both sides helped to improve relations/USA begins to sell the USSR wheat in 1970s

Any other valid point of knowledge

NATIONAL 5 HISTORY 2018

Section 1, Context A, The Wars of Independence, 1286–1328

1. *Candidates can be credited in a number of ways **up to a maximum of 6 marks.***

Candidates must make a number of points that make the issue plain or clear, for example by showing connections between factors or causal relationships between events or ideas. These should be key reasons but there is no need for any evaluation or prioritising of these reasons.

Up to a **maximum of 6 marks in total**, **1 mark** should be given for each accurate, relevant reason, and a **second mark** should be given for reasons that are developed. Candidates may achieve full marks by providing six straightforward reasons, three developed reasons (or a combination of these).

Possible reasons may include:
1. Margaret was a child – problematic as others would have to rule or lead on her behalf/an adult ruler would be better/problematic as many children died before adulthood
2. Margaret was female – problematic as many thought a king would be a stronger ruler/better able to control the nobles/better able to lead an army in to battle
3. Margaret would need a husband – problematic as a Scottish husband could cause rivalry in Scotland/a foreign husband could mean that Scotland was controlled by a foreign country
4. Some nobles did not support Margaret – problematic as the monarch needed the support of the nobles to be able to have strong government
5. Margaret was from Norway which meant that some saw her as a foreigner and worried that she would have divided loyalties
6. Balliols and Bruces thought they had a rightful claim to the throne – problematic as rivalry increased/threat of civil war increased
7. if Margaret died there was no direct heir left.

Any other valid reason.

2. *Candidates can be credited in a number of ways **up to a maximum of 6 marks.***

Candidates must make a judgement about the extent to which the source provides a full description or explanation of a given event or development.

Up to a **maximum of 6 marks** in total, **1 mark** should be awarded for each valid point selected from the source or each valid point of significant omission provided. Candidates should be awarded **up to 3 marks** for their identification of points from the source which support their judgement. Candidates should be awarded **up to 4 marks** for their identification of points of significant omission, based on their own knowledge, that support their judgement.

A **maximum of 2 marks** may be awarded for answers in which no judgement has been made **or** which refer only to the source.

Possible points which may be identified from the source include:
1. John's parliament agreed that homage and fealty should be withdrawn
2. they (Scotland) concluded a treaty with France

3. the Scots invaded England

4. Edward slaughtered most of the citizens of Berwick

Possible points of significant omission may include:

5. John Balliol had accepted Edward I as his overlord

6. John Balliol was bullied by King Edward (eg summoned to pay wine bill)

7. John Balliol refused King Edward's order to join him in the war against France

8. King Edward defeated John Balliol at Dunbar/pursued Balliol north

9. King Edward forced John Balliol to surrender to him (at Montrose)

10. King Edward stripped John Balliol of his crown and title.

Any other valid point of significant omission.

3. *Candidates can be credited in a number of ways **up to a maximum of 9 marks.***

Candidates must make a judgement about the extent to which different factors contributed to an event or development, or its impact. They are required to provide a balanced account of the influence of different factors and come to a reasoned conclusion based on the evidence presented.

Up to **5 marks** can be given for relevant, factual, key points of knowledge used to support factors, with **1 mark** given for each point (but **one mark should be deducted** if the process is not clear in at least two factors). **If only one factor is presented, a maximum of 3 marks should be given for relevant points of knowledge. A further 4 marks** can be given for providing the answer in a structured way and coming to a reasoned conclusion.

Possible factors:	Key points of knowledge to support this factor may include:
English mistakes	1. the English were overconfident which meant that they underestimated the Scots/victory at Dunbar created the belief that they were superior 2. the English were missing experienced commanders/Hugh de Cressingham had little military experience/Earl of Surrey was in poor health 3. English army was smaller than the army they had at Dunbar which helped the Scots 4. poor planning – Cressingham rejected the option of crossing using a ford/crossing by the bridge was a difficult manoeuvre 5. Cressingham wanted the battle to be over quickly to save money which meant that they rushed decisions 6. choice of battlefield not suited to cavalry 7. plans chaotic – two false starts revealed plans to the Scots/English slow to get organised/slept in/knighting ceremony 8. army forced into a bottleneck/bridge too narrow for cavalry and no chance of escape
Scottish strengths	9. Scots positioned on high ground giving them an advantage/Abbey Craig 10. tactics – schiltrons impossible to break with cavalry charge/moved as a unit/mobility a surprise for the English
leadership of Wallace and Murray	11. chose battleground well/surveyed land/knew marshy ground would not be suited to the English cavalry 12. timing was superb – attacked quickly so English were trapped/if had attacked too early vanguard would not have got across bridge
any other relevant factor	13. any other valid reason.

Up to **4 marks** should be given for presenting the answer in a structured way, leading to a conclusion which addresses the question, as follows:

1 mark for an introduction (which places the question in its historical context or outlines relevant factors). **1 mark** for the answer being presented in a structured way (with knowledge being organised in support of different factors). **1 mark** for a conclusion with a valid judgement (or overall summary). **1 mark** for a reason in support of the judgement (a summary cannot be supported).

4. *Candidates can be credited in a number of ways **up to a maximum of 5 marks.***

Candidates must evaluate the extent to which a source is useful by commenting on evidence such as the author, type of source, purpose, timing, content or omission. For a mark to be given, the candidate must identify an aspect of the source and make a comment which shows why this aspect makes the source more or less useful.

A **maximum of 4 marks** can be given for evaluative comments relating to the author, type of source, purpose and timing. A **maximum of 2 marks** may be given for evaluative comments relating to the content of the source. A **maximum of 2 marks** may be given for evaluative comments relating to points of significant omission.

Examples of aspects of the source and relevant comments:

Aspect		Possible comment(s)
Author	Scottish writer	Useful as he lived during the time of King Robert/collected stories about King Robert.
Type of source	Chronicle	Useful as they tend to be detailed.
Purpose	To record	Less useful as may have been written to glorify King Robert and therefore be exaggerated for dramatic effect.
Timing	1335	Useful as primary source from the 14th century.

Content	Possible comment(s)
Some of King Robert's followers hurried to the castle with ladders and secretly climbed over the stone wall and took the castle.	Useful as it is accurate (Bruce and his followers did capture castles held by the English).
Then they slaughtered all they found.	Useful as it is accurate (Bruce and his followers did kill many English soldiers who were garrisoned in Scotland/treated English brutally).

The king had the castle wall broken down, destroyed the well and then the whole castle/moved onto Perth with his army and soon set siege to it.	Useful as it is accurate (Bruce did destroy castles so that the English could not return to them).

Possible points of significant omission may include:

1. King Robert used guerrilla tactics (e.g. ambushed groups of English soldiers)
2. King Robert won the support of powerful nobles (e.g. Angus MacDonald)
3. English soldiers were demoralised by the capture of garrisons
4. King Robert defeated the English at Bannockburn.

Any other valid point of significant omission.

Section 1, Context B, Mary Queen of Scots, and the Scottish Reformation, 1542–1587

5. *Candidates can be credited in a number of ways **up to a maximum of 6 marks.***

Candidates must make a number of points that make the issue plain or clear, for example by showing connections between factors or causal relationships between events or ideas. These should be key reasons but there is no need for any evaluation or prioritising of these reasons.

Up to a **maximum of 6 marks in total**, **1 mark** should be given for each accurate, relevant reason, and a **second mark** should be given for reasons that are developed. Candidates may achieve full marks by providing six straightforward reasons, three developed reasons (or a combination of these).

Possible reasons may include:

1. the Church could be easily influenced through bribery by rich nobles which affected the authority of the Church
2. Abbots and Bishops insisted that funds from parishes were sent to them (often abroad) which meant that local churches suffered
3. local parish priests were often poorly educated which meant they lacked knowledge of scripture and were not able to say mass accurately
4. some of the clergy were married with children which caused criticism as they were supposed to be celibate
5. illegitimate children of the nobility and royalty were appointed to offices within the Church which caused resentment (e.g. James V's illegitimate sons)
6. attempts at reform before the 1560s were criticised for being too limited
7. senior clergy spent Church finances to fund luxurious lifestyles which many people saw as corrupt
8. Protestant ideas were growing in Scotland which was a threat to the practices of the Catholic Church (e.g. sale of pardons)
9. the Lords of the Congregation, a group of Protestant Lords, united against Mary of Guise and were planning to establish a Protestant Reformation in Scotland, which challenged the authority of the Catholic Queen and Church
10. the Catholic Church faced condemnation for its persecution of Protestant followers (e.g. George Wishart who was burned as a heretic in 1546)
11. the Catholic Church was closely connected to France which aroused resentment in Scotland.

Any other valid reason.

6. *Candidates can be credited in a number of ways **up to a maximum of 6 marks.***

Candidates must make a judgement about the extent to which the source provides a full description or explanation of a given event or development.

Up to a **maximum of 6 marks** in total, **1 mark** should be awarded for each valid point selected from the source or each valid point of significant omission provided.

Candidates should be awarded **up to 3 marks** for their identification of points from the source which support their judgement. Candidates should be awarded **up to 4 marks** for their identification of points of significant omission, based on their own knowledge, that support their judgement. A **maximum of 2 marks** may be awarded for answers in which no judgement has been made **or** which refer only to the source.

Possible points which may be identified from the source include:

1. [Moray] had to cope with the fact that Mary still had supporters who wanted to return her to the throne even after her abdication
2. Moray spent his time securing Protestantism in Scotland by passing laws to strengthen the religion
3. in 1572 Morton became regent and also strongly supported Protestantism
4. he forced ministers to declare loyalty to the King as Governor of the Kirk

Possible points of significant omission may include:

5. Moray passed laws of the Reformation Parliament in 1560 which favoured the Kirk
6. Moray took strong action against Catholic priests
7. Moray was murdered in Linlithgow in 1570 by one of Mary's supporters
8. Morton had strong support from Elizabeth I for his religious policies
9. Morton was a strong regent who restored law and order and increased taxes
10. Morton was executed in 1581 due to his complicity in the murder of Darnley.

Any other valid point of significant omission.

7. *Candidates can be credited in a number of ways **up to a maximum of 9 marks.***

Candidates must make a judgement about the extent to which different factors contributed to an event or development, or its impact. They are required to provide a balanced account of the influence of different factors and come to a reasoned conclusion based on the evidence presented.

Up to **5 marks** can be given for relevant, factual, key points of knowledge used to support factors, with **1 mark** given for each point (but **one mark should be deducted** if the process is not clear in at least two factors). **If only one factor is presented, a maximum of 3 marks should be given for relevant points of knowledge. A further 4 marks** can be given for providing the answer in a structured way and coming to a reasoned conclusion.

Possible factors:	Key points of knowledge to support this factor may include:
relations with the nobility	1. many nobles were suspicious of Mary on her return from France as they thought she would replace them with Frenchmen 2. the nobles resented taking orders from a woman 3. during her first few years, Mary used her half-brother, Lord James Stewart, and Maitland of Lethington to help govern Scotland which annoyed their rivals 4. in March 1565, Moray, Argyll and Châtelherault agreed to rebel because of Mary's marriage to Darnley, resulting in the Chaseabout Raid
marital relationships	5. Darnley's behaviour of drinking and womanising reflected badly on Mary 6. Mary's relationship with Riccio was under suspicion, some suspected they were having an affair/he was a foreign spy 7. Mary was suspected of involvement in Darnley's murder 8. Mary's marriage to Bothwell was heavily criticised and lost Mary support because he was a suspect in Darnley's death
religious policy	9. Scotland was a Protestant country and when the Catholic Mary returned from France the new Kirk was suspicious that she may wish to return Scotland to a Catholic country 10. John Knox never believed that Mary accepted the Protestant religion in Scotland and encouraged opposition to her amongst Protestant followers
relationship with Elizabeth	11. Mary was undermined by Elizabeth's support of Scottish nobles in rebellion against her 12. Mary's religion encouraged English Catholics to plot against Elizabeth which further undermined their relationship
any other relevant factor	13. any other valid reason.

Up to **4 marks** should be given for presenting the answer in a structured way, leading to a conclusion which addresses the question, as follows:

1 mark for an introduction (which places the question in its historical context or outlines relevant factors). **1 mark** for the answer being presented in a structured way (with knowledge being organised in support of different factors). **1 mark** for a conclusion with a valid judgement (or overall summary). **1 mark** for a reason in support of the judgement (a summary cannot be supported).

8. *Candidates can be credited in a number of ways up to a maximum of 5 marks.*

Candidates must evaluate the extent to which a source is useful by commenting on evidence such as the author, type of source, purpose, timing, content or omission. For a mark to be given, the candidate must identify an aspect of the source and make a comment which shows why this aspect makes the source more or less useful.

A maximum of 4 marks can be given for evaluative comments relating to the author, type of source, purpose and timing. A maximum of 2 marks may be given for evaluative comments relating to the content of the source. A maximum of 2 marks may be given for evaluative comments relating to points of significant omission.

Examples of aspects of the source and relevant comments:

Aspect		Possible comment(s)
Author	Lady-in-waiting to Mary	Useful because she was an eyewitness.
Type of source	Diary	Useful because it is an honest, personal account.
Purpose	To record	Useful because it is a private account (and likely to be truthful).
Timing (either /or)	1587	Useful because it was written at the time of Mary's execution.
	1587	Not useful because it was not written at the time of Mary's execution.

Content	Possible comment(s)
The Queen quickly, and with great courage, knelt down and showed no signs of faltering.	Useful because it is accurate (Mary did show courage during her execution).
The executioner kept interrupting her prayers/ when she was eventually finished she laid her head on the block.	Useful because it is accurate (the executioner did attempt to interrupt Mary's prayers).
The executioner struck her a great blow on the neck, which was not however, entirely severed.	Useful because it is accurate (the first blow failed to cut off her head).

Possible points of significant omission may include:
1. Mary removed her black dress to reveal a red petticoat which was a symbol of Catholic martyrdom
2. two blows were needed to cut off Mary's head
3. the executioner raised up her head to show the crowd and her wig came away to reveal her grey hair cut short to her scalp
4. Mary's small dog was found under her skirts soaked in her blood/the dog had to be removed by force then it laid on her shoulder.

Any other valid point of significant omission.

Section 1, Context C, The Treaty of Union, 1689—1715

9. *Candidates can be credited in a number of ways up to a maximum of 6 marks.*

Candidates must make a number of points that make the issue plain or clear, for example by showing connections between factors or causal relationships between events or ideas. These should be key reasons but there is no need for any evaluation or prioritising of these reasons.

Up to a **maximum of 6 marks in total**, **1 mark** should be given for each accurate, relevant reason, and a **second mark** should be given for reasons that are developed. Candidates may achieve full marks by providing six straightforward reasons, three developed reasons (or a combination of these).

Possible reasons may include:
1. no one involved in setting up the scheme had ever been to Darien to carry out research and so were unaware of just how unsuitable for a colony the site was
2. the very high temperatures made things difficult for Scots who were not used to such heat
3. Darien has heavy rainfall/200 inches a year and this proved not to be conducive to the establishment of a settlement
4. Darien was full of diseases which posed dangers to the settlers (e.g. malaria, yellow fever)
5. the failure to take enough food on the journey contributed to the high casualty rate (e.g. 44 died during voyage) during the initial voyage
6. on the second expedition the casualty rate was even higher (e.g. 160 died during the voyage because of unclean water/rotting food)
7. not enough investment was made in the scheme as King William did not allow English or foreign investment
8. when the Scots got into difficulty King William forbade nearby English colonies to offer assistance
8. the Spanish attacked the settlement and forced the Scots to surrender
10. the Scots asked for high prices and so failed to trade
11. the Scots took the wrong goods for trading (e.g. Bibles, wigs, heavy cloths).

Any other valid reason.

10. *Candidates can be credited in a number of ways **up to a maximum of 6 marks**.*

Candidates must make a judgement about the extent to which the source provides a full description or explanation of a given event or development.

Up to a **maximum of 6 marks** in total, **1 mark** should be awarded for each valid point selected from the source or each valid point of significant omission provided.

Candidates should be awarded **up to 3 marks** for their identification of points from the source which support their judgement. Candidates should be awarded **up to 4 marks** for their identification of points of significant omission, based on their own knowledge, that support their judgement.

A **maximum of 2 marks** may be awarded for answers in which no judgement has been made **or** which refer only to the source.

Possible points which may be identified from the source include:
1. its opponents said that taxes would be sure to rise if the Union went ahead
2. they also claimed that as Scots would be in a minority in a new British Parliament/their voices would always be drowned out by the English
3. some Presbyterians warned that Union would force unwelcome changes on the Church of Scotland
4. opponents of the Union also argued that Union would give the English too much control over Scotland's trade

Possible points of significant omission may include:
5. it was argued that in the aftermath of Union, Scottish businesses would not be able to compete with stronger English businesses
6. Episcopalians in Scotland opposed Union as it would secure the Hanoverian succession (and only a return to the Stuart dynasty could restore episcopacy to the Scottish church)
7. Union would lead to the end of Scotland's identity as an independent nation
8. Union would be wrong as a majority of the Scottish people opposed it
9. Royal burghs feared the end of their special privileges
10. many claimed Scotland's distinctive legal system would be under threat.

Any other valid point of significant omission.

11. *Candidates can be credited in a number of ways up to a maximum of 9 marks.*

Candidates must make a judgement about the extent to which different factors contributed to an event or development, or its impact. They are required to provide a balanced account of the influence of different factors and come to a reasoned conclusion based on the evidence presented.

Up to **5 marks** can be given for relevant, factual, key points of knowledge used to support factors, with **1 mark** given for each point (but **one mark should be deducted if the process is not clear in at least two factors). If only one factor is presented, a maximum of 3 marks should be given for relevant points of knowledge. A further 4 marks** can be given for providing the answer in a structured way and coming to a reasoned conclusion.

Possible factors:	Key points of knowledge to support this factor may include:
support of Squadrone Volante	1. role of the Squadrone crucial as had they failed to support Union it might have failed in Parliament given the opposition of the Country Party 2. many in the Squadrone supported Union as they were Presbyterians and believed this was the best way to protect the Kirk 3. many in the Squadrone were motivated by greed as they believed support for Union would give them control over the distribution of the Equivalent
pressure from England	4. England used the Aliens Act to make it clear there would be severe economic difficulties for Scotland should they resist Union 5. Queen Anne was determined for Union to take place and was ably assisted by political figures (e.g. Queensberry) 6. English troops were on the border during the negotiations to focus the mind of the Scots/fear of English army after recent victories (e.g. Blenheim, Ramillies)

bribery	7. pensions, promotions and jobs were all offered to encourage support for Union (e.g. the Earl of Glasgow distributed £20,000 to encourage support for Union) 8. Hamilton may have been bribed by the Court Party
division among the opposition	9. disagreement amongst opponents of Union (e.g. Catholics and extreme Presbyterians) meant they were unable to act together to prevent it 10. the Opposition was poorly led by the unpredictable Hamilton/he refused to participate in planned walkout of parliament
any other relevant factor	11. any other valid reason.

Up to **4 marks** should be given for presenting the answer in a structured way, leading to a conclusion which addresses the question, as follows:

1 mark for an introduction (which places the question in its historical context or outlines relevant factors). **1 mark** for the answer being presented in a structured way (with knowledge being organised in support of different factors). **1 mark** for a conclusion with a valid judgement (or overall summary). **1 mark** for a reason in support of the judgement (a summary cannot be supported).

12. *Candidates can be credited in a number of ways **up to a maximum of 5 marks.***

Candidates must evaluate the extent to which a source is useful by commenting on evidence such as the author, type of source, purpose, timing, content or omission. For a mark to be given, the candidate must identify an aspect of the source and make a comment which shows why this aspect makes the source more or less useful.

A maximum of **4 marks** can be given for evaluative comments relating to the author, type of source, purpose and timing. A maximum of **2 marks** may be given for evaluative comments relating to the content of the source. A maximum of **2 marks** may be given for evaluative comments relating to points of significant omission.

Examples of aspects of the source and relevant comments:

Aspect		Possible comment(s)
Author	Scottish Lord	Useful as it is a first-hand account by a Scottish Lord in Parliament who wanted to end Union.
Type of source	Parliamentary Journal (speech)	Useful as this is part of an official account.
Purpose	To record	Useful as it provides detail of Scottish grievances.
Timing	June 1713	Useful as it was written soon after the Union (by which time Scots were able to judge its effects).

Content	Possible comment(s)
Permission should be given to bring in a Bill to end the Union.	Useful as it is accurate (many Scots did desire to end Union at this time).
Each Kingdom should have its Rights and Privileges restored to what they had been at the time when the Union was first passed.	Useful as it is accurate (many Scots were annoyed at the infringement of their rights).
Charging Scotland with a Malt Tax is in violation of the 14th Article of the Treaty of Union.	Useful as it is accurate (many Scots were angry at the levying of this tax in contravention of the terms of Union).

Possible points of significant omission may include:
1. there was dissatisfaction with the length of time it took to pay the Equivalent
2. anger over higher customs duties led to an increase in smuggling
3. anti-Union feeling important in explaining the level of support for the Jacobites in 1715
4. there was anger after the Scottish Privy Council was abolished in 1708.

Any other valid point of significant omission.

Section 1, Part D, Migration and Empire, 1830–1939

13. *Candidates can be credited in a number of ways **up to a maximum of 5 marks.***

Candidates must evaluate the extent to which a source is useful by commenting on evidence such as the author, type of source, purpose, timing, content or omission. For a mark to be given, the candidate must identify an aspect of the source and make a comment which shows why this aspect makes the source more or less useful.

A maximum of **4 marks** can be given for evaluative comments relating to the author, type of source, purpose and timing. A maximum of **2 marks** may be given for evaluative comments relating to the content of the source. A maximum of **2 marks** may be given for evaluative comments relating to points of significant omission.

Examples of aspects of the source and relevant comments:

Aspect		Possible comment(s)
Author	Peter Rusgis	Useful as he was the son of an immigrant so he would have first-hand knowledge of why people immigrated to Scotland.
Type of source	Interview	Useful because they tend to be factual and detailed.
Purpose	To record/ inform	Useful as he would want to record his father's story as accurately as possible.
Timing	1910	Useful because it was written when immigrants were coming to Scotland from Eastern Europe.

Content	Possible comment(s)
Neither of them wanted to be forced into the Russian army as this would have meant they were away from home for several years.	Useful as it is accurate (young men did flee from Lithuania to escape conscription into the Russian army).
They were both frightened as conditions were bad in the Russian army/Scotland seemed a safe destination.	Useful as it is accurate (people did flee from places like Lithuania because of fear).
My father had also heard that there were plenty of jobs in Scotland.	Useful as it is accurate (many immigrants did come to Scotland as there were plenty of jobs available).

Possible points of significant omission may include:
1. Irish Catholics came to escape hunger/because Scotland was geographically close/family connections/fares to Scotland were cheap/wages were higher in Scotland
2. Italian immigrants came to Scotland to escape poverty/ to work in family businesses/to escape drought/to earn money to send back to Italy
3. Jewish immigrants came to escape persecution/pogroms in Russia
4. Irish Protestants came in response to job adverts/to work in shipyards.

Any other valid point of significant omission.

14. *Candidates can be credited in a number of ways **up to a maximum of 6 marks.***

Candidates must make a judgement about the extent to which the source provides a full description or explanation of a given event or development.

Up to a **maximum of 6 marks** in total, **1 mark** should be awarded for each valid point selected from the source or each valid point of significant omission provided.

Candidates should be awarded **up to 3 marks** for their identification of points from the source which support their judgement. Candidates should be awarded **up to 4 marks** for their identification of points of significant omission, based on their own knowledge, that support their judgement.

A **maximum of 2 marks** may be awarded for answers in which no judgement has been made **or** which refer only to the source.

Possible points which may be identified from the source include:
1. Italians established many popular businesses (such as ice-cream parlours, cafés and fish and chip shops)
2. there was tension between the Catholic Italians and the Protestant Scots (e.g. Italian cafés being open on a Sunday)
3. the café owners were also criticised by local people who claimed the cafés sometimes encouraged unruly behaviour
4. there was little integration between the Scots and Italians

Possible points of significant omission may include:
5. immigrants were unpopular with the Scottish workers as they were accused of taking jobs/being strike breakers/ keeping wages down
6. immigrants and Scots competed for available housing/ pushed housing costs up
7. Catholic Irish faced hostility from the Church of Scotland
8. Protestant Irish assimilated more easily as they shared the same religion with the Scots

9. Jews set up businesses which provided services for the Scots (e.g. watchmakers, tobacconists)
10. Jews did face some anti-Semitism.

Any other valid point of significant omission.

15. *Candidates can be credited in a number of ways **up to a maximum of 9 marks.***

Candidates must make a judgement about the extent to which different factors contributed to an event or development, or its impact. They are required to provide a balanced account of the influence of different factors and come to a reasoned conclusion based on the evidence presented.

Up to **5 marks** can be given for relevant, factual, key points of knowledge used to support factors, with **1 mark** given for each point (but **one mark should be deducted** if the process is not clear in at least two factors). **If only one factor is presented, a maximum of 3 marks should be given for relevant points of knowledge. A further 4 marks** can be given for providing the answer in a structured way and coming to a reasoned conclusion.

Possible factors:	Key points of knowledge to support this factor may include:
attractions of new lands	1. the promise of cheap land/ opportunity to own land/more fertile land
	2. climate perceived as better to that in Scotland
	3. employment opportunities/higher wages
	4. encouragement from relatives/ friends
the clearances	5. many people evicted from their homes/made homeless so had to move
	6. some landlords assisted tenants by paying their passage if they agreed to leave
difficulties of earning a living	7. collapse of kelp industry/fall in demand for black cattle/collapse of herring trade after Russian Revolution in 1917
	8. overpopulation led to the subdivision of land/not enough good land to support family/pay rent
	9. failure of potato crop/blight/hunger
poor living standards	10. rural housing – blackhouses/ croft houses offer primitive accommodation
	11. urban housing – tenements often squalid. Lacking basic amenities in 1920s and 1930s
Government	12. Government assistance to emigrate/assistance of charities (e.g. Barnardos)
any other relevant factor	13. any other valid reason.

Up to **4 marks** should be given for presenting the answer in a structured way, leading to a conclusion which addresses the question, as follows:

1 mark for an introduction (which places the question in its historical context or outlines relevant factors). **1 mark** for the answer being presented in a structured way (with knowledge being organised in support of different factors).

1 mark for a conclusion with a valid judgement (or overall summary). **1 mark** for a reason in support of the judgement (a summary cannot be supported).

16. *Candidates can be credited in a number of ways up to a maximum of 6 marks.*

Candidates must make a number of points that make the issue plain or clear, for example by showing connections between factors or causal relationships between events or ideas. These should be key reasons but there is no need for any evaluation or prioritising of these reasons.

Up to a **maximum of 6 marks in total**, **1 mark** should be given for each accurate, relevant reason, and a **second mark** should be given for reasons that are developed. Candidates may achieve full marks by providing six straightforward reasons, three developed reasons (or a combination of these).

Possible reasons may include:
1. Scots who emigrated often had skills which were in demand in their homeland which meant they prospered (e.g. they were experienced farmers/granite workers/handloom weavers/seamen)
2. Scots were often relatively well educated which meant they could often adopt leadership roles in their new communities which meant they did well (e.g. education/politics/finance)
3. Scots gained a reputation as being hardworking which meant that employers were often keen to hire them
4. many Scots had an entrepreneurial attitude and set up their own businesses which meant that there were examples of Scots who became very rich
5. Scots were innovative and played key roles in the modernisation of their new homelands (e.g. developing railroads/telegraph systems/introducing new farming methods)
6. many Scots moved to areas where there were existing Scots communities which meant they had families and friends to support them/felt at home/were able to settle quickly (e.g. Otago in New Zealand and Nova Scotia)
7. Scots were experienced in finance and banking which meant that these skills were much in demand in their new homelands
8. many Scots were experienced miners which meant they were successful in the Australian Gold Rush
9. the Canadian Fur Trade was dominated by Scots so Scots were recruited for Hudson Bay Company which meant that other Scots were given key positions
10. the Presbyterian church in New Zealand was able to offer support/was familiar to them which helped Scots create a stronger community than other immigrants.

Any other valid reason.

Section 1, Context E, The Era of the Great War, 1900–1928

17. *Candidates can be credited in a number of ways up to a maximum of 9 marks.*

Candidates must make a judgement about the extent to which different factors contributed to an event or development, or its impact. They are required to provide a balanced account of the influence of different factors and come to a reasoned conclusion based on the evidence presented.

Up to **5 marks** can be given for relevant, factual, key points of knowledge used to support factors, with **1 mark** given for each point (but **one mark should be deducted** if the process is not clear in at least two factors). **If only one factor is presented, a maximum of 3 marks should be given for relevant points of knowledge. A further 4 marks** can be

given for providing the answer in a structured way and coming to a reasoned conclusion.

Possible factors:	Key points of knowledge to support this factor may include:
machine gun	1. machine gun's casualty rate was much higher than that of regular rifles/the machine gun had the capability to fire 400-600 rounds per minute 2. the machine gun had a longer range than regular rifles/the use of cross fire made the machine gun deadly 3. it was the most effective defensive weapon in the trenches/but lacked mobility 4. at times less effective as barrel overheated and jammed
the tank	5. destroyed barbed wire defences/crossed no man's land easily 6. bullet proof/shielded infantry during an attack on enemy trenches 7. very slow/often got stuck in the mud or broke down
gas	8. (chlorine/phosgene/mustard) – created panic and killed/wounded many by choking/blinding 9. less effective as it was weather dependent/impact of gas masks
artillery	10. killed/wounded the most men from long range
rifle	11. crucial ever-present infantry weapon/useful due to its mobility when the soldiers were attacking
aeroplanes	12. some success in reconnaissance/bombing enemy trenches
any other relevant factor	13. any other valid reason.

Up to **4 marks** should be given for presenting the answer in a structured way, leading to a conclusion which addresses the question, as follows:

1 mark for an introduction (which places the question in its historical context or outlines relevant factors). **1 mark** for the answer being presented in a structured way (with knowledge being organised in support of different factors). **1 mark** for a conclusion with a valid judgement (or overall summary). **1 mark** for a reason in support of the judgement (a summary cannot be supported).

18. *Candidates can be credited in a number of ways up to a maximum of 6 marks.*

Candidates must make a judgement about the extent to which the source provides a full description or explanation of a given event or development.

Up to a **maximum of 6 marks** in total, **1 mark** should be awarded for each valid point selected from the source or each valid point of significant omission provided.

Candidates should be awarded **up to 3 marks** for their identification of points from the source which support their judgement. Candidates should be awarded **up to 4 marks** for their identification of points of significant omission, based on their own knowledge, that support their judgement.

A **maximum of 2 marks** may be awarded for answers in which no judgement has been made **or** which refer only to the source.

Possible points which may be identified from the source include:

1. it stated that no-one was allowed to talk about the navy or the army in public places
2. you were also not allowed to spread rumours about military matters
3. you could not trespass on railway lines or bridges
4. British Summer Time was introduced to give more daylight hours for extra work.

Possible points of significant omission may include:

5. no-one was allowed to melt down gold or silver
6. no-one was allowed to light bonfires or fireworks
7. no-one was allowed to use invisible ink when writing abroad
8. no-one was allowed to ring church bells
9. the government could censor newspapers/letters
10. opening hours in pubs were cut/beer was watered down/customers in pubs were not allowed to buy a round of drinks.

Any other valid point of significant omission.

19. *Candidates can be credited in a number of ways **up to a maximum of 5 marks.***

Candidates must evaluate the extent to which a source is useful by commenting on evidence such as the author, type of source, purpose, timing, content or omission. For a mark to be given, the candidate must identify an aspect of the source and make a comment which shows why this aspect makes the source more or less useful.

A maximum of **4 marks** can be given for evaluative comments relating to the author, type of source, purpose and timing. A maximum of **2 marks** may be given for evaluative comments relating to the content of the source. A maximum of **2 marks** may be given for evaluative comments relating to points of significant omission.

Examples of aspects of the source and relevant comments:

	Aspect	Possible comment(s)
Author	David Lloyd George	Useful as he is the PM and has first-hand/eyewitness knowledge of the work done by women.
Type of source	Newspaper interview	Useful as interviews tend to be both factual and detailed.
Purpose	To inform/persuade	Useful as it praises the work done by women/provides detailed account of women's war work.
Timing	22 August 1918	Useful as it was written in the last year of the war.

Content	Possible comment(s)
female volunteers came forward to work in administrative offices of all kinds.	Useful as it is accurate (women did volunteer to do various jobs on the home front).
women working in hospitals.	Useful as it is accurate (many women did become nurses).
The heroines who have flocked to work behind the front lines as ambulance drivers.	Useful as it is accurate (many women did work behind the front lines).

Possible points of significant omission may include:

1. women worked in munition factories
2. the land army/on the land
3. on the trains as railway guards and ticket collectors/buses and tram conductors/emergency services like police/firefighters
4. some women also worked heavy or precision machinery in engineering/shipyards.

Any other valid point of significant omission.

20. *Candidates can be credited in a number of ways **up to a maximum of 6 marks.***

Candidates must make a number of points that make the issue plain or clear, for example by showing connections between factors or causal relationships between events or ideas. These should be key reasons but there is no need for any evaluation or prioritising of these reasons.

Up to a **maximum of 6 marks in total**, **1 mark** should be given for each accurate, relevant reason, and a **second mark** should be given for reasons that are developed. Candidates may achieve full marks by providing six straightforward reasons, three developed reasons (or a combination of these).

Possible reasons may include:

1. militancy created lots of bad publicity which made achieving the vote much less likely/portrayed women as unfit to vote
2. Suffragettes smashed shop windows which angered business owners
3. Suffragettes interrupted political meetings which annoyed politicians
4. Emily Davison's actions at the Derby outraged the nation
5. Suffragettes slashing paintings upset many people
6. attacking politicians made many people view Suffragettes as too immature to vote
7. chaining themselves to public buildings made many view Suffragettes as a nuisance
8. arson attacks (e.g. racecourses, post boxes) turned many against the cause
9. use of letter bombs made many think women were not responsible enough to vote
10. acid attacks (e.g. golf clubs) turned many against the cause
11. some Suffragettes viewed as unpatriotic for not supporting the war effort.

Any other valid reason.

Section 2, Context A, The Creation of the Medieval Kingdoms. 1066–1406

21. *Candidates can be credited in a number of ways **up to a maximum of 4 marks.***

They may take different perspectives on the events and may describe a variety of different aspects of the events. Candidates must make a number of relevant, factual points. These should be key points. These do not have to be in any particular order.

1 mark should be given for each accurate relevant key point of knowledge. **A second mark** should be given for each point that is developed, up to a maximum of **4 marks**. Candidates may achieve full marks by providing four straightforward points, by making two developed points (or a combination of these).

Possible points of knowledge may include:

1. the king kept some land for himself and gave the rest to the nobility/other important members of society
2. barons received land from the king and in return provided knights to fight in the king's army

3. knights received land from the barons and in return fought for the king on behalf of the barons
4. peasants received some land and in return worked on their overlord's land/or provided other services
5. barons had to pay homage for their land
6. knights could pay money to their lord instead of providing military service (e.g. Scutage)
7. the Church was also part of the feudal system and could be asked to provide services in return for land.

Any other valid point of knowledge.

22. *Candidates can be credited in a number of ways up to a maximum of 4 marks.*

Candidates must interpret the evidence and make direct comparisons between sources. Candidates are expected to compare content directly on a point-by-point basis. They may compare the details in the sources and/or compare the viewpoints overall.

A simple comparison will indicate what points of detail or viewpoint the sources agree or disagree on and should be given **1 mark**. A developed comparison of the points of detail or overall viewpoint should be given a **second mark**. Candidates may achieve full marks by making four simple comparisons, two developed comparisons (or by a combination of these).

Possible points of comparison may include:

Overall the sources agree about the violent murder of Archbishop Becket.

Source A	Source B
The knights attempted to arrest Becket but he refused to leave, claiming he was ready to die for God.	The knights attempted to seize Archbishop Becket but he would not move, stating he was willing to be a martyr for the Church.
Becket was dragged from the altar and in the scuffle that followed, was attacked by the knights.	Becket was thrown to the floor and assaulted by the knights.
(In an act of horror) one of the knights drew his sword and sliced off the crown of Becket's head.	To make sure he was dead, one of the knights held Becket down and cut off the top of his head.

23. *Candidates can be credited in a number of ways up to a maximum of 6 marks.*

Candidates must make a judgement about the extent to which the source provides a full description or explanation of a given event or development.

Up to a **maximum of 6 marks in total**, **1 mark** should be given for each valid point selected from the source or each valid point of significant omission provided.

Candidates should be given **up to 3 marks** for their identification of points from the source that support their judgement. Candidates should be given **up to 4 marks** for their identification of points of significant omission, based on their own knowledge, that support their judgement.

A maximum of 2 marks may be given for answers in which no judgement has been made or which refer only to the source.

Possible points which may be identified from the source include:
1. monasteries played a vital role in the wool trade (creating work for people and boosting the economy)

2. monasteries were also centres of learning (especially for boys preparing for a career in the Church)
3. pilgrims often stayed there overnight
4. the sick were also frequent visitors (hoping to be treated at the monastic infirmary)

Possible points of significant omission may include:
5. key places of worship (e.g. prayed for the souls of the dead)
6. monastic libraries held chronicles which were of great historical importance
7. monastic fields were used to grow herbs for medicine/only source of medical treatment for many people
8. monasteries involved in developing other industries (e.g. brewing, fishing)
9. monasteries provided food for the needy.

Any other valid point of significant omission.

24. *Candidates can be credited in a number of ways up to a maximum of 6 marks.*

Candidates must make a number of points that make the issue plain or clear, for example by showing connections between factors or causal relationships between events or ideas. These should be key reasons but there is no need for any evaluation or prioritising of these reasons.

Up to a **maximum of 6 marks in total**, **1 mark** should be given for each accurate, relevant reason, and a **second mark** should be given for reasons that are developed. Candidates may achieve full marks by providing six straightforward reasons, three developed reasons (or a combination of these).

Possible reasons may include:
1. the increase in population meant there was a greater demand for manufactured goods made in towns
2. the workforce needed somewhere to live and so moved to towns
3. peasants moved to towns because they could improve their social position there
4. towns were supported by kings which helped them to grow (e.g. right to hold a market)
5. kings/barons could levy taxes and obtain cash from them and so encouraged their growth
6. towns were supported by barons which helped them to grow (e.g. did not stop peasants from moving there/rented land instead)
7. towns were attractive to people because it was safer to live together inside a town's walls
8. towns were attractive to merchants who moved there so they could set up guilds.

Any other valid reason.

25. *Candidates can be credited in a number of ways up to a maximum of 9 marks.*

Candidates must make a judgement about the extent to which different factors contributed to an event or development, or its impact. They are required to provide a balanced account of the influence of different factors and come to a reasoned conclusion based on the evidence presented.

Up to **5 marks** can be awarded for relevant, factual, key points of knowledge used to support factors, with **1 mark** given for each point (but **one mark should be deducted** if the process is not clear in at least two factors). **If only one factor is presented, a maximum of 3 marks should be awarded** for relevant points of knowledge. **A further 4 marks** can be awarded for providing the answer in a structured way and coming to a reasoned conclusion.

Possible factors:	Key points of knowledge to support this factor may include:
Black Death	1. the peasants were unhappy because the Statute of Labourers law in 1351 said that no peasant could ever be paid more than he was before the Black Death 2. the peasants were angry because since the Black Death some peasants had been able to buy their freedom from their lord but many were still villeins and were not free
The Hundred Years' War	3. England had been at war with France for nearly 50 years (the peasants were tired of paying for the war) 4. the war had been going badly since 1369, the peasants feared the French might invade
King Richard II	5. King Richard II was still young (the peasants believed he was being badly advised by his commissioners) 6. the peasants disliked the King's commissioners because they were enforcing the collection of new taxes (eg in Essex and Kent)
poll taxes	7. the peasants were worried because they could not pay the new poll taxes (which had been introduced in 1377, 1379 and 1381) 8. the peasants were angry with the 1381 poll tax because every person over 15 had to pay 4d
the Church	9. the peasants resented having to work on the Church's land for free 10. the peasants were angry when John Ball, a priest who supported them, was jailed
any other relevant factor	11. any other valid reason.

Up to **4 marks** should be given for presenting the answer in a structured way, leading to a conclusion which addresses the question, as follows:

1 mark for an introduction (which places the question in its historical context or outlines relevant factors). **1 mark** for the answer being presented in a structured way (with knowledge being organised in support of different factors). **1 mark** for a conclusion with a valid judgement (or overall summary). **1 mark** for a reason in support of the judgement (a summary cannot be supported).

Section 2, Context B, War of the Three Kingdoms, 1603–1651

26. *Candidates can be credited in a number of ways up to a maximum of 9 marks.*

Candidates must make a judgement about the extent to which different factors contributed to an event or development, or its impact. They are required to provide a balanced account of the influence of different factors and come to a reasoned conclusion based on the evidence presented.

Up to **5 marks** can be awarded for relevant, factual, key points of knowledge used to support factors, with **1 mark** given for each point (but **one mark should be deducted** if the correct process is not clear in at least two factors).

If only one factor is presented, a maximum of 3 marks should be awarded for relevant points of knowledge. A further 4 marks can be awarded for providing the answer in a structured way and coming to a reasoned conclusion.

Possible factors:	Key points of knowledge to support this factor may include:
religion	1. Millenary Petition (1603) which requested changes to practices in Church of England was rejected by James 2. licensing of Bancroft's Canons (brought changes to clergy and Prayer Book) annoyed the clergy 3. James gave Bishops more control in the Church which worried Puritans (Direction of Preachers 1622)
revenue/ finance	4. Parliament viewed James as being extravagant with money (eg spending on favourites/spending on coronation) 5. Parliament was dismissed in 1610 because of arguments over finances 6. arguments over impositions (extra customs tax) and subsidies led to parliament's dismissal in 1614 7. quarrels over the sale of monopolies
King's personality	1. many in parliament were offended by James' belief in the Divine Right of Kings 2. James was criticised for neglecting the business of government in favour of leisure pursuits
any other relevant factor	3. any other valid reason.

Up to **4 marks** should be given for presenting the answer in a structured way, leading to a conclusion which addresses the question, as follows:

1 mark for an introduction (which places the question in its historical context or outlines relevant factors). **1 mark** for the answer being presented in a structured way (with knowledge being organised in support of different factors). **1 mark** for a conclusion with a valid judgement (or overall summary). **1 mark** for a reason in support of the judgement (a summary cannot be supported).

27. *Candidates can be credited in a number of ways up to a maximum of 6 marks.*

Candidates must make a judgement about the extent to which the source provides a full description or explanation of a given event or development.

Up to a **maximum of 6 marks in total**, **1 mark** should be given for each valid point selected from the source or each valid point of significant omission provided.

Candidates should be given **up to 3 marks** for their identification of points from the source that supports their judgement. Candidates should be given **up to 4 marks** for their identification of points of significant omission, based on their own knowledge, that support their judgement.

A maximum of **2 marks** may be given for answers in which no judgement has been made or which refer only to the source.

Possible points which may be identified from the source include:
1. the King's plans were undermined by lack of funds
2. the Scottish forces organised themselves quickly and efficiently

3. English forces lacked experienced commanders
4. the English army that finally gathered on the Scottish border in mid-1639 was untrained and poorly equipped.

Possible points of significant omission may include:

5. there was a lack of support for the war among the King's subjects
6. in 1640, King Charles attempted a second campaign against the Scots, but once again, the army he raised was inadequate
7. many of the English soldiers deserted on the march to the north because they were untrained and poorly-disciplined
8. by August 1640, the King's forces had mustered in Yorkshire and Northumberland, most of them poorly-armed, unpaid and underfed
9. the Earl of Strafford coerced the Irish parliament into granting funds to raise an Irish army but it was not ready in time to take part in the campaign against Scotland
10. the Scots were able to occupy Newcastle/morale in the English army was shattered.

Any other valid point of significant omission.

28. *Candidates can be credited in a number of ways up to a maximum of 6 marks.*

Candidates must make a number of points that make the issue plain or clear, for example by showing connections between factors or causal relationships between events or ideas. These should be key reasons but there is no need for any evaluation or prioritising of these reasons.

Up to a **maximum of 6 marks in total**, **1 mark** should be given for each accurate, relevant reason, and a **second mark** should be given for reasons that are developed. Candidates may achieve full marks by providing six straightforward reasons, three developed reasons (or a combination of these).

Possible reasons may include:

1. King Charles I believed in the Divine Right of Kings which annoyed Parliament because they objected to the power it gave him
2. Charles' period of Personal Rule (1629-1640) increased opposition because he ruled without consulting Parliament for 11 years
3. Charles' personality caused problems because he was considered extravagant and Parliament accused him of wasting money
4. the foreign policy of Charles I (e.g. war with Spain was unpopular and caused opposition in Parliament because they mostly failed)
5. the money raising methods of Charles (forced loans, Ship Money, Tonnage and Poundage) led to opposition as they were deemed unfair
6. Charles attempted to reform the Church by introducing religious policies which were opposed by Parliament and Puritans because they believed they were returning to more Catholic-like ceremonies
7. Charles showed favouritism to some individuals at court (e.g. Buckingham, who was distrusted by Parliament leading to distrust of Charles).

Any other valid reason.

29. *Candidates can be credited in a number of ways up to a maximum of 4 marks.*

They may take different perspectives on the events and may describe a variety of different aspects of the events. Candidates must make a number of relevant, factual points.

These should be key points. These do not have to be in any particular order.

1 mark should be given for each accurate relevant key point of knowledge. **A second mark** should be given for each point that is developed, up to a maximum of **4 marks**. Candidates may achieve full marks by providing four straightforward points, by making two developed points (or a combination of these).

Possible points of knowledge may include:

1. on 23 July 1637 in St Giles Cathedral, the Sunday service used the New Prayer Book introduced by Charles I
2. the Dean of the Cathedral began to read from the book but was shouted down by some women in the congregation (shouting 'the mass has come amongst us')
3. the Bishop of Edinburgh climbed the pulpit to try and appease the crowd
4. members of the congregation began to throw Bibles at him
5. Jenny Geddes threw a stool at the Bishop (shouting 'how dare you say mass in ma lug')
6. bailiffs attempted to restore order and threw the rioters out
7. the service continued but rioters were banging on doors outside and throwing stones at the windows.

Any other valid point of knowledge.

30. *Candidates can be credited in a number of ways up to a maximum of 4 marks.*

Candidates must interpret the evidence and make direct comparisons between sources. Candidates are expected to compare content directly on a point-by-point basis. They may compare the details in the sources and/or compare the viewpoints overall.

A simple comparison will indicate what points of detail or viewpoint the sources agree or disagree on and should be given **1 mark**. A developed comparison of the points of detail or overall viewpoint should be given a **second mark**. Candidates may achieve full marks by making four simple comparisons, two developed comparisons (or by a combination of these).

Possible points of comparison may include:

Overall the sources agree on the reasons why people joined sides on the outbreak of the civil war.

Source B	Source C
The King's supporters included the gentry because they saw him as defender of the social order.	However, for some religion did not matter, they were more attracted by the Parliamentarians' attitudes to challenging the class system.
Others supported him because of religious reasons with more conservative Protestants and some Catholics defending his religious policies.	The Parliamentarians were against the King's religious policies and many Puritans joined them to fight against changes to the church.
Then there were those who joined up purely because they sincerely believed in the cause of the King, which was to maintain his royal authority.	A few joined the civil war only to make money but the majority believed in the royal cause.

Section 2, Context C, The Atlantic Slave Trade, 1770–1807

31. *Candidates can be credited in a number of ways up to a maximum of 9 marks.*

Candidates must make a judgement about the extent to which different factors contributed to an event or development, or its impact. They are required to provide a balanced account of the influence of different factors and come to a reasoned conclusion based on the evidence presented.

Up to **5 marks** can be awarded for relevant, factual, key points of knowledge used to support factors, with **1 mark** given for each point (but **one mark should be deducted** if the correct process is not clear in at least two factors). **If only one factor is presented, a maximum of 3 marks should be awarded** for relevant points of knowledge. **A further 4 marks** can be awarded for providing the answer in a structured way and coming to a reasoned conclusion.

Possible factors:	Key points of knowledge to support this factor may include:
tribal conflict	1. Africans became slaves by being captured as prisoners of war 2. African chiefs captured slaves from rival kingdoms to trade for goods (e.g. cloth, iron tools, weapons and alcohol) 3. Kingdom of Dahomey sent raiding parties to capture slaves to sell onto Europeans 4. demand for more slaves led to increased hatred and violence between tribes/within tribes/made worse by the introduction of guns
destruction of society	5. the loss of the youngest men and women in society meant that Africa fell behind the rest of the world (estimated that around 10 million people were transported from Africa over the eighteenth century)/villages often destroyed/deserted 6. farm land or hunting areas being abandoned because it was too far from the village to be safe/impact on food supply 7. parents were encouraged to sell children to pay family debts 8. African chiefs changed laws to make being sold into slavery a more common punishment 9. Slave trade led to loss of/destruction of culture
slave factories	1. development of European 'factories' on the coast to control the slave trade led to terrible treatment for captured Africans 2. captured Africans deemed unfit were often left abandoned at slave factories
any other relevant factor	3. any other valid reason.

Up to **4 marks** should be given for presenting the answer in a structured way, leading to a conclusion which addresses the question, as follows:

1 mark for an introduction (which places the question in its historical context or outlines relevant factors). **1 mark** for the answer being presented in a structured way (with knowledge being organised in support of different factors). **1 mark** for a conclusion with a valid judgement (or overall summary). **1 mark** for a reason in support of the judgement (a summary cannot be supported).

32. *Candidates can be credited in a number of ways up to a maximum of 6 marks.*

Candidates must make a judgement about the extent to which the source provides a full description or explanation of a given event or development.

Up to a **maximum of 6 marks** in total, **1 mark** should be awarded for each valid point selected from the source or each valid point of significant omission provided.

Candidates should be awarded **up to 3 marks** for their identification of points from the source which support their judgement. Candidates should be awarded **up to 4 marks** for their identification of points of significant omission, based on their own knowledge, that support their judgement.

A **maximum of 2 marks** may be awarded for answers in which no judgement has been made **or** which refer only to the source.

Possible points which may be identified from the source include:
1. slave produced goods such as sugar and coffee were imported into British ports helping them to become rich and powerful trading centres
2. work was provided in many ports as men were employed as sailors, shipbuilders and dock workers
3. the profits made from the slave trade were also invested in the development of other British industries
4. wealthy colonial families built huge mansions in many of the British cities where they traded

Possible points of significant omission may include:
5. many important government buildings in British cities were constructed using the profits of the slave trade
6. Glasgow's economy benefited from the tobacco trade
7. slave cotton provided work for the mills of Lancashire
8. the slave trade had raised struggling ports to rich and prosperous trading centres (e.g. Bristol, London, Liverpool)
9. banking and insurance businesses grew.

Any other valid point of significant omission.

33. *Candidates can be credited in a number of ways up to a maximum of 4 marks.*

They may take different perspectives on the events and may describe a variety of different aspects of the events.

Candidates must make a number of relevant, factual points. These should be key points. These do not have to be in any particular order.

1 mark should be awarded for each accurate relevant key point of knowledge. **A second mark** should be awarded for each point that is developed, up to a maximum of **4 marks.** Candidates may achieve full marks by providing four straightforward points, by making two developed points (or any combination of these).

Possible points of knowledge may include:
1. flogging with a whip
2. beatings (for working slowly)
3. branded with hot iron
4. forced to wear heavy iron chains
5. iron muzzles

6. thumbscrews
7. execution (as an example to other slaves, e.g. burning slaves alive)
8. mutilation (e.g. cutting off feet of runaways).

Any other valid point of knowledge.

34. *Candidates can be credited in a number of ways up to a maximum of 4 marks.*

Candidates must interpret the evidence and make direct comparisons between sources. Candidates are expected to compare content directly on a point-by-point basis. They may compare the details in the sources and/or compare the viewpoints overall.

A **simple comparison** will indicate what points of detail or viewpoint the sources agree or disagree on and **should be awarded 1 mark**. A **developed comparison** of the points of detail or overall viewpoint **should be awarded a second mark**. Candidates may achieve full marks by making four simple comparisons, two developed comparisons (or by any combination of these).

Possible points of comparison may include:

Overall the sources agree about the methods that were used by the abolitionists.

Source B	Source C
(Personal accounts changed public opinion as) the dreadful experiences of the slaves during the Middle Passage were told by survivors.	Some slaves (such as Olaudah Equiano) published autobiographies sharing their experiences (and changing the views of the public).
Many slavers backed these up, giving similar accounts about the horrors of the trade.	John Newton, former slaver, published a pamphlet outlining the horrific conditions on the slave trade and confirming slave accounts.
Abolitionists such as Clarkson toured the country with equipment used on slaves (to show the public how badly they were treated).	Clarkson travelled around Britain with instruments such as manacles and thumbscrews (to gain support for the cause).

35. *Candidates can be credited in a number of ways up to a maximum of 6 marks.*

Candidates must make a number of points that make the issue plain or clear, for example by showing connections between factors or causal relationships between events or ideas. These should be key reasons but there is no need for any evaluation or prioritising of these reasons.

Up to a **maximum of 6 marks** in total, **1 mark** should be awarded for each accurate, relevant reason, and a **second mark** should be awarded for reasons that are developed. Candidates may achieve full marks by providing six straightforward reasons, three developed reasons (or any combination of these).

Possible reasons may include:
1. the slave trade brought wealth to Britain, so was popular with those who were wealthy
2. the slave trade brought employment to Britain (e.g. shipyards, ports, mills, manufacturing) so was supported by many involved in these industries

3. cities profited from the slave trade (e.g. Bristol, Liverpool and Glasgow), so many in these cities wished to see slavery continue
4. the products of the slave trade were in great demand (e.g. cotton, tobacco and sugar) and many believed that slavery was needed in order to meet demand for these products
5. involvement in the slave trade helped Britain to remain a world power, so many continued to support slavery
6. the slave trade was seen as a valuable training ground for the Royal Navy, so it was supported
7. many MPs had financial interests in the slave trade, so wished to see it continue
8. many MPs were being bribed to ensure that they continued to give their support for the continuation of the trade
9. the slave trade still enjoyed the support of the King
10. taxes from slave produced goods were essential to fund the war with France.

Any other valid reason.

Section 2, Context D, Changing Britain, 1760–1914

36. *Candidates can be credited in a number of ways up to a maximum of 9 marks.*

Candidates must make a judgement about the extent to which different factors contributed to an event or development, or its impact. They are required to provide a balanced account of the influence of different factors and come to a reasoned conclusion based on the evidence presented.

Up to **5 marks** can be awarded for relevant, factual, key points of knowledge used to support factors, with **1 mark** given for each point (but **one mark should be deducted** if the process is not clear in at least two factors). **If only one factor is presented, a maximum of 3 marks should be awarded** for relevant points of knowledge. A **further 4 marks** can be awarded for providing the answer in a structured way and coming to a reasoned conclusion.

Possible factors:	Key points of knowledge to support this factor may include:
better sanitation	1. wash houses and public baths helped improve hygiene 2. provision of fresh, clean water reduced the threat of disease 3. improved sewerage systems/proper drainage reduced spread of germs/diseases
medical advances	4. smallpox vaccination (1798) helped prevent deaths from this illness 5. 1897 – cholera vaccine was developed, helping to protect people from deadly cholera epidemics 6. chloroform (after 1847/Simpson) helped to prevent deaths from shock during surgery 7. carbolic acid (Lister 1867) helped prevent spread of infection during/after surgery
better medical care	8. cleaner hospitals (thanks to Florence Nightingale) led to better treatment/survival rates 9. better training for doctors and nurses led to better medical care 10. properly trained midwives meant that more mothers and babies survived

Public Health Acts	11. local authorities empowered to improve living conditions (eg 1848, 1875)
any other relevant factor.	12. any other valid reason.

Up to **4 marks** should be given for presenting the answer in a structured way, leading to a conclusion which addresses the question, as follows:

1 mark for an introduction (which places the question in its historical context or outlines relevant factors). **1 mark** for the answer being presented in a structured way (with knowledge being organised in support of different factors). **1 mark** for a conclusion with a valid judgement (or overall summary). **1 mark** for a reason in support of the judgement (a summary cannot be supported).

37. *Candidates can be credited in a number of ways up to a maximum of 4 marks.*

Candidates must interpret the evidence and make direct comparisons between sources. Candidates are expected to compare content directly on a point-by-point basis. They may compare the details in the sources and/or compare the viewpoints overall.

A simple comparison will indicate what points of detail or viewpoint the sources agree or disagree on and should be given **1 mark**. A developed comparison of the points of detail or overall viewpoint should be given a **second mark**. Candidates may achieve full marks by making four simple comparisons, two developed comparisons (or by a combination of these).

Possible points of comparison may include:

Overall the sources agree about the harsh rules and punishments in textile factories.

Source A	Source B
Any person coming to work late shall be fined.	being fined for things such as being late.
Any person found talking with the other workers instead of working shall be fined.	There were other fines too, for offences such as talking, whistling or singing.
Any person found smoking on the premises shall be instantly dismissed.	Mill owners also had the power to sack on the spot any employee who was found to be breaking the rules.

38. *Candidates can be credited in a number of ways up to a maximum of 6 marks.*

Candidates must make a judgement about the extent to which the source provides a full description or explanation of a given event or development.

Up to a **maximum of 6 marks in total**, **1 mark** should be given for each valid point selected from the source or each valid point of significant omission provided.

Candidates should be given **up to 3 marks** for their identification of points from the source that support their judgement. Candidates should be given **up to 4 marks** for their identification of points of significant omission, based on their own knowledge, that support their judgement.

A **maximum of 2 marks** may be given for answers in which no judgement has been made or which refer only to the source.

Possible points which may be identified from the source include:
1. (1842 Mines Act) stated that no-one under 15 could be in charge of operating machinery/winding gear
2. (after 1850) all mine owners had to report accidents that led to death
3. (the 1862 Mines Act) made single shaft mines illegal
4. (1872 Mines Act) gave miners the right to appoint inspectors from among themselves

Possible points of significant omission may include:
5. (1842 Mines Act stated that) no women or children under 10 could work underground
6. (1842 Mines Act) replaced people dragging coal underground with ponies
7. (1842 Mines Act) appointed a Mines Inspector
8. (1860 Mines Act) increased the age of boys that were allowed to work underground to 12
9. (1872 Mines Act) stated that fans had to be installed to improve ventilation
10. (in 1872) naked flames were made illegal/all mines had to use safety lamps.

Any other valid point of significant omission.

39. *Candidates can be credited in a number of ways up to a maximum of 6 marks.*

Candidates must make a number of points that make the issue plain or clear, for example by showing connections between factors or causal relationships between events or ideas. These should be key reasons but there is no need for any evaluation or prioritising of these reasons.

Up to a **maximum of 6 marks in total**, **1 mark** should be given for each accurate, relevant reason, and a **second mark** should be given for reasons that are developed. Candidates may achieve full marks by providing six straightforward reasons, three developed reasons (or a combination of these).

Possible reasons may include:
1. raw materials and finished products could be transported quickly and cheaply which meant that factories/industry was boosted by the railways
2. perishable foods (such as fish or milk) could be transported to cities quickly which meant that diets improved/these industries were boosted
3. railways were reached more parts of Britain, which meant that canals/roads/turnpikes went into decline
4. national railway timetables had to be made which meant that time had to be standardised across Britain
5. sporting teams could now play teams from further away which meant that national sporting leagues developed
6. railway travel was affordable which meant that the working classes could travel further than before/cheap holidays
7. railway travel was quick/cheap (e.g. suburbs developed as people could commute to work)
8. railways meant that national daily newspapers were possible for the first time
9. railways meant cheap and extensive postal service was now possible nationwide
10. politicians could use trains to travel which meant that travel was easier between parliament and constituency/ there were now national election campaigns
11. railways created new jobs (e.g. navvies and conductors) which reduced unemployment
12. the railway network was extensive which meant that some people complained that Britain's countryside was ruined.

Any other valid reason.

40. *Candidates can be credited in a number of ways **up to a maximum of 4 marks.***

They may take different perspectives on the events and may describe a variety of different aspects of the events. Candidates must make a number of relevant, factual points. These should be key points. These do not have to be in any particular order.

1 mark should be given for each accurate relevant key point of knowledge. **A second mark** should be given for each point that is developed, up to a maximum of **4 marks**. Candidates may achieve full marks by providing four straightforward points, by making two developed points (or a combination of these).

Possible points of knowledge may include:
1. all men (over 21) to have the vote/universal manhood suffrage
2. voting should take place by secret ballot
3. constituencies should be of equal size
4. MPs should be paid
5. the property qualification for becoming an MP should be abolished
6. annual parliamentary elections.

Any other valid point of knowledge.

Section 2, Context E, The Making of Modern Britain, 1880–1951

41. *Candidates can be credited in a number of ways **up to a maximum of 6 marks.***

Candidates must make a number of points that make the issue plain or clear, for example by showing connections between factors or causal relationships between events or ideas. These should be key reasons but there is no need for any evaluation or prioritising of these reasons.

Up to a **maximum of 6 marks in total**, **1 mark** should be given for each accurate, relevant reason, and a **second mark** should be given for reasons that are developed. Candidates may achieve full marks by providing six straightforward reasons, three developed reasons (or a combination of these).

Possible reasons may include:
1. reports of Booth and Rowntree highlighted the need for government intervention to tackle poverty
2. children were too young to be able to work and provide for themselves so deserved help if they were poor
3. children were often born into poverty which was no fault of their own so they deserved help
4. many children had to work instead of going to school so help for their families may enable them to go to school
5. the old were often unable to work and support themselves so they deserved some help
6. the old often ended up in the workhouse as they had been unable to save for their old age so it was seen as fair that they should receive some help from the state
7. the sick were unable to work and usually there was no sick pay so they deserved some help
8. medical treatment had to be paid for which many could not afford so they deserved some help
9. many of the unemployed were seasonally unemployed so they deserved help at certain times of year
10. finding work was difficult/employment was often irregular/workers often lost their jobs with no warning so they deserved some help.

Any other valid reason.

42. *Candidates can be credited in a number of ways **up to a maximum of 9 marks.***

Candidates must make a judgement about the extent to which different factors contributed to an event or development, or its impact. They are required to provide a balanced account of the influence of different factors and come to a reasoned conclusion based on the evidence presented.

Up to **5 marks** can be awarded for relevant, factual, key points of knowledge used to support factors, with **1 mark** given for each point (but **one mark should be deducted** if the correct process is not clear in at least two factors). **If only one factor is presented, a maximum of 3 marks should be awarded** for relevant points of knowledge. **A further 4 marks** can be awarded for providing the answer in a structured way and coming to a reasoned conclusion.

Possible factors:	Key points of knowledge to support this factor may include:
free school meals	1. often the only meal that children had in a day, making them healthier 2. helped poor families, as meals were paid for through local taxes 3. children's health deteriorated during the school holidays, showing how important school meals were 4. not made compulsory until 1914 so many children did not benefit/children were benefitted after 1914
medical inspections	5. only identified problems at first/did not provide treatment (although did put pressure on government to act) 6. led to further reform/prompted the introduction of school clinics in 1912 providing free treatment
Children's Charter	7. banned children under 16 from buying tobacco and children under 18 from buying alcohol so improved child health 8. juvenile remand homes/courts/prisons/probation officers meant that child criminals were no longer treated like adult criminals 9. abolished the death penalty for children which was fairer 10. fires in homes had to be guarded helping to prevent children from being burned in accidents 11. children could be removed from parents who did not take care of them improving their welfare
any other relevant factor	1. any other valid reason.

Up to **4 marks** should be given for presenting the answer in a structured way, leading to a conclusion which addresses the question, as follows:

1 mark for an introduction (which places the question in its historical context or outlines relevant factors). **1 mark** for the answer being presented in a structured way (with knowledge being organised in support of different factors). **1 mark** for a conclusion with a valid judgement (or overall summary). **1 mark** for a reason in support of the judgement (a summary cannot be supported).

43. *Candidates can be credited in a number of ways up to a maximum of 4 marks.*

Candidates must interpret the evidence and make direct comparisons between sources. Candidates are expected to compare content directly on a point-by-point basis. They may compare the details in the sources and/or compare the viewpoints overall.

A simple comparison will indicate what points of detail or viewpoint the sources agree or disagree on and should be given **1 mark**. A developed comparison of the points of detail or overall viewpoint should be given a **second mark**. Candidates may achieve full marks by making four simple comparisons, two developed comparisons (or by a combination of these).

Possible points of comparison may include:

Overall the sources agree about the benefits of the 1911 National Insurance Act.

Source A	Source B
Insured workers received 10 shillings per week for the first 26 weeks of illness and 5 shillings a week after that.	The 1911 Act also gave insured workers 10 shillings a week for the first six months of sickness and this benefit was then halved until they were fit to return to work.
They were also entitled to free visits to the doctor and medicine.	Insured workers were also provided with free medical care.
there was a maternity grant for insured workers of 30 shillings.	When insured workers had a baby they were given a grant of 30 shillings.

44. *Candidates can be credited in a number of ways up to a maximum of 6 marks.*

Candidates must make a judgement about the extent to which the source provides a full description or explanation of a given event or development.

Up to a **maximum of 6 marks in total**, **1 mark** should be given for each valid point selected from the source or each valid point of significant omission provided.

Candidates should be given **up to 3 marks** for their identification of points from the source that support their judgement. Candidates should be given **up to 4 marks** for their identification of points of significant omission, based on their own knowledge, that support their judgement.

A **maximum of 2 marks** may be given for answers in which no judgement has been made or which refer only to the source.

Possible points which may be identified in the source include:
1. the war brought people together/created a sense of community/made people determined to create a better Britain
2. the government intervened in people's lives more/moved away from 'laissez-faire'
2. rationing was brought in/the Ministry of Food was created (to make sure everyone got a fair share of food)
4. family allowances were introduced before 1945

Possible points of significant omission may include:
5. evacuation raised awareness of levels of poverty/created a determination to tackle poverty amongst children

6. bombing levelled the social classes which created a sense of shared suffering and helped to change people's attitudes
7. the Beveridge Report sold hundreds of thousands of copies/created a public expectation of reform
8. some of the 'Giants' were tackled before the end of the war such as 'Ignorance' with the 1944 Butler Act
9. people accepted more government involvement in their lives because of things such as conscription.

Any other valid point of significant omission.

45. *Candidates can be credited in a number of ways up to a maximum of 4 marks.*

They may take different perspectives on the events and may describe a variety of different aspects of the events. Candidates must make a number of relevant, factual points. These should be key points. These do not have to be in any particular order.

1 mark should be given for each accurate relevant key point of knowledge. **A second mark** should be given for each point that is developed, up to a maximum of **4 marks**. Candidates may achieve full marks by providing four straightforward points, by making two developed points (or a combination of these).

Possible points of knowledge may include:
1. National Insurance was extended to prevent all workers from falling into poverty when they were sick or unemployed
2. National Insurance extended pensions for the old
3. National Insurance was universal/comprehensive (people were covered from the cradle to the grave)
4. National Assistance was available as a safety-net for those not covered by National Insurance
5. a National Health Service was introduced
6. many industries were nationalised
7. housing was improved with prefabs
8. housing was improved by the building of New Towns.

Any other valid point of knowledge.

Section 3, Context A, The Cross and the Crescent: the Crusades, 1071–1192

46. *Candidates can be credited in a number of ways up to a maximum of 5 marks.*

Candidates must evaluate the extent to which a source is useful by commenting on evidence such as the author, type of source, purpose, timing, content or omission. For a mark to be given, the candidate must identify an aspect of the source and make a comment which shows why this aspect makes the source more or less useful.

A maximum of **4 marks** can be given for evaluative comments relating to the author, type of source, purpose and timing.

A maximum of **2 marks** may be given for evaluative comments relating to the content of the source.

A maximum of **2 marks** may be given for evaluative comments relating to points of significant omission.

Examples of aspects of the source and relevant comments:

Aspect		Possible comment(s)
Author	Modern historian	Useful as he is a well-informed expert.
Type of source	Textbook	Useful because it will have been thoroughly researched.

Purpose	To inform	Useful as it gives detailed information/a balanced account.
Timing	1960	Useful as it is written with the benefit of hindsight.

Content	Possible comment(s)
Most castles were built to defend a location.	Useful as it is accurate (castles were used mainly for protection).
Castles had a Great Hall, where weddings and feasts were held to celebrate special occasions.	Useful as it is accurate (Great Halls were used to entertain).
Castles provided a place for knights to stay when carrying out guard duty for their lord.	Useful as it is accurate (most castles had barracks used by knights/soldiers).

Possible points of significant omission may include:
1. castles were used as a home by the king/lord
2. Great Hall used as a court to try criminals
3. castles had a store room for supplies (e.g. crops)
4. castles were used as an administrative centre from which to control the surrounding land/village.

Any other valid point of significant omission.

47. *Candidates can be credited in a number of ways **up to a maximum of 6 marks.***

Candidates must make a number of points that make the issue plain or clear, for example by showing connections between factors or causal relationships between events or ideas. These should be key reasons but there is no need for any evaluation or prioritising of these reasons.

Up to a **maximum of 6 marks in total**, **1 mark** should be given for each accurate, relevant reason, and a **second mark** should be given for reasons that are developed. Candidates may achieve full marks by providing six straightforward reasons, three developed reasons (or a combination of these).

Possible reasons may include:
1. the People's Crusade had behaved badly whilst in the Byzantine Empire and Byzantine troops had attacked them
2. the Crusaders blamed Emperor Alexius for the failure of the People's Crusade
3. some Crusaders were unhappy Emperor Alexius had forced them to take an oath of loyalty/to give back any land they captured
4. Emperor Alexius withheld supplies until the oath was taken, angering the Crusaders
5. the Crusaders felt betrayed by Emperor Alexius when he negotiated with the Muslims inside Nicaea/took the city behind the Crusaders' backs
6. Baldwin broke his oath/took Edessa which upset Emperor Alexius
7. Emperor Alexius did not arrive at Antioch to help the Crusaders when they were besieged by the Muslims
8. Bohemond broke his oath/kept Antioch for himself angering Emperor Alexius.

Any other valid reason.

48. *Candidates can be credited in a number of ways **up to a maximum of 6 marks.***

Candidates must make a judgement about the extent to which the source provides a full description or explanation of a given event or development.

Up to a **maximum of 6 marks in total, 1 mark** should be given for each valid point selected from the source or each valid point of significant omission provided.

Candidates should be given **up to 3 marks** for their identification of points from the source that support their judgement. Candidates should be given **up to 4 marks** for their identification of points of significant omission, based on their own knowledge, that support their judgement.

A **maximum of 2 marks** may be given for answers in which no judgement has been made or which refer only to the source.

Possible points which may be identified from the source include:
1. Bohemond bribed a Muslim guard who agreed to let the Crusaders into the city
2. in the middle of the night, 60 of Bohemond's men scaled the city walls
3. quickly they reached the battlements and captured three towers
4. the two main gates were opened and the rest of the Crusader army rushed in.

Possible points of significant omission may include:
5. the Crusaders appeared to withdraw to give the defenders a false sense of security
6. the Crusaders used ropes/ladders to climb the walls
7. the Crusaders slaughtered the inhabitants of the city
8. native Christians inside the city joined the Crusaders in the attack
9. the citadel was not initially captured.

Any other valid point of significant omission.

49. *Candidates can be credited in a number of ways **up to a maximum of 4 marks.***

They may take different perspectives on the events and may describe a variety of different aspects of the events. Candidates must make a number of relevant, factual points. These should be key points. These do not have to be in any particular order.

1 mark should be given for each accurate relevant key point of knowledge. **A second mark** should be given for each point that is developed, up to a maximum of **4 marks**. Candidates may achieve full marks by providing four straightforward points, by making two developed points (or a combination of these).

Possible points of knowledge may include:
1. the Crusaders were trapped at Hattin and cut off from any water supplies
2. Saladin surrounded the Crusaders with burning brushwood and dry grass, blinding them
3. the Muslim cavalry attacked the Crusaders with arrows
4. some Crusaders broke through the Muslim lines but were then cut off from the main army and forced to retreat
5. many Crusaders were killed in battle/others were captured
6. the Knights Templars/Hospitallers were singled out for execution
7. other Crusaders were sold into slavery
8. King Guy was forced to surrender/taken prisoner by Saladin.

Any other valid point of knowledge.

50. *Candidates can be credited in a number of ways **up to a maximum of 4 marks.***

Candidates must interpret the evidence and make direct comparisons between sources. Candidates are expected to compare content directly on a point-by-point basis. They may compare the details in the sources and/or compare the viewpoints overall.

A **simple comparison** will indicate what points of detail or viewpoint the sources agree or disagree on and **should be awarded 1 mark**. A **developed comparison** of the points of detail or overall viewpoint **should be awarded a second mark**. Candidates may achieve full marks by making four simple comparisons, two developed comparisons (or by any combination of these).

Possible points of comparison may include:

Overall the sources disagree about the relationship between Saladin and the Muslims.

Source C	Source D
Many Muslims were unhappy with Saladin's leadership and were close to leaving his army.	Thousands of Muslims from Syria and Egypt flocked to join Saladin's forces.
Saladin had been out-fought by the Crusaders at Arsuf and the Muslims believed his poor tactics at Jaffa had cost them victory.	At Jaffa Saladin successfully held off an attack led by Richard I and saved the grateful Muslims from defeat.
Saladin also upset the Muslims at Jerusalem by showing mercy to the Crusaders and refusing to kill them.	Saladin was so highly respected by the Muslims that even when he let the Crusaders go free at Jerusalem, not one Muslim complained.

Section 3, Context B, 'Tea and Freedom': the American Revolution, 1774–1783

51. *Candidates can be credited in a number of ways up to a maximum of 4 marks.*

They may take different perspectives on the events and may describe a variety of different aspects of the events. Candidates must make a number of relevant, factual points. These should be key points. These do not have to be in any particular order.

1 mark should be awarded for each accurate relevant key point of knowledge. **A second mark** should be awarded for each point that is developed, up to a maximum of **4 marks**. Candidates may achieve full marks by providing four straightforward points, by making two developed points (or any combination of these).

Possible points of knowledge may include:
1. arguments began at Custom House between colonists and a British sentry over Townshend Acts (taxes)
2. the British soldiers came to the aid of a sentry dealing with an increasingly angry crowd
3. the crowd failed to disperse when ordered to do so
4. shots were fired to disperse crowd
5. five people died
6. seven people were wounded
7. the British officer in charge, Captain Preston, was arrested for manslaughter.

Any other valid point of knowledge.

52. *Candidates can be credited in a number of ways up to a maximum of 6 marks.*

Candidates must make a number of points that make the issue plain or clear, for example by showing connections

between factors or causal relationships between events or ideas. These should be key reasons but there is no need for any evaluation or prioritising of these reasons.

Up to a **maximum of 6 marks** in total, **1 mark** should be awarded for each accurate, relevant reason, and a **second mark** should be awarded for reasons that are developed. Candidates may achieve full marks by providing six straightforward reasons, three developed reasons (or any combination of these).

Possible reasons may include:
1. colonists were angered by the presence of British troops following the defeat of the French in 1763
2. colonists were angered by George III's desire to exert greater control over colonies
3. frustration over Britain's refusal to allow the colonies to expand westward
4. growing anger over continued taxation of colonies without direct representation in the British parliament
5. anger over imposition of British taxes (e.g. Sugar Act, Stamp Act, The Tea Act, Quartering Acts, Intolerable Acts)
6. the Boston Massacre increased tension between Britain and the colonists
7. the Boston Tea Party increased tension between Britain and the colonists
8. formation of the Continental Congress in 1774
9. fighting at Lexington and Concord in April 1775 led to formation of Continental Army under leadership of George Washington in June 1775.

Any other valid reason.

53. *Candidates can be credited in a number of ways up to a maximum of 5 marks.*

Candidates must evaluate the extent to which a source is useful by commenting on evidence such as the author, type of source, purpose, timing, content or omission. For a mark to be awarded, the candidate must identify an aspect of the source **and** make a comment which shows why this aspect makes the source more or less useful.

A maximum of **4 marks** can be awarded for evaluative comments relating to the author, type of source, purpose and timing.

A maximum of **2 marks** may be awarded for evaluative comments relating to the content of the source.

A maximum of **2 marks** may be awarded for evaluative comments relating to points of significant omission.

Examples of aspects of the source and relevant comments:

Aspect		Possible comment(s)
Author	Written by a modern historian	Useful because he is a well-informed expert.
Type of source	Textbook	Useful as it is likely to have been thoroughly researched.
Purpose	To inform	Useful as it provides detailed information about the conflict/less useful as it only informs us about Ticonderoga.
Timing	2005	Useful because it was written with the benefit of hindsight.

Content	Possible comment(s)
The Battle of Fort Ticonderoga gave the colonists a surprising but important victory over the British.	Useful because it is accurate (this was an unexpected victory for the colonists).
The location of the fort was vital as its position protected New York and the New England colonies from British invasion from Canada.	Useful because it is accurate (the location was advantageous to colonists).
The main reason that the colonists wanted the fort was because they would gain control over cannons, munitions and armaments/ these cannons were later moved to Boston.	Useful because it is accurate (the colonists did seize a significant amount of weaponry from the fort).

Possible points of significant omission may include:
1. Green Mountain Boys (local militia group) took over fort for the colonists
2. Battles of Lexington/Concord are considered the start of the conflict
3. Battle of Bunker Hill many British soldiers died causing further escalation of conflict.

Any other valid point of significant omission.

54. *Candidates can be credited in a number of ways **up to a maximum of 6 marks.***

Candidates must make a judgement about the extent to which the source provides a full description or explanation of a given event or development. Up to a **maximum of 6 marks** in total, **1 mark** should be awarded for each valid point selected from the source or each valid point of significant omission provided.

Candidates should be awarded **up to 3 marks** for their identification of points from the source which support their judgement. Candidates should be awarded **up to 4 marks** for their identification of points of significant omission, based on their own knowledge, that support their judgement.

A **maximum of 2 marks** may be awarded for answers in which no judgement has been made **or** which refer only to the source.

Possible points which may be identified from the source include:
1. the British army had around 8,500 men and were vastly outnumbered by the militia they were fighting
2. their uniform made them easy targets
3. it (uniform) was also unsuitable for fighting in North America
4. British troops were not used to guerrilla warfare (fighting enemies whose main tactics were to hide behind walls and trees, open fire then move away)

Possible points of significant omission may include:
5. the British army was drilled to fight in formation
6. soldiers carried smooth-bore muskets that took time to load down the barrel and these guns were not very accurate
7. soldiers also had bayonets for close quarter combat
8. some British officers were ignorant and lazy and made poor military decisions which caused confusion
9. the British underestimated the colonists which led to higher casualties (e.g. Bunker Hill).

Any other valid point of significant omission.

55. *Candidates can be credited in a number of ways **up to a maximum of** 4 marks.*

Candidates must interpret the evidence and make direct comparisons between sources. Candidates are expected to compare content directly on a point-by-point basis. They may compare the details in the sources and/or compare the viewpoints overall.

A **simple comparison** will indicate what points of detail or viewpoint the sources agree or disagree on and **should be awarded 1 mark**. A **developed comparison** of the points of detail or overall viewpoint **should be awarded a second mark**. Candidates may achieve full marks by making four simple comparisons, two developed comparisons (or by any combination of these).

Possible points of comparison may include:

Overall the sources disagree about attitudes towards the Declaration of Independence in 1776.

Source C	Source D
King George III was accused by many colonists of indefensible crimes such as imposing taxes which colonists had not agreed to and damaging their trade.	Many colonists supported King George III's policies, arguing that his taxes were justified.
The worst charge was that he was responsible for an unfair justice system.	The King was most upset by the accusation that he had stopped America from having a just legal system as the British felt it was the fairest available.
The Declaration of Independence was inspirational for all Americans, both black and white.	The Declaration was criticised by many as it made no comment on the large number of slaves in America.

Section 3, Context C, USA, 1850–1880

56. *Candidates can be credited in a number of ways **up to a maximum of 5 marks.***

Candidates must evaluate the extent to which a source is useful by commenting on evidence such as the author, type of source, purpose, timing, content or omission. For a mark to be given, the candidate must identify an aspect of the source and make a comment which shows why this aspect makes the source more or less useful.

A maximum of **4 marks** can be given for evaluative comments relating to the author, type of source, purpose and timing.

A maximum of **2 marks** may be given for evaluative comments relating to the content of the source.

A maximum of **2 marks** may be given for evaluative comments relating to points of significant omission.

Examples of aspects of the source and relevant comments:

Aspect		Possible comment(s)
Author	Modern historians	Useful because they are well-informed experts.
Type of source	Textbook	Useful because it will have researched the issue thoroughly.

Purpose	To inform	Useful because it is a detailed explanation of the reasons for Westward expansion.
Timing	1998	Useful because it has been written with the benefit of hindsight.

Content	Possible comment(s)
Thousands of former soldiers wanted to rebuild their lives.	Useful as it is accurate (many ex-soldiers did go West to rebuild their lives).
Many of the newly freed black slaves were looking for a new life.	Useful as it is accurate (many former slaves did want to leave the South for a new life in the West).
The Homestead Act in 1862 encouraged people to move West/allowed each family to settle on 160 acres of land.	Useful as it is accurate (many settlers did move West because of the promise of free land).

57. *Candidates can be credited in a number of ways up to a maximum of 4 marks.*

They may take different perspectives on the events and may describe a variety of different aspects of the events. Candidates must make a number of relevant, factual points. These should be key points. These do not have to be in any particular order.

1 mark should be given for each accurate relevant key point of knowledge. **A second mark** should be given for each point that is developed, up to a maximum of **4 marks**. Candidates may achieve full marks by providing four straightforward points, by making two developed points (or a combination of these).

Possible points of knowledge may include:
1. very few reliable maps/unreliable routes/poor roads/no bridges
2. harsh and unpredictable weather
3. homesteaders became ill/caught diseases and were unable to receive medical attention
4. cases of accidents/run over by wagon wheels
5. dangers crossing rivers/crossing mountain ranges
6. attacked by animals
7. threat from Native Americans
8. possibility of running out of food/water.

Any other valid point of knowledge.

58. *Candidates can be credited in a number of ways up to a maximum of 6 marks.*

Candidates must make a number of points that make the issue plain or clear, for example by showing connections between factors or causal relationships between events or ideas. These should be key reasons but there is no need for any evaluation or prioritising of these reasons.

Up to a **maximum of 6 marks in total, 1 mark** should be given for each accurate, relevant reason, and a **second mark** should be given for reasons that are developed. Candidates may achieve full marks by providing six straightforward reasons, three developed reasons (or a combination of these).

Possible reasons may include:
1. people supported the Republicans because they appeared to be the anti-slavery party

2. people supported the Republicans because they advocated the return to high protective tariffs
3. people supported the Republicans because they wished to give free grants of land to Western settlers
4. people supported the Republicans because they appeared to be the party of big business and the North was developing in this way
5. people supported the Republicans because they were successful at securing majorities in the Senate so could implement their policies
6. people supported the Republicans because Lincoln was an able leader
7. European immigrants supported the Republicans because they opposed slavery/tended to settle in the northern cities
8. split in Democrats along North/South lines drove some northern Democrats to the Republicans.

Any other valid reason.

59. *Candidates can be credited in a number of ways up to a maximum of 6 marks.*

Candidates must make a judgement about the extent to which the source provides a full description or explanation of a given event or development.

Up to a **maximum of 6 marks in total, 1 mark** should be given for each valid point selected from the source or each valid point of significant omission provided.

Candidates should be given **up to 3 marks** for their identification of points from the source that support their judgement. Candidates should be given **up to 4 marks** for their identification of points of significant omission, based on their own knowledge, that support their judgement.

A **maximum of 2 marks** may be given for answers in which no judgement has been made or which refer only to the source.

Possible points which may be identified from the source include:
1. they gave newly freed slaves the right to own and inherit property
2. former slaves also had the right to legal protection
3. the Black Codes tried to prevent them from using their right to vote in elections
4. Black Codes banned newly freed slaves from certain jobs/made sure that they could only earn very low wages

Possible points of significant omission may include:
5. ex-slaves could not run their own business
6. ex-slaves were not allowed to bear arms
7. ex-slaves were allowed to marry in some states
8. ex-slaves were forced to be tried in separate courts
8. ex-slaves were not allowed to strike or leave their jobs
10. ex-slaves could not testify in court against whites.

Any other valid point of significant omission.

60. *Candidates can be credited in a number of ways up to a maximum of 4 marks.*

Candidates must interpret the evidence and make direct comparisons between sources. Candidates are expected to compare content directly on a point-by-point basis. They may compare the details in the sources and/or compare the viewpoints overall.

A **simple comparison** will indicate what points of detail or viewpoint the sources agree or disagree on and **should be awarded 1 mark**. A **developed comparison** of the points of detail or overall viewpoint **should be awarded a second** mark. Candidates may achieve full marks by making four simple comparisons, two developed comparisons (or by any combination of these).

Possible points of comparison may include:

Overall both sources disagree about the reaction of Native Americans to their treatment by the US Government.

Source C	Source D
We cannot accept being forced to live on land which is not suitable to our needs.	Most accepted the change from being hunters to farmers/The only option for us was life on a reservation which had some advantages.
There is no climate or soil which is equal to our previous home.	We were given adequate amounts of land on which to grow crops.
Our people are decreasing in numbers here, and will continue to decrease unless they are allowed to return to their native land.	Food rations were sufficient and the Native American population increased.

Section 3, Context D, Hitler and Nazi Germany, 1919–139

61. *Candidates can be credited in a number of ways **up to a maximum of 4 marks.***

They may take different perspectives on the events and may describe a variety of different aspects of the events. Candidates must make a number of relevant, factual points. These should be key points. These do not have to be in any particular order.

1 mark should be given for each accurate relevant key point of knowledge. **A second mark** should be given for each point that is developed, up to a maximum of **4 marks**. Candidates may achieve full marks by providing four straightforward points, by making two developed points (or a combination of these).

Possible points of knowledge may include:
1. (on the night of 8 November 1923) Hitler and 600 supporters burst into a political meeting at the local Beer Hall
2. Hitler stood on a chair and fired a shot in the air and announced a revolution had begun/made an impassioned speech and gained support of those in hall
3. Hitler forced the Bavarian leaders present to agree to rebel
4. Ludendorff then let them go home and they ordered the army/police to end the rebellion
5. the next day (9 November 1923) Hitler and his Nazis went into Munich on what they thought would be a triumphal march to take power
6. police and army reinforcements blocked the path of the rebels
7. 16 Nazis and 4 policemen were killed in an exchange of gunfire
8. Hitler was injured and fled/was arrested two days later.

Any other valid point of knowledge.

62. *Candidates can be credited in a number of ways **up to a maximum of 6 marks.***

Candidates must make a number of points that make the issue plain or clear, for example by showing connections between factors or causal relationships between events or

ideas. These should be key reasons but there is no need for any evaluation or prioritising of these reasons.

Up to a **maximum of 6 marks in total**, **1 mark** should be given for each accurate, relevant reason, and a **second mark** should be given for reasons that are developed. Candidates may achieve full marks by providing six straightforward reasons, three developed reasons (or a combination of these).

Possible reasons may include:
1. Versailles was very unpopular in Germany and Hitler's promise to ignore/tear it up got him a lot of support
2. Germans were disgusted by a series of weak, short-lived coalitions so they supported Hitler who seemed a strong and determined leader
3. opponents of the Nazis were not united so there was no one who was prepared or able to fight to stop Hitler
4. Hitler's promises to end unemployment were very popular
5. people wanted someone to blame, and looked to extreme solutions – Hitler offered them both, and Nazi success in the elections grew
6. the financial support of wealthy businessmen gave Hitler the money to run his propaganda and election campaigns
7. Nazi propaganda persuaded the German masses to believe that Hitler was their last hope
8. Hitler promised everybody something, so the Nazis had widespread appeal
9. parades of uniformed SA/Brownshirts impressed Germans/led to many young men joining the Nazis
10. Hitler was a brilliant speaker/he was a good organiser and politician (his self-belief persuaded people to believe in him)
11. failure of Weimar to deal with economic problems (e.g. hyperinflation/Great Depression) helped to create support for the Nazis.

Any other valid reason.

63. *Candidates can be credited in a number of ways **up to a maximum of 5 marks.***

Candidates must evaluate the extent to which a source is useful by commenting on evidence such as the author, type of source, purpose, timing, content or omission. For a mark to be given, the candidate must identify an aspect of the source and make a comment which shows why this aspect makes the source more or less useful.

A maximum of **4 marks** can be given for evaluative comments relating to the author, type of source, purpose and timing. A maximum of **2 marks** may be given for evaluative comments relating to the content of the source. A maximum of **2 marks** may be given for evaluative comments relating to points of significant omission.

Examples of aspects of the source and relevant comments:

Aspect		Possible comment(s)
Author	Historians	Useful as they are well-informed experts.
Type of source	Textbook	Useful because it will have researched the issue thoroughly.
Purpose	To inform	Useful as it provides detailed information/less useful as it only refers to Kristallnacht.
Timing	2000	Useful as it is a written with the benefit of hindsight.

Content	Possible comment(s)
attacks on Jewish shops, homes and synagogues	Useful as it is accurate (many Jewish shops and businesses were destroyed or looted).
100 Jews were murdered	Useful as it is accurate (many Jews were killed).
20,000 sent to concentration camps	Useful as it is accurate (many Jews were sent to camps).

Possible points of significant omission may include:
1. Jews were forced out of jobs (e.g. civil service)/ boycotts of Jewish shops
2. the Nuremburg Laws were passed in 1935 (e.g. Jews no longer allowed to be German citizens/Jews not allowed to have sexual relationships with non-Jews/Jews not allowed to marry non-Jews)
3. Jews beaten up on streets/separate park benches for Jews
4. Jews banned from state schools/cinemas/public places.

Any other valid point of significant omission.

64. *Candidates can be credited in a number of ways **up to a maximum of 6 marks.***

Candidates must make a judgement about the extent to which the source provides a full description or explanation of a given event or development.

Up to a **maximum of 6 marks in total, 1 mark** should be given for each valid point selected from the source or each valid point of significant omission provided.

Candidates should be given **up to 3 marks** for their identification of points from the source that support their judgement. Candidates should be given **up to 4 marks** for their identification of points of significant omission, based on their own knowledge, that support their judgement.

A **maximum of 2 marks** may be given for answers in which no judgement has been made or which refer only to the source.

Possible points which may be identified from the source include:
1. some workers protested by refusing to give Nazi salutes
2. others rebelled by not turning up for work at all
3. some even damaged factory machinery or equipment
4. one worker planted a bomb in a Munich beer hall where Hitler was scheduled to speak

Possible points of significant omission may include:
5. anti-Nazi activity among some urban youth groups (e.g. 'Edelweiss Pirates' who sang insulting parodies of Hitler Youth anthems and sometimes beat up members/ the Pirates also engaged in petty resistance, such as vandalism of Nazi propaganda or buildings)
6. university halls and campuses were notable sources of anti-government criticism and protest
7. Christian churches (both Catholic and Protestant) opposed the imposition of Nazi ideology on German life (e.g. **the Confessional Church** was formed by **Martin Niemöller** in 1934 with 6,000 ministers)
8. some in the military despised Hitler and there were occasional plots and discussions about removing him from power
9. many SPD members went 'underground', forming a resistance group called *Roter Strosstrupp* ('Red Strike Troops')/by late 1933 this group had around 3,000 members

10. following the Reichstag fire (more than 30,000) KPD members continued with underground resistance.

Any other valid point of significant omission.

65. *Candidates can be credited in a number of ways **up to a maximum of 4 marks.***

Candidates must interpret the evidence and make direct comparisons between sources. Candidates are expected to compare content directly on a point-by-point basis. They may compare the details in the sources and/or compare the viewpoints overall.

A **simple comparison** will indicate what points of detail or viewpoint the sources agree or disagree on and **should be awarded 1 mark**. A **developed comparison** of the points of detail or overall viewpoint **should be awarded a second mark.** Candidates may achieve full marks by making four simple comparisons, two developed comparisons (or by any combination of these).

Possible points of comparison may include:

Overall the sources disagree about attitudes towards youth organisations for girls in Nazi Germany.

Source C	Source D
For girls, the organisation prepared them for motherhood which most accepted.	Girls (aged 10-14 years) joined the Young Maidens where they were taught how to become good mothers but many resented this.
Girls had to run 60 metres in 14, seconds/throw a ball 12 metres/know how to somersault and they enjoyed the competitiveness.	Compulsory route marches and swimming contests were disliked by many girls.
When they turned 14, they had lessons on sewing and cooking which most found very useful.	There were also classes on needlework and housework which many considered unnecessary.

Section 3, Context E, Red Flag: Lenin and the Russian Revolution, 1894–1921

66. *Candidates can be credited in a number of ways **up to a maximum of 4 marks.***

They may take different perspectives on the events and may describe a variety of different aspects of the events. Candidates must make a number of relevant, factual points. These should be key points. These do not have to be in any particular order.

1 mark should be given for each accurate relevant key point of knowledge. **A second mark** should be given for each point that is developed, up to a maximum of **4 marks.** Candidates may achieve full marks by providing four straightforward points, by making two developed points (or a combination of these).

Possible points of knowledge may include:
1. Tsar was an autocrat/nobody was able to challenge his position
2. the Okhrana (Secret Police) was used to identify and spy on enemies of the state
3. political opponents routinely imprisoned/exiled (e.g. to Siberia)
4. the army was used as an effective means of enforcing the Tsar's power

5. the Russian Orthodox Church reinforced the Tsar's authority
6. the Russian legal system was designed to maintain autocracy and the power of the Tsar
7. the Civil Service was used by the Tsar to control everyday life (e.g. censorship)
8. Russification used to control non-Russian peoples.

Any other valid point of knowledge.

67. *Candidates can be credited in a number of ways **up to a maximum of 6 marks.***

Candidates must make a judgement about the extent to which the source provides a full description or explanation of a given event or development.

Up to a **maximum of 6 marks in total, 1 mark** should be given for each valid point selected from the source or each valid point of significant omission provided.

Candidates should be given **up to 3 marks** for their identification of points from the source that support their judgement. Candidates should be given **up to 4 marks** for their identification of points of significant omission, based on their own knowledge, that support their judgement.

A **maximum of 2 marks** may be given for answers in which no judgement has been made or which refer only to the source.

Possible points which may be identified from the source include:
1. in January, a wave of strikes began throughout the country involving 400,000 people
2. the Tsar's uncle was assassinated in February
3. protestors took to the streets (demanding freedom of speech, an elected parliament and the right to form political parties)
4. national minorities who were opposed to the Tsarist regime also rose up to demand political and economic reforms

Possible points of significant omission may include:
5. Father Gapon organised a peaceful protest to deliver a petition to the Tsar
6. march on Winter Palace leading to Bloody Sunday
7. in October, a General Strike took place in Moscow and quickly spread to other cities
8. railway strike in October led to a halt of the transport system upon which food distribution depended
9. some naval mutinies (e.g. Battleship Potemkin)
10. large scale peasant riots throughout October/November in many parts of the country/land seizure by peasants of what they saw as their land.

Any other valid point of significant omission.

68. *Candidates can be credited in a number of ways **up to a maximum of 6 marks.***

Candidates must make a number of points that make the issue plain or clear, for example by showing connections between factors or causal relationships between events or ideas. These should be key reasons but there is no need for any evaluation or prioritising of these reasons.

Up to a **maximum of 6 marks in total**, **1 mark** should be given for each accurate, relevant reason, and a **second mark** should be given for reasons that are developed. Candidates may achieve full marks by providing six straightforward reasons, three developed reasons (or a combination of these).

Possible reasons may include:
1. working class discontent over poor living/working conditions/ shortages led to them wanting a change
2. the Tsar was blamed for the military defeats of the First World War after he took control of the army/by February 1917 he had lost the confidence of the Russian people as they wanted change
3. people had expected the First World War to be over long before 1917/people were war weary and believed the Tsar would not agree to a cessation of fighting so they looked for change
4. Russian peasants were still aggrieved due to the land issue/strain of the First World War hit the peasantry and they wanted change
5. severe economic problems such as high taxes/inflation and price rises led to a general demand for change
6. the Tsar was seen as a weak ruler who relied on the Tsarina/Rasputin and a close group of ministers which people grew to dislike and demanded change
7. the Tsarina was viewed with suspicion due to her German heritage and so people did not trust her
8. discontent at lack of political power by growing middle class/dislike of privileged status e.g. nobility, church.

Any other valid reason.

69. *Candidates can be credited in a number of ways **up to a maximum of 5 marks.***

Candidates must evaluate the extent to which a source is useful by commenting on evidence such as the author, type of source, purpose, timing, content or omission. For a mark to be given, the candidate must identify an aspect of the source and make a comment which shows why this aspect makes the source more or less useful.

A maximum of **4 marks** can be given for evaluative comments relating to the author, type of source, purpose and timing. A maximum of **2 marks** may be given for evaluative comments relating to the content of the source. A maximum of **2 marks** may be given for evaluative comments relating to points of significant omission.

Examples of aspects of the source and relevant comments:

Aspect		Possible comment(s)
Author	Modern historian	Useful as he is a well-informed expert.
Type of source	Textbook	Useful because it will have researched the issue thoroughly.
Purpose	To inform	Useful as it is a detailed explanation of the reasons for the failure of the Provisional Government.
Timing	1963	Useful as the author has the benefit of hindsight.

Content	Possible comment(s)
They did not overcome the difficulties facing Russia.	Useful as it is accurate (the Provisional Government was not successful at solving the key problems Russia faced).
The Provisional Government also continued the war, even though the Russian people were completely against it and the army became much less willing to fight.	Useful as it is accurate (Provisional Government failed to end the war which increased criticism).

The Provisional Government failed to solve the issue of land settlements which also angered the peasants.	Useful as it is accurate (the Provisional Government made no definitive land settlement).

70. *Candidates can be credited in a number of ways up to a maximum of 4 marks.*

Candidates must interpret the evidence and make direct comparisons between sources. Candidates are expected to compare content directly on a point-by-point basis. They may compare the details in the sources and/or compare the viewpoints overall.

A **simple comparison** will indicate what points of detail or viewpoint the sources agree or disagree on and **should be awarded 1 mark.** A **developed comparison** of the points of detail or overall viewpoint **should be awarded a second mark.** Candidates may achieve full marks by making four simple comparisons, two developed comparisons (or by any combination of these).

Possible points of comparison may include:

Overall the sources disagree about the effects that the Civil War had on Russian peasants.

Source C	Source D
My troops entered the village and put all the Bolshevik traitors to death, this was the usual punishment.	They looked on the death penalty as an emergency measure, which was only used when absolutely necessary.
Then the rest of the population was ordered to deliver, without payment, all of their grain.	The Whites adopted a policy of grain requisitioning, sending soldiers, usually armed, to get a share of the grain out of peasants' barns.
We left them with their cattle and horses.	They also took farm animals and horses to help them win the war.

Section 3, Context F, Mussolini and Fascist Italy, 1919–1939

71. *Candidates can be credited in a number of ways up to a maximum of 5 marks.*

Candidates must evaluate the extent to which a source is useful by commenting on evidence such as the author, type of source, purpose, timing, content or omission. For a mark to be given, the candidate must identify an aspect of the source and make a comment which shows why this aspect makes the source more or less useful.

A maximum of **4 marks** can be given for evaluative comments relating to the author, type of source, purpose and timing. A maximum of **2 marks** may be given for evaluative comments relating to the content of the source. A maximum of **2 marks** may be given for evaluative comments relating to points of significant omission.

Examples of aspects of the source and relevant comments:

Aspect		Possible comment(s)
Author	Modern historians	Useful as they are well-informed experts.
Type of source	Textbook	Useful because it will have researched the issue thoroughly.

Purpose	To inform	Useful as it provides detailed information.
Timing	1998	Useful as it is written with the benefit of hindsight.

Content	Possible comment(s)
They appealed to many small landowners who had been harmed by Socialist local government and were worried about a Socialist revolution.	Useful as it is accurate (the Fascists did exploit the fear of Socialism).
Young people were attracted to Fascism as it seemed to offer the prospect of adventure and action.	Useful as it is accurate (Fascism did have dynamic appeal for the young).
The Fascists also gained working class support as they kept some of their original radical social policies such as fair wages and prices.	Useful as it is accurate (the Fascists did appeal to the workers).

Possible points of significant omission may include:
1. many were attracted by Mussolini's oratory
2. Fascism presented itself as a patriotic movement and so appealed to nationalists
3. Fascism appealed to ex-soldiers by promising recognition of their service
4. the promise of an eight-hour day appealed to many.

Any other valid point of significant omission.

72. *Candidates can be credited in a number of ways up to a maximum of 4 marks.*

They may take different perspectives on the events and may describe a variety of different aspects of the events. Candidates must make a number of relevant, factual points. These should be key points. These do not have to be in any particular order.

1 mark should be given for each accurate relevant key point of knowledge. **A second mark** should be given for each point that is developed, up to a maximum of **4 marks**. Candidates may achieve full marks by providing four straightforward points, by making two developed points (or a combination of these).

Possible points of knowledge may include:
1. control of newspapers
2. control of radio
3. use of mass rallies
4. display of posters
5. use of sport to promote Fascist ideals
6. L'Unione Cinematografica Eductavia produced documentaries and newsreels to be shown at cinemas
7. subsidies provided to Italian film makers who made patriotic films
8. schools used to indoctrinate pupils with Fascist ideals.

Any other valid point of knowledge.

73. *Candidates can be credited in a number of ways up to a maximum of 6 marks.*

Candidates must make a judgement about the extent to which the source provides a full description or explanation of a given event or development.

Up to a **maximum of 6 marks in total, 1 mark** should be given for each valid point selected from the source or each valid point of significant omission provided.

Candidates should be given **up to 3 marks** for their identification of points from the source that support their judgement. Candidates should be given **up to 4 marks** for their identification of points of significant omission, based on their own knowledge, that support their judgement.

A **maximum of 2 marks** may be given for answers in which no judgement has been **made or which refer only to the source.**

Possible points which may be identified from the source include:
1. young people learned horse riding skills
2. many youngsters went skiing in the Italian Alps
3. every member had to swear a personal oath of loyalty to Mussolini
4. most towns had rallies on a Saturday afternoon between 3.30 and 6.00 pm.

Possible points of significant omission may include:
5. military drill
6. attending propaganda lectures
7. singing Fascist hymns/songs
8. watching propaganda films
9. taking part in parades
10. girls did sewing, flower arranging and gardening.

Any other valid point of significant omission.

74. *Candidates can be credited in a number of ways **up to a maximum of 6 marks.***

Candidates must make a number of points that make the issue plain or clear, for example by showing connections between factors or causal relationships between events or ideas. These should be key reasons but there is no need for any evaluation or prioritising of these reasons.

Up to a **maximum of 6 marks in total**, **1 mark** should be given for each accurate, relevant reason, and a **second mark** should be given for reasons that are developed. Candidates may achieve full marks by providing six straightforward reasons, three developed reasons (or a combination of these).

Possible reasons may include:
1. to avenge the defeat at Adowa in 1896
2. to consolidate Italy's position in East Africa (where they had had a presence since the 1880s)
3. to increase Italian prestige/to show that Italy was capable of acting as an imperial power like Britain and France
4. a successful war abroad could rally support at home
5. to put Italy in a position to exploit Abyssinian resources
6. to develop export markets for Italian businesses
7. to demonstrate to Hitler that Italy was a powerful nation (and therefore a valuable ally)
8. Mussolini believed that Britain and France would not act to stop him.

Any other valid reason.

75. *Candidates can be credited in a number of ways **up to a maximum of 4 marks.***

Candidates must interpret the evidence and make direct comparisons between sources. Candidates are expected to compare content directly on a point-by-point basis. They may compare the details in the sources and/or compare the viewpoints overall.

A **simple comparison** will indicate what points of detail or viewpoint the sources agree or disagree on and **should be awarded 1 mark**. A **developed comparison** of the points of detail or overall viewpoint **should be awarded a second**

mark. Candidates may achieve full marks by making four simple comparisons, two developed comparisons (or by any combination of these).

Possible points of comparison may include:

Overall the sources disagree on opposition to the Fascist regime.

Source C	Source D
Opposition to the Fascist government in Italy was quite effective.	There was opposition to the Fascists, but it never posed a threat to the regime.
the regime was not popular amongst large numbers of people.	most supported Mussolini's foreign and economic policies.
The opposition groups were only occasionally infiltrated by the police and their informers.	When opposition groups did appear they were unable to operate without interference from the police.

Section 3, Context G, Free at Last? Civil Rights in the USA, 1918–1968

76. *Candidates can be credited in a number of ways **up to a maximum of 4 marks.***

They may take different perspectives on the events and may describe a variety of different aspects of the events. Candidates must make a number of relevant, factual points. These should be key points. These do not have to be in any particular order.

1 mark should be given for each accurate relevant key point of knowledge. **A second mark** should be given for each point that is developed, up to a maximum of **4 marks**. Candidates may achieve full marks by providing four straightforward points, by making two developed points (or a combination of these).

Possible points of knowledge may include:
1. on first arrival to America, immigrants were taken to Ellis Island where they faced a physical examination and possible return
2. immigrants found it difficult to find accommodation/ often had to pay high rent
3. overcrowded housing/some large families sometimes with 10 or 12 people had only one room to live in
4. housing which lacked adequate heating/cold and damp housing/ housing without sanitation/running water
5. many immigrants were poorly educated/non-English speaking and struggled to find work
6. many immigrants found that the only work that was available to them was unskilled and low paid
7. many immigrants faced prejudice and discrimination from the American public (e.g. ethnicity, religious tensions, political views)
8. immigrants were often viewed as criminals.

Any other valid point of knowledge.

77. *Candidates can be credited in a number of ways **up to a maximum of 5 marks.***

Candidates must evaluate the extent to which a source is useful by commenting on evidence such as the author, type of source, purpose, timing, content or omission. For a mark to be given, the candidate must identify an aspect of the source and make a comment which shows why this aspect makes the source more or less useful.

A maximum of **4 marks** can be given for evaluative comments relating to the author, type of source, purpose and timing. A maximum of **2 marks** may be given for evaluative comments relating to the content of the source. A maximum of **2 marks** may be given for evaluative comments relating to points of significant omission.

Examples of aspects of the source and relevant comments:

Aspect		Possible comment(s)
Author	Modern historians	Useful because they are well-informed experts.
Type of source	Textbook	Useful because it will have researched the issue thoroughly.
Purpose	To inform	Useful because it provides detailed information.
Timing	2013	Useful as it is written with the benefit of hindsight.

Content	Possible comment(s)
Black children were forbidden to attend school with white children.	Useful as it is accurate (education was segregated).
At work, black Americans collected their pay separately from whites.	Useful as it is accurate (employment was segregated).
There were also strict bans on whites and blacks marrying.	Useful as it is accurate (marriage between black and white Americans was forbidden).

Possible points of significant omission may include:
1. separate train carriages/separate seating on buses
2. separate restaurants/separate seating areas in restaurants
3. separate leisure and sporting facilities
4. separate toilets, drinking fountains and restrooms.

Any other valid point of significant omission.

78. *Candidates can be credited in a number of ways up to a maximum of 6 marks.*

Candidates must make a number of points that make the issue plain or clear, for example by showing connections between factors or causal relationships between events or ideas. These should be key reasons but there is no need for any evaluation or prioritising of these reasons.

Up to a **maximum of 6 marks in total**, **1 mark** should be given for each accurate, relevant reason, and a **second mark** should be given for reasons that are developed. Candidates may achieve full marks by providing six straightforward reasons, three developed reasons (or a combination of these).

Possible reasons may include:
1. many white Americans supported the protestors
2. restaurants and cafés across America could not afford the bad publicity and loss of business/by the summer of 1960 there were almost no more segregated lunch counters in the South
3. the success of the sit-ins proved that blacks had economic power and could use it to end segregation
4. sit-ins attracted a great amount of media attention and sympathy for the civil rights movement/night after night TV viewers across America saw peaceful students being mistreated

5. the sit-ins led to the formation of the Students Non-Violent Co-ordinating Committee (SNCC) which provided student volunteers for marches and other protests
6. the use of the sit-in tactic spread to protest against other forms of racial segregation (e.g. wade-ins at segregated swimming pools/pray-ins at segregated churches)
7. sit-ins gave other black Americans (e.g. students/young people) the confidence and determination to campaign for civil rights.

Any other valid reason.

79. *Candidates can be credited in a number of ways up to a maximum of 6 marks.*

Candidates must make a judgement about the extent to which the source provides a full description or explanation of a given event or development.

Up to a **maximum of 6 marks in total**, **1 mark** should be given for each valid point selected from the source or each valid point of significant omission provided.

Candidates should be given **up to 3 marks** for their identification of points from the source that support their judgement. Candidates should be given **up to 4 marks** for their identification of points of significant omission, based on their own knowledge, that support their judgement.

A **maximum of 2 marks** may be given for answers in which no judgement has been made or which refer only to the source.

Possible points which may be identified in the source include:
1. Martin Luther King led a protest march through Birmingham (against the discrimination and inequality faced by black Americans in the city)
2. the march was led by children/with over 30,000 demonstrators taking part
3. Chief of Police, Bull Connor, ordered the arrest of protestors (many children aged 6 to 18 were jailed)
4. on the following day water cannons were used to disperse the marchers

Possible points of significant omission may include:
5. many protestors were beaten/injured by police (many of them were children)
6. dogs were also used by the police to attack the protestors
7. on the third day, the firemen refused to turn on their hoses/many of the police refused orders to attack the marchers
8. the march continued into a fourth day
9. the businessmen of Birmingham, worried about the impact on trade, offered to desegregate restrooms, lunch counters and drinking fountains within 90 days
10. the Ku Klux Klan was furious at the offer from the businessmen and firebombed black churches, houses and businesses.

Any other valid point of significant omission.

80. *Candidates can be credited in a number of ways up to a maximum of 4 marks.*

Candidates must interpret the evidence and make direct comparisons between sources. Candidates are expected to compare content directly on a point-by-point basis. They may compare the details in the sources and/or compare the viewpoints overall.

A **simple comparison** will indicate what points of detail or viewpoint the sources agree or disagree on and **should be awarded 1 mark**. A **developed comparison** of the points of detail or overall viewpoint **should be awarded a second mark.** Candidates may achieve full marks by making four simple comparisons, two developed comparisons (or by any combination of these).

Possible points of comparison may include:

Overall the sources disagree about the beliefs of Malcolm X.

Source C	Source D
Malcolm was a racist who hated white Americans (in much the same way that members of the KKK hated black Americans).	Malcolm didn't hate white Americans, he just distrusted them (not because of their skin colour but because of the way they treated his people).
His answer to the discrimination faced by black Americans was to call for segregation of the races (to separate black Americans from the 'white enemy').	Malcolm X never once argued for segregation of white Americans from black Americans.
In promoting 'Black is Beautiful', Malcolm argued that black Americans were a superior people to other races.	Malcolm never believed that black people were superior to anyone else.

Section 3, Context H, Appeasement and the Road to War, 1918–1939

81. *Candidates can be credited in a number of ways **up to a maximum of 6 marks.***

Candidates must make a number of points that make the issue plain or clear, for example by showing connections between factors or causal relationships between events or ideas. These should be key reasons but there is no need for any evaluation or prioritising of these reasons.

Up to a **maximum of 6 marks in total, 1 mark** should be given for each accurate, relevant reason, and a **second mark** should be given for reasons that are developed. Candidates may achieve full marks by providing six straightforward reasons, three developed reasons (or a combination of these).

Possible reasons may include:
1. Germans were angered at having no say in the terms of the Treaty, calling it a 'DIKTAT' or dictated peace
2. Germans felt that Germany was unjustly blamed for starting the war (War Guilt Clause)
3. Germans resented having to pay reparations
4. anger towards the Treaty was further heightened by the economic difficulties Germany faced in the 1920s (hyperinflation)
5. Germans were angered that land lost in the Treaty led to Germans living under foreign rule
6. the loss of German colonies was felt to be unfair
7. resentment towards the Treaty was further heightened as the territorial terms were not based on Wilson's 14 points/self-determination
8. Germans believed that the reduction in the armed forces left their country vulnerable to attack by foreign nations.

Any other valid reason.

82. *Candidates can be credited in a number of ways **up to a maximum of 6 marks.***

Candidates must make a judgement about the extent to which the source provides a full description or explanation of a given event or development.

Up to a **maximum of 6 marks in total, 1 mark** should be given for each valid point selected from the source or each valid point of significant omission provided.

Candidates should be given **up to 3 marks** for their identification of points from the source that support their judgement. Candidates should be given **up to 4 marks** for their identification of points of significant omission, based on their own knowledge, that support their judgement.

A **maximum of 2 marks** may be given for answers in which no judgement has been made or which refer only to the source.

Possible points which may be identified from the source include:
1. the League improved health by starting a global campaign to exterminate mosquitoes and the spread of malaria
2. when Czechoslovakia and Poland fought over Teschen, the League resolved the conflict by splitting the area between the two countries
3. in 1921 it held a vote to settle a disagreement between Germany and Poland over control of Silesia
4. when Greece invaded Bulgaria in 1925, the League successfully ordered Greece to withdraw.

Possible points of significant omission may include:
5. the League helped prisoners of war return to their homes in the years following the end of the First World War
6. the League settled a dispute between Sweden and Finland over the Aaland Islands in 1921 (e.g. after an investigation it decided that the islands should belong to Finland)
7. the League fought worldwide slavery (e.g. slave trade in Africa and Burma, freed 200,000 slaves)
8. the League assisted refugees (e.g. set up camps, provided food, built farms and homes)
9. the League of Nations tackled the illegal drugs trade (e.g. blacklisting large German, Dutch, French and Swiss companies which were involved in the sale of illegal drugs)
10. the League worked to prevent the spread of leprosy.

Any other valid point of significant omission.

83. *Candidates can be credited in a number of ways **up to a maximum of 4 marks.***

They may take different perspectives on the events and may describe a variety of different aspects of the events. Candidates must make a number of relevant, factual points. These should be key points. These do not have to be in any particular order.

1 mark should be given for each accurate relevant key point of knowledge. A second mark should be given for each point that is developed, up to a maximum of **4 marks.** Candidates may achieve full marks by providing four straightforward points, by making two developed points (or a combination of these).

Possible points of knowledge may include:
1. Hitler introduced conscription to the German army (e.g. by the end of 1935 the German army totalled over 500,000 men)
2. Hitler ordered industry to begin the production of tanks
3. Hitler had built up an air force by the end of 1934
4. the Anglo-German Naval agreement was signed giving Germany permission to build up its navy/to a level that was 35% of Britain's naval strength
5. in March 1936, Hitler sent 20,000 German troops to reoccupy the demilitarised zone of the Rhineland

6. in March 1938, Hitler ordered German troops to march across the border with Austria
7. under threat of a German invasion of Czechoslovakia, Britain, France and Italy signed the Munich agreement in September 1938 giving Germany permission to annexe the Sudetenland.

Any other valid point of knowledge.

84. *Candidates can be credited in a number of ways* **up to a maximum of 5 marks.**

Candidates must evaluate the extent to which a source is useful by commenting on evidence such as the author, type of source, purpose, timing, content or omission. For a mark to be given, the candidate must identify an aspect of the source and make a comment which shows why this aspect makes the source more or less useful.

A maximum of **4 marks** can be given for evaluative comments relating to the author, type of source, purpose and timing. A maximum of **2 marks** may be given for evaluative comments relating to the content of the source. A maximum of **2 marks** may be given for evaluative comments relating to points of significant omission.

Examples of aspects of the source and relevant comments:

Aspect		Possible comment(s)
Author	Modern historians	Useful because they are well-informed experts.
Type of source	Textbook	Useful because it will have researched the issue thoroughly.
Purpose	To inform	Useful because it provides detailed information.
Timing	2006	Useful as it is written with the benefit of hindsight.

Content	Possible comment(s)
This policy can be traced back to the way Germany was treated at Versailles, with many in Britain later regretting how harsh the Treaty had been.	Useful as it is accurate (many British people felt that Hitler was merely righting the wrongs of the unjust Treaty of Versailles).
After the horrors of the Great War, public opinion influenced British governments more than ever before because people longed for peace.	Useful as it is accurate (there was a growing pacifist feeling amongst the British public).
the British economy was depressed throughout the 1930s and appeasement was an attractive way of avoiding expensive conflict.	Useful as it is accurate (the British economy faced difficulties in the interwar period).

Possible points of significant omission may include:
1. Britain lacked allies (e.g. Empire countries unwilling, USA isolationist and France not trusted)
2. Germany had rearmed with a powerful army, navy and air force so Britain felt too weak to challenge
3. there was fear of war due to the likely destruction caused by bombing from the air
4. by appeasing Hitler Britain bought itself time to rearm and strengthen the military.

Any other valid point of significant omission.

85. *Candidates can be credited in a number of ways* **up to a maximum of 4 marks.**

Candidates must interpret the evidence and make direct comparisons between sources. Candidates are expected to compare content directly on a point-by-point basis. They may compare the details in the sources and/or compare the viewpoints overall.

A **simple comparison** will indicate what points of detail or viewpoint the sources agree or disagree on and **should be awarded 1 mark**. A **developed comparison** of the points of detail or overall viewpoint **should be awarded a second mark**. Candidates may achieve full marks by making four simple comparisons, two developed comparisons (or by any combination of these).

Possible points of comparison may include:

Overall both sources disagree about the reaction of Neville Chamberlain to Germany's occupation of Czechoslovakia in March 1939.

Source C	Source D
However, Chamberlain's reaction to the German occupation of Czechoslovakia was weak.	The German occupation of Czechoslovakia marks the moment that Chamberlain finally took strong action against Hitler.
Although Hitler was clearly in breach of the promises he had previously made, Chamberlain would not accuse him of breaking the terms of the Munich Agreement.	Chamberlain made it very clear to Hitler that he believed the promises he had made at Munich had been broken.
Chamberlain never had any intention of fighting Germany at this point and he continued trying to negotiate a peaceful settlement with Hitler.	Chamberlain put Britain on a war footing and was ready and willing to fight with Germany if necessary.

Section 3, Context I, World War II, 1939–1945

86. *Candidates can be credited in a number of ways* **up to a maximum of 6 marks.**

Candidates must make a number of points that make the issue plain or clear, for example by showing connections between factors or causal relationships between events or ideas. These should be key reasons but there is no need for any evaluation or prioritising of these reasons.

Up to a **maximum of 6 marks in total**, **1 mark** should be given for each accurate, relevant reason, and a **second mark** should be given for reasons that are developed. Candidates may achieve full marks by providing six straightforward reasons, three developed reasons (or a combination of these).

Possible reasons may include:
1. two German army groups invaded, from Slovakia in the south and Prussia in the north which meant that the Polish forces were surrounded
2. the German air force attacked and destroyed the Polish air force in the air and on the ground which meant they quickly established air supremacy
3. German bombers attacked road and rail junctions, as well as concentrations of Polish troops which meant Polish counter-attack and communications were compromised
4. towns and villages were bombed to spread terror among civilians and generate a fleeing mass of refugees which

blocked the roads and prevented reinforcements from arriving at the front

5. dive-bombers (Junkers) destroyed any strong points in the German path meaning that counter-attack was almost impossible

6. Anglo-French military aid could not reach Poland in time to help

7. the Soviet Union had signed a non-aggression pact with Germany in August 1939 and helped Germany defeat Poland by seizing a third of all Polish territory by mid-September

8. the Polish army was weaker than the German army (e.g. 30 Polish divisions faced 40 German ones/12 of the Polish divisions were cavalry)

9. the German army was more mechanised (e.g. while the Germans deployed 3,200 tanks, the Polish only had 600).

Any other valid reason.

87. *Candidates can be credited in a number of ways* **up to a maximum of 5 marks.**

Candidates must evaluate the extent to which a source is useful by commenting on evidence such as the author, type of source, purpose, timing, content or omission. For a mark to be given, the candidate must identify an aspect of the source and make a comment which shows why this aspect makes the source more or less useful.

A maximum of 4 marks can be given for evaluative comments relating to the author, type of source, purpose and timing. A maximum of 2 marks may be given for evaluative comments relating to the content of the source. A maximum of 2 marks may be given for evaluative comments relating to points of significant omission.

Examples of aspects of the source and relevant comments:

Aspect		Possible comment(s)
Author	Modern historian	Useful because he is a well-informed expert.
Type of source	Textbook	Useful because it will have been thoroughly researched.
Purpose	To inform	Useful because it provides detailed information.
Timing	2011	Useful because it is written with the benefit of hindsight.

Content	Possible comment(s)
The German plan was to attack through Holland and Belgium, with the main blow against France to be launched a little later through the Ardennes.	Useful because it is accurate (the plan was to attack France through the Ardennes).
Contrary to a generally held belief, the Germans had fewer tanks than the Allies (2,500 against 3,500) at this point.	Useful because it is accurate (the German tanks were fewer in number than the French).
The German tanks were concentrated into Panzer formations but the French tanks were scattered rather than organised into powerful formations like the Germans.	Useful because it is accurate (the German tank formations were stronger than the French).

Possible points of significant omission may include:

1. German troops used Blitzkrieg tactics and unleashed their surprise attack

2. the French had most of their forces on the Maginot Line further south

3. the Germans launched a major offensive on Paris on 9th June/on 13th June Paris was declared an open city

4. the French government fled to Bordeaux/the first German troops entered the French capital on 14th June.

Any other valid point of significant omission.

88. *Candidates can be credited in a number of ways* **up to a maximum of 6 marks.**

Candidates must make a judgement about the extent to which the source provides a full description or explanation of a given event or development. Up to a **maximum of 6 marks in total**, **1 mark** should be given for each valid point selected from the source or each valid point of significant omission provided.

Candidates should be given **up to 3 marks** for their identification of points from the source that support their judgement. Candidates should be given **up to 4 marks** for their identification of points of significant omission, based on their own knowledge, that support their judgement.

A **maximum of 2 marks** may be given for answers in which no judgement has been made or which refer only to the source.

Possible points which may be identified in the source include:

1. 37 bombers from the USS *Enterprise* engaged in a dive-bombing attack on two Japanese aircraft carriers

2. within minutes both ships were on fire due to the explosion of fuel lines and aircraft petrol tanks

3. within six hours the remaining two Japanese carriers had also been destroyed

4. by the time the battle ended, 3,057 Japanese had died

Possible points of significant omission may include:

5. the Americans were able to confirm the target of the Japanese was Midway by intercepting radio communications

6. the American attack was a combined assault, mixing torpedo bombers with dive bombers escorted by fighters

7. earlier the US torpedo bombers flew in at low level but were badly damaged by Japanese Zero fighters/47 out of 51 American torpedo planes were shot down

8. the dive-bombers from the USS *Enterprise* were lost, but found their target by following a Japanese destroyer, which was steaming at high speed to re-join the carriers after driving off an American submarine

9. the Japanese did not have radar, relying instead on the human eye to spot the threat

10. Japanese losses were much greater than the US (the Japanese lost four carriers, a heavy cruiser and 270 aircraft - the US lost one carrier and 130 aircraft).

Any other valid point of significant omission.

89. *Candidates can be credited in a number of ways* **up to a maximum of 4 marks.**

They make take different perspectives on the events and may describe a variety of different aspects of the events. Candidates must make a number of relevant, factual points. These should be key points. These do not have to be in any particular order.

1 mark should be given for each accurate relevant key point of knowledge. **A second mark** should be given for each point that is developed, up to a maximum of **4 marks**. Candidates may achieve full marks by providing four straightforward points, by making two developed points (or a combination of these).

Possible points of knowledge may include:
1. on arrival the inmates were separated (men and women were kept apart, children stayed with their mothers) had their heads shaved and were given a striped uniform
2. every day there was a roll call (sometime the prisoners would have to stand in rows for hours on end in all weathers)
3. before roll call the inmates had to share unsanitary toilet facilities and wash in dirty water with no soap or change of clothes
4. inmates were given meagre rations (e.g. watery soup, a piece of bread and some imitation coffee once a day)
5. depending on the type of camp, prisoners were assigned to a whole range of different duties (e.g. some remained inside the camp working on a variety of jobs, from administration tasks to heavy manual labour)
6. most prisoners worked outside the camps in one of the many factories, construction projects, farms or coal mines (they would quite often have to walk several kilometres to their place of work)
7. punishments for breaking rules were harsh and could result in death
8. sleeping quarters were cramped and overcrowded bunk beds.

Any other valid point of knowledge.

90. *Candidates can be credited in a number of ways up to a maximum of 4 marks.*

Candidates must interpret the evidence and make direct comparisons between sources. Candidates are expected to compare content directly on a point-by-point basis. They may compare the details in the sources and/or compare the viewpoints overall.

A **simple comparison** will indicate what points of detail or viewpoint the sources agree or disagree on and **should be awarded 1 mark**. A **developed comparison** of the points of detail or overall viewpoint **should be awarded a second mark**. Candidates may achieve full marks by making four simple comparisons, two developed comparisons (or by any combination of these).

Possible points of comparison may include:

Overall the sources disagree about the Normandy landings in June 1944.

Source C	Source D
The Normandy landings, which pushed German forces out of north-west Europe, are often remembered as a predominantly American operation.	Despite being led by an American General, D-Day was a huge Allied effort with Britain taking the lead in planning and resourcing it.
The German forces were defeated in northern France due to the better tactical skills of the Allies.	The German forces were not easy to defeat, nevertheless the Allies prevailed due to their superior resources.
However, despite the Allies becoming bogged down in Normandy, they eventually secured one of history's most memorable victories.	The rapid Allied advance through France was faster than the German advance through France four years earlier.

Section 3, Context J, The Cold War, 1945–1989

91. *Candidates can be credited in a number of ways up to a maximum of 6 marks.*

Candidates must make a number of points that make the issue plain or clear, for example by showing connections between factors or causal relationships between events or ideas. These should be key reasons but there is no need for any evaluation or prioritising of these reasons.

Up to a **maximum of 6 marks in total**, **1 mark** should be given for each accurate, relevant reason, and a **second mark** should be given for reasons that are developed. Candidates may achieve full marks by providing six straightforward reasons, three developed reasons (or a combination of these).

Possible reasons may include:
1. to protect Western Europe from a potential Soviet attack
2. to resist the spread of Communism to Western Europe
3. to provide for a system of collective security
4. to strengthen the American military presence in Europe
5. to ensure that smaller member countries would be less vulnerable to Soviet influence or attack (in case the Soviets tried to pick off countries one by one)
6. to make good on the Truman doctrine, which stated that the US would resist the spread of Communism
7. in 1948 Czechoslovakia became Communist and this prompted action as it saw the disappearance of the last democracy in Eastern Europe
8. the Berlin blockade seemed to indicate a new aggressive intent from the Soviets and NATO was established to try and counter this
9. as a US response to British requests to do more to aid the countries of Western Europe
10. the US hoped that NATO would integrate West Germany into the European system and thus reduce the likelihood of future conflict.

Any other valid reason.

92. *Candidates can be credited in a number of ways up to a maximum of 5 marks.*

Candidates must evaluate the extent to which a source is useful by commenting on evidence such as the author, type of source, purpose, timing, content or omission. For a mark to be given, the candidate must identify an aspect of the source and make a comment which shows why this aspect makes the source more or less useful.

A maximum of **4 marks** can be given for evaluative comments relating to the author, type of source, purpose and timing. A maximum of **2 marks** may be given for evaluative comments relating to the content of the source. A maximum of **2 marks** may be given for evaluative comments relating to points of significant omission.

Examples of aspects of the source and relevant comments:

Aspect		Possible comment(s)
Author	Modern historian	Useful as he is a well-informed expert.
Type of source	Textbook	Useful because it will have researched the issue thoroughly.
Purpose	To inform	Useful as it provides detailed information.
Timing	1997	Useful as it is written with the benefit of hindsight.

Content	Possible comment(s)
In 1962 Castro agreed to the placing of 64 nuclear missiles on 9 bases in Cuba.	Useful as it is accurate (Castro did allow several Soviet bases to be set up in Cuba).
In October, 43,000 Soviet servicemen arrived in Cuba, along with hundreds of tanks and anti-aircraft missiles, to operate and defend the bases.	Useful as it is accurate (a considerable number of Soviet military personnel were based in Cuba).
The equipment was unloaded at night, and the servicemen arrived on cruise ships dressed as holidaymakers.	Useful as it is accurate (Soviets did try to disguise their intentions).

Possible points of significant omission may include:

1. an American U2 spy plane took photographs of the missile sites
2. the Americans responded with a naval blockade of Cuba
3. US armed forces moved to DefCon2
4. Krushchev agreed to remove the missiles (if the US did the same in Turkey).

Any other valid point of significant omission.

93. *Candidates can be credited in a number of ways* **up to a maximum of 6 marks.**

Candidates must make a judgement about the extent to which the source provides a full description or explanation of a given event or development.

Up to a **maximum of 6 marks in total, 1 mark** should be given for each valid point selected from the source or each valid point of significant omission provided.

Candidates should be given **up to 3 marks** for their identification of points from the source that support their judgement. Candidates should be given **up to 4 marks** for their identification of points of significant omission, based on their own knowledge, that support their judgement.

A **maximum of 2 marks** may be given for answers in which no judgement has been made or which refer only to the source.

Possible points which may be identified in the source include:

1. the Americans used napalm which caused horrific burns on its victims
2. anti-personnel bombs exploded in mid-air and spewed out thousands of pellets and needles onto the land below
3. helicopters were also used to transport platoons in and out of the jungle very quickly
4. Operation Flaming Dart was a bombing campaign targeting North Vietnamese bases in 1965

Possible points of significant omission may include:

5. Agent Orange was sprayed on crops/jungle
6. search and destroy missions aimed to kill any Vietcong found in villages
7. peasants were forced to leave Vietcong controlled areas and live in strategic hamlets
8. 'Zippo' raids were launched to burn villages
9. Operation Rolling Thunder involved a massive bombing campaign on North Vietnam by B52 Bombers
10. Operation Phoenix saw the CIA kill or capture suspected Vietcong and sympathetic civilians.

Any other valid point of significant omission.

94. *Candidates can be credited in a number of ways* **up to a maximum of 4 marks.**

They may take different perspectives on the events and may describe a variety of different aspects of the events. Candidates must make a number of relevant, factual points. These should be key points. These do not have to be in any particular order.

1 mark should be given for each accurate relevant key point of knowledge. **A second mark** should be given for each point that is developed, up to a maximum of **4 marks.** Candidates may achieve full marks by providing four straightforward points, by making two developed points (or a combination of these).

Possible points of knowledge may include:

1. guerilla warfare (launched surprise attacks before quickly disappearing)
2. use of the Ho Chi Minh trail to supply their armies
3. staying very close to the Americans so they could not use air or artillery backup without killing their own men (**'Hanging onto the belts'** of the Americans)
4. use of booby traps/landmines
5. mingling in with peasants to prevent identification
6. the Tet Offensive was an attack on South Vietnamese cities
7. location of bases in swamps and forests
8. use of tunnels and underground bases.

Any other valid point of knowledge.

95. *Candidates can be credited in a number of ways* **up to a maximum of 4 marks.**

Candidates must interpret the evidence and make direct comparisons between sources. Candidates are expected to compare content directly on a point-by-point basis. They may compare the details in the sources and/or compare the viewpoints overall.

A **simple comparison** will indicate what points of detail or viewpoint the sources agree or disagree on and **should be awarded 1 mark.** A **developed comparison** of the points of detail or overall viewpoint **should be awarded a second mark.** Candidates may achieve full marks by making four simple comparisons, two developed comparisons (or by any combination of these).

Possible points of comparison may include:

Overall the sources disagree on the attitudes towards strategic arms limitation treaties.

Source C	Source D
Both countries believed that these treaties would limit the threat of nuclear destruction.	Many were concerned that agreements such as this would not reduce the threat of nuclear war.
There was a desire in both countries to save money rather than spending it on more weapons.	Nixon and Brezhnev did not care about how much this would cost.
There was a belief that arms reduction could lead to increased cooperation between the two superpowers.	Both countries continued to view each other with suspicion and were reluctant to cooperate on areas such as joint space missions.

Acknowledgements

Permission has been sought from all relevant copyright holders and Hodder Gibson is grateful for the use of the following:

Source A: National Health Service leaflet, May 1948 (INF 2/66, page 15) www.nationalarchives.gov.uk/wp-content/uploads/2014/03/inf-2-66-f151.jpg. Contains public sector information licensed under the Open Government Licence v3.0 (www.nationalarchives.gov.uk/doc/open-government-licence/version/3/) (2017 page 12);
Source B: An extract adapted from 'The Glorious Cause: The American Revolution, 1763–1789', by Robert Middlekauff. Copyright © 1982, 2005 by Oxford University Press, Inc (2017 page 16);
Source A: An extract adapted from 'The Night of the Long Knives' by C.N. Trueman, taken from www.historylearningsite.co.uk/nazi-germany/the-night-of-the-long-knives/ © The History Learning Site, 9 Mar 2015 & 16 Aug 2016 (2017 page 20);
Source B: An extract adapted from 'The Savage Years: Tales From the 20th Century' by Rupert Colley © 2015 Rupert Colley (2017 page 20);
Source C: An extract adapted from 'Nazi Education' by C.N. Trueman, taken from www.historylearningsite.co.uk/nazi-germany/nazi-education/© The History Learning Site, 9 Mar 2015 & 16 Aug 2016 (2017 page 21);
Source A: An extract adapted from 'The Russian Revolution' by Anthony Wood. Published by Routledge. Copyright © 1976, 1986, Taylor & Francis (2017 page 22);
Source D: An extract from 'Lordship to Patronage: Scotland, 1603–1745' (New History of Scotland) by Rosalind Mitchison, published by Edinburgh University Press, 1990 (2017 SQP page 9);
Source B: An extract from 'Empires and Citizens: Pupil's Book 2' by Ben Walsh, published by Nelson Thornes 2004 (2017 SQP page 17);
Source A: An extract from 'Top Causes of the Civil War' by Martin Kelly, ThoughtCo, Sep. 13, 2017 (thoughtco.com/top-causes-of-the-civil-war-104532) (2017 SQP page 28);
Source C: Extract from 'Civil Rights in the USA, 1863–1890' by David Paterson, Susan Willoughby and Doug Willoughby, published by Heinemann Educational Publishers, 2001 © David Paterson, Susan Willoughby and Doug Willoughby. Reproduced by permission of Pearson Education Limited (2017 SQP page 29);
Source C: An extract from 'Europe's Changing Economy in the Second Half of the Nineteenth Century' by Sidney Pollard © Sempringham; www.ehistory.org.uk (2017 SQP page 35);
Source C: An extract from 'Laughter Wasn't Rationed: Remembering the War Years in Germany' by Dorothea (von Schwanenfluegel) Lawson, 1999 © Tricor Press (2017 SQP page 41);
Source A: An extract adapted from 'Scotland: A History, 8000 B.C.–A.D. 2000' by Fiona J. Watson, published by Tempus Publishing Ltd (2018 page 4);
Source A: An extract adapted from 'Germany 1919–45' by Martin Collier & Philip Pedley, published by Heinemann Educational Publishers, 2000 © Martin Collier & Philip Pedley. Reproduced by permission of Pearson Education Limited (2018 page 30);
Source C: An extract adapted from 'Hitler Youth Movement' by C.N. Trueman, taken from www.historylearningsite.co.uk/nazi-germany/hitler-youth-movement/ © The History Learning Site, 9 Mar 2015 (2018 page 31);
Source A: An extract adapted from 'How to Pass National 5 History' by John Kerr and Jerry Teale, published by Hodder Gibson, 2013 (2018 page 36);
Source A: An extract adapted from 'The Fall of France' by Dr Gary Sheffield from www.bbc.co.uk/history/worldwars/wwtwo/fall_france_01.shtml © BBC (2018 page 40);
Source B: An extract adapted from 'The Battle of Midway' by Andrew Lambert from www.bbc.co.uk/history/worldwars/wwtwo/battle_midway_01.shtml © BBC (2018 page 40).